THE BOND OF PEACE

Exploring generous orthodoxy

Edited by Graham Tomlin and Nathan Eddy

First published in Great Britain in 2021

Society for Promoting Christian Knowledge
36 Causton Street
London SW1P 4ST
www.spck.org.uk

British Library Cataloguing-in-Publication Data
A catalogue record for this book is available from the British Library

ISBN 978–0–281–08283–4
eBook ISBN 978–0–281–08284–1

Typeset by Fakenham Prepress Solutions, Fakenham, Norfolk NR21 8NL
First printed in Great Britain by Ashford Colour Press
Subsequently digitally printed in Great Britain

eBook by Fakenham Prepress Solutions, Fakenham, Norfolk NR21 8NL

Produced on paper from sustainable forests

In grateful memory of Al McDonald

Contents

Contents

Contributors

Simon Cuff is Lecturer in Theology at St Mellitus College, and Honorary Assistant Priest at St Cyprian's, Clarence Gate. He is Vice-Chair of the Ecumenical Council for Corporate Responsibility, Fellow of the Centre for Theology and Community, a contributing editor to the St Mary Magdalen School of Theology, trustee of Migrants Organise, member of the editorial board of *Crucible*, and helps convene the Sacramental Evangelism Network. He is the author of *Love in Action: Catholic Social Teaching for Every Church* (2019) and *Only God Will Save Us: The Nature of God and the Christian Life* (2020).

David F. Ford OBE is a Lay Reader in the Church of England, Regius Professor of Divinity Emeritus in the University of Cambridge, and a Fellow of Selwyn College. He co-founded the interfaith practice of scriptural reasoning, and now co-chairs the Rose Castle Foundation, chairs the Cambridge Friendship Trust (Lyn's House), and is a trustee of the National Society of the Church of England. Among his writings are *The Gospel of John: A Theological Commentary* (2021); *A Kind of Upside-Downness: Learning Disabilities and Transformational Community*, co-edited with Deborah Hardy Ford and Ian Randall (2020); *Christian Wisdom: Desiring God and Learning in Love* (2007); and *The Shape of Living* (2000).

Tom Greggs FRSE is the Marischal (1616) Chair and Head of Divinity at the University of Aberdeen. He was formerly the Professor of Systematic Theology at the University of Chester. Educated at the Universities of Oxford and Cambridge, Tom is a Methodist Preacher who serves on the Methodist Church's Faith and Order Committee as well as the Faith and Order Commission of the World Council of Churches. His publications include *The Breadth of Salvation* (2020); *Dogmatic Ecclesiology Vol. 1: The*

Priestly Catholicity of the Church (2019); *Theology against Religion* (2011); and *New Perspectives for Evangelical Theology* (2009).

Lincoln Harvey is Vicar of The Annunciation, Marble Arch, in the Diocese of London. He was previously Assistant Dean and Lecturer in Systematic Theology at St Mellitus College. Lincoln is the author of numerous articles and books, including *A Brief Theology of Sport* (2014) and *Jesus in the Trinity: A Beginner's Guide to the Theology of Robert Jenson* (2020).

Willie James Jennings is Associate Professor of Systematic Theology and Africana Studies at Yale University Divinity School. He is the author of *The Christian Imagination: Theology and the Origins of Race* (2010); *Acts: A Commentary, The Revolution of the Intimate* (2017); and *After Whiteness: An Education in Belonging* (2020). He is an ordained Baptist minister and has served as interim pastor for several North Carolina churches.

Michael J. Leyden is the Dean of Emmanuel Theological College and Honorary Canon of Chester Cathedral. He was a member of the St Mellitus College staff team for eight years, and for three of those he was Director of St Mellitus College North West. Michael's academic interest is at the interface of doctrine, ethics and liturgy. As well as various articles and chapters, he is the author of *Faithful Living: Discipleship, Creed and Ethics* (2019) and the forthcoming companion volume, *Living Eucharistically: Discipleship, Communion and Ethics*.

Fleming Rutledge is a sought-after speaker, theologian and preacher. A prolific writer, she is the author most recently of *Means of Grace: A Year of Weekly Devotions* (2021) and *Three Hours: Sermons for Good Friday* (2019). She was one of the first women ordained in The Episcopal Church (USA). Born in Virginia, she lives in Rye Brook, New York. Her writings can be found at <www.generousorthodoxy.org>.

Mark Scarlata is Tutor and Lecturer in Old Testament Studies at St Mellitus College. He received his PhD from Cambridge University, which was published as *Outside of Eden: Cain in the Ancient Versions of Gen. 4.1–16* (2012). He has published widely in the Pentateuch, with recent books that include *The Abiding Presence: A Theological Commentary on Exodus* (2017) and *Sabbath Rest: The Beauty of God's Rhythm for a Digital Age* (2019). He is currently working in Leviticus with forthcoming titles: *A Journey through Leviticus: Holiness, Sacrifice and the Rock Badger* and *The Theology of Leviticus*. Mark is also the Vicar-Chaplain at St Edward, King and Martyr, Cambridge, where he serves as priest and director of the St Edward's Institute for Christian Thought.

James K. A. Smith is Professor of Philosophy at Calvin University in Grand Rapids, Michigan, where he holds the Gary and Henrietta Byker Chair in Applied Reformed Theology and Worldview. He also serves as the editor-in-chief of *Image*, a quarterly journal of art and literature at the intersection of art, faith and mystery. He is the author of a number of award-winning books, including *Desiring the Kingdom* (2009); *How (Not) to Be Secular* (2014); *You Are What You Love: The Spiritual Power of Habit* (2016); and *On the Road with Saint Augustine* (2019).

Steve Smith is Tutor and Lecturer in New Testament Studies at St Mellitus College, London. He is the author of *The Fate of the Jerusalem Temple in Luke-Acts: An Intertextual Approach to Jesus' Laments over Jerusalem and Stephen's Speech* (2016), and co-editor of *Methodology in the Use of the Old Testament in the New: Context and Criteria* (2019).

Katherine Sonderegger is the William Meade Chair of Systematic Theology at Virginia Theological Seminary. Her areas of expertise include systematic theology, Barth, medieval studies, feminist studies and reformed theology. She is the author of *Systematic Theology, Vol. 2: The Doctrine of the Holy Trinity* (2021), *Systematic Theology, Vol. 1* (2015) and *That Jesus Christ Was Born a Jew: Karl Barth's 'Doctrine of Israel'* (1992).

Hannah Steele is Director of St Mellitus College London, and Lecturer in Missiology. She is the author of *New World, New Church? The Theology of the Emerging Church Movement* (2017) and *Living His Story: Revealing* *the Extraordinary Love of God in Ordinary Ways* (2020), which was the Archbishop of Canterbury's Lent book in 2021.

Jane Williams is McDonald Professor in Christian Theology at St Mellitus College, where she has taught since its foundation. She is the author of a number of books, including, *The Art of Advent* (2018); *The Merciful Humility of God* (2018); *Why Did Jesus Have to Die?* (2016).

Abbreviations

BDAG	William Arndt, Frederick W. Danker, Walter Bauer and F. W. Gringrich (eds), *A Greek–English Lexicon of the New Testament and Other Early Christian Literature*, 3rd edn, Chicago, IL: University of Chicago Press, 2000
Bibint	*Biblical Interpretation*
CBQ	*Catholic Biblical Quarterly*
CD	Karl Barth, *Church Dogmatics*, ed. G. W. Bromiley and T. F. Torrance, 4 vols in 13 parts, Edinburgh: T & T Clark, 1956–75. Reprint, Peabody, MA: Hendrickson, 2010
ConBNT	Coneictanea Biblica, New Testament Series
EuroJTh	*European Journal of Theology*
EvQ	*Evangelical Quarterly*
ExAud	*Ex Auditu*
ExpTim	*Expository Times*
IJST	*International Journal of Systematic Theology*
Inst	John Calvin, *Institutes of the Christian Religion*, ed. John Thomas McNeill, trans. Ford Lewis Battles, 2 vols, Philadelphia, PA: Westminster Press, 1960
IVP	InterVarsity Press
JBL	*Journal of Biblical Literature*
JETS	*Journal of the Evangelical Theological Society*
JSNT	*Journal for the Study of the New Testament*
JSNTSup	*Journal for the Study of the New Testament Supplement Series*
NRSV	New Revised Standard Version
NTL	New Testament Library
ProEccl	*Pro Ecclesia*
PRSt	*Perspectives in Religious Studies*
SNTA	Studiorum Novi Testamentum Auxilia

SNTSMS	Society of New Testament Studies Monograph Series
TynBul	*Tyndale Bulletin*
WJW	John Wesley, *Works of John Wesley*, 14 vols, Kansas City, MO: Beacon Hill, 1978
ZAW	*Zeitschrift für die alttestamentliche Wissenschaft*

Introduction

The phrase 'generous orthodoxy' has gained a great deal of traction in church life in recent years. It seems to have offered a description of Christian faith and life which is attractive for many, as it combines a commitment to specific Christian identity, given by the reference to 'orthodoxy', but also avoids some of the narrowness and rigidity that this notion can sometimes seem to imply, with its use of the qualifying adjective 'generosity'. The term has been used in many different ways by many different people, and as so often, when a term is used very widely with various different meanings, its specificity and precision can begin to get blurred.

This book is one of a number of resources to emerge from a project, generously sponsored by the McDonald Agape Foundation, which aimed to bring more clarity and definition to the idea. The project grew out of St Mellitus College, a new experiment in theological education which began in London in 2007 and grew very rapidly to be based in a number of centres across the UK, with further affiliated partner institutions in places such as Kuala Lumpur and Bermuda. Early on, the college had adopted 'generous orthodoxy' as a phrase to describe its attempt to hold together the different traditions of the Church in its own theological and worshipping life. The essays in this book are based on a series of lectures given by visiting scholars to the college, a symposium on the theme, which brought together a number of theologians from around the world in March 2019, and some reflections by existing and former members of staff.

'Generous orthodoxy' may perhaps be best known as the title of a book published in 2004 by Brian McLaren. McLaren wasn't the first to use the phrase, however. As several authors in this volume recognize, most scholars trace it back to the work of Hans Frei at Yale Divinity School in the 1970s and 80s, who in turn often credited the idea, if not the phrase, to the work of a previous scholar at Yale, under whom he had studied, Professor Robert Calhoun, and his unpublished lectures on the history of Christian doctrine.

The phrase occurs in an article written by Frei in 1987 as a response to a previous article written by the evangelical scholar Carl Henry. In the article, Frei writes:

> my own vision of what might be propitious for our day, split as we are, not so much into denominations as into schools of thought, is that we need a kind of generous orthodoxy which would have in it an element of liberalism, and an element of evangelicalism. I don't know if there is a voice between these two, as a matter of fact. If there is, I would like to pursue it.

Frei thought of the phrase as a way of bringing together evangelical and liberal perspectives. Yet that is not the only divide that the notion can address. In this volume we see how the phrase might help the Church develop new ways of addressing diversity in worship, find new approaches to ecclesiology and missiology, as well as help to develop a theological understanding of the variety of traditions across the Church, and assist in bringing them together creatively and harmoniously.

Listening to the lectures and reading through the essays, what struck me was the christological focus of so many of them. Many of the essays identify the heart of generous orthodoxy as Christ himself, the one who shows us the distinct face of God, who has a face – a distinct character and nature – and who, in and through Christ, extends a welcome of radical generosity to the whole of his creation.

David Ford begins by drawing our attention back to Hans Frei and his focus on the story of Jesus. Ford brings before us a Christ who is himself the future of the world and therefore offers us a kind of 'reliable surprise' – not random or erratic but utterly faithful, yet at the same time free to surprise us rather than becoming tediously familiar. As we seek to understand the nature of this 'reliably surprising' figure, Jane Williams goes on to focus on the Nicene Creed and its historical background. In a discussion of the debates over the teaching of Arius, she offers a vision of creeds as both defining a form of orthodoxy that delineates the nature of the God whom we worship and at the same time recognizes that this very God invites us into a world of gift and response which has generosity at its very heart. Creeds are boundaries that define borders, but they also enrich our participation in the heart of reality. They lay out pathways of life shaped by the nature of God as seen in the face of Jesus Christ, telling us who the God is whom Christians worship and seek to shape their life around.

Jamie Smith takes this incarnational focus further in an illuminating discussion of how Nicene orthodoxy and its incarnational way of seeing the world bring about a renewed imagination. He sees at the heart of true orthodoxy an aesthetic revolution that sanctifies matter and thus goes beyond the 'banal materialism of modernity (that) evacuates the material of significance'. He also focuses on the prophetic nature of Christian orthodoxy in naming evil for what it is and hoping for the good despite it. As such, generous orthodoxy has something to offer the world – a new way of seeing, a new way to be human.

One hundred and twenty-six years after Nicaea came the Council of Chalcedon, building on Nicaea's clarification of the relationship between the Father and the Son, to define the relationship between the humanity and divinity of Christ. Katherine Sonderegger mounts a rich and fascinating case that the metaphysical categories of Chalcedon are not a betrayal of the simple personal or historical concepts of primitive Christianity, but are in fact best suited to describe the heart of a truly generous orthodoxy, which centres on the deity of Christ. This is the revolutionary idea that Jesus reveals to us the very nature of reality: 'He, this very One, come to birth in Mary, is the Architect, the Truth and Logic of the cosmic spheres; He is the very Ratio and Verbum of everything that is.' God lives a human life – a life that therefore reveals the true nature of humanity and divinity, and draws them together, once and for all, in his person.

Fleming Rutledge takes us from the Incarnation to the resurrection in a stirring reminder that at the heart of a generous orthodoxy is the conviction that Jesus is alive and powerful – even today. She declares how God speaks into the world and how the divine Word does not simply describe reality but brings it into being. We see this primarily in Christ, but also in a strange paradoxical way it even happens when that Word is taken up and preached in the frail words of the preacher in the life of the Church.

Steve Smith then brings a New Testament and eschatological angle to this discussion of the christological focus of generous orthodoxy. In a close reading of the Letter to the Ephesians he shows how the question of the shape of the Church (orthodoxy) and the question of how differences within that Church are held together (generosity) have the same answer: Christ. It is a mutual allegiance to Christ, expressed in different cultural forms that points forward to the eschatological vision of unity in Christ.

As we move from Christology to ecclesiology, Tom Greggs reflects on the nature of the Church as born of the Holy Spirit. This pneumatological understanding of the Church defines it, not as focused on its own life and survival but as essentially turned outwards towards God and the world. This inevitably involves a Spirit-inspired generosity towards each other in the Church, recognizing the unity of the Church as a given, and a striving for unity rather than uniformity. Simon Cuff builds on this ecclesiological focus to remind us that the early Church held more variety and difference than we sometimes imagine. Right from the very beginning there was, therefore, a need for forbearance and patience with other members within the Church. The unity of the Church is found in Christ and in the range of responses to the one Christ that we find there.

The discussion then moves on to the worshipping life of the Church. In a rich discussion of the theme, Michael Leyden echoes Tom Greggs's focus on the Holy Spirit to offer a pneumatological understanding of worship where the Spirit leads us to the worship of Jesus. Worshipping Jesus in the Spirit inevitably recognizes the possibility of the Spirit's work in forms and traditions other than the one with which we might be familiar. As we encounter difference within the Church, it invites us to ask the question, 'What is the Holy Spirit doing here among these people?' Orthodoxy at the same time helps us to recognize what is of Christ in other forms of worship that may be unfamiliar. Lincoln Harvey goes on to explore this issue of the variety of styles of worship in the Church and concentrates on the essentially personal rather than institutional nature of the Church, focused in the office of the bishop, who authorizes different forms of worship through the apostolic charge to ensure the continuing faithfulness to the Church's core identity.

The last three chapters in the book begin to look outwards, both historically and geographically, to raise some real points of tension but also opportunity in the idea of generous orthodoxy. Willie Jennings draws attention to the essential marginality of the Church, in that Gentiles were initially allowed in to the story of Israel, a story that is not their own. However, very quickly, Gentile Christianity took centre stage, moved the story of Israel to the edges, and therefore learned habits of hubris which in turn led to the colonial mentality that emerged in the modern world. He draws the Church back from that deformed orthodoxy to a posture of humility and true remembering, which can prevent orthodoxy becoming a badge of superiority or domination.

Mark Scarlata takes his cue from Old Testament prophets as well as Jesus himself to explore the idea of generous orthodoxy as 'crossing borders to bless the other' as a way of encountering those with different beliefs or practices, an approach that can bear fruit both with regard to internal relations within the Church yet also even outside it, as Christians encounter others who do not share their faith in Christ.

The final chapter focuses on the missional implications of generous orthodoxy. Hannah Steele's meditation on the great commission reveals its essential generosity in the Church's call to go out to embrace the world and share the gifts of God with that world, and yet its essential orthodoxy in being focused on Christ alone as the true revelation of the nature of God. The unity that a generous orthodoxy brings enables pioneers and traditionalists to learn from one another and models the kind of unity that Jesus prayed for so that the world might believe.

The book thus moves from Christology to ecclesiology, through worship to mission. In doing so it expands the idea of generous orthodoxy into a rich means of exploring both the spaciousness and the specific identity of Christian faith in all its variety and harmony. It shows how the phrase is not so much an oxymoron, a rigid orthodoxy softened by a generous spirit, or a profligate generosity that is hemmed in by a strict orthodoxy. Instead, it proposes a version of Christian orthodoxy which reveals the very capaciousness of that orthodoxy and therefore sees generosity as of the very essence of orthodoxy and orthodoxy as the essence of generosity.

I am deeply grateful for the assistance of my co-editor, Nathan Eddy, who managed the lecture series and helped with the gathering and editing of this volume. I'm also thankful for staff colleagues at St Mellitus College, especially Andy Emerton, the Dean of the College, during the period when this project was underway, for his support and encourgament. Peter McDonald of the McDonald Agape Foundation was an unfailing source of support and strength throughout the project. This volume is dedicated to the memory of Al McDonald, his father, without whose wisdom, desire to enable Christian scholarship and rich generosity this thoroughly enjoyable and enriching venture could not have taken place at all. The Ephesian Christians were urged to 'lead a life worthy of the calling to which you have been called, with all humility and gentleness, with patience, bearing with one another in love, making every effort to maintain the unity of the Spirit in the bond of peace'. The goal of this book, and the project of which it is a part, is to inspire and enable the Church to do just that.

Graham Tomlin

1

Jesus: Reliably surprising, generously orthodox

DAVID F. FORD

It is appropriate that a book on generously orthodox Christian theology should begin with Jesus. If generous orthodoxy, or any other account of faith and understanding, is to have any Christian validity it must ring true with who Jesus is and what he has done and continues to do.

As this book was brought together, generous orthodoxy was initally described as an approach to theology that 'has deep roots in the Scriptures and the great tradition of Christian orthodoxy, wants to learn from the riches of the whole church and is always expectant for the Holy Spirit who makes all things new'. That suggests something of good theology's depth – here, scriptural depth; its length – the long tradition of Christian orthodoxy; its breadth – the riches of the whole Church; and its height – the Holy Spirit poured out from on high on all flesh. The imagery of the Spirit in Scripture in fact reaches in all directions: in spatial imagery, the wind of the Spirit blows where it will from any direction, the water of the Spirit wells up from the depths to eternal life; and, in temporal terms, the Spirit inspires the prophets and others in the past, is the foretaste of what is to come, and in the present can lead into all the truth, give all sorts of gifts, produce the fruit of 'love, joy, peace, patience, kindness, goodness, faithfulness, gentleness and self-control' (Galatians 5.22–23), unite us with Jesus and with each other in love and peace, and, in short, is the ultimate reality of generous abundance. As the Gospel of John says, the Spirit is given 'without measure' (John 3.34).

And Jesus is intrinsic to each of these elements of a generous orthodoxy.

7

As regards Scripture, it is not just that he is the central figure of the New Testament, and not just that the Old Testament was his own Scripture, shaping him deeply; in addition, what scholars call the intertextuality between the two is so pervasive that one simply cannot adequately understand the New Testament witness to Jesus without going deeper and deeper into the Old Testament. My favourite work of New Testament scholarship in recent years is *Echoes of Scripture in the Gospels* by Richard Hays. It is a profound inquiry into how the New Testament is illuminated by its multiple, rich echoes of the Old Testament in stories, imagery, terms, titles, patterns and a God-centred figural imagination.

If the Church today is to be orthodox it needs to be as deeply immersed in the Old Testament as Jesus was. The sad fact is that the Old Testament is often neglected, sometimes omitted from readings in services, and, in my experience, seldom preached on. One of the most powerful and convincing advocates of the immense importance of the Old Testament is Ellen Davis, a colleague of Richard Hays at Duke University. Her book *Wondrous Depth: Preaching the Old Testament* is a scholarly and passionate call to preach the Old Testament, together with some superb examples of her own sermons.[1] Her more recent collection, *Preaching the Luminous Word: Biblical Sermons and Homiletical Essays*, has some of the best sermons I have ever read or heard.[2] Best of all is her recent major work, *Opening Israel's Scriptures*, which moves through the whole Old Testament/Hebrew Bible in short, wise and theologically rich chapters.[3] Both Davis and Hays figure high on my list of outstanding exemplars of generous orthodoxy.

As regards the long tradition of Christian orthodoxy, for the first half millennium or so the main doctrinal debates in the Church circled around Jesus. They led to the Council of Nicaea in 325, and its decision on the full divinity of Jesus as being of one substance (*homoousios*) with the Father; the Council of Chalcedon (451), and its definition of the full humanity in relation to the full divinity of Jesus; and parallel developments in decisions about the Holy Spirit that together led to the orthodox

---

1 Ellen F. Davis, *Wondrous Depth: Preaching the Old Testament* (Louisville, KY: Westminster John Knox Press, 2005).

2 Ellen F. Davis with Austin McIver Dennis, *Preaching the Luminous Word: Biblical Sermons and Homiletical Essays* (Grand Rapids, MI: Eerdmans, 2016).

3 Ellen F. Davis, *Opening Israel's Scriptures* (Oxford: Oxford University Press, 2019).

doctrine of the Trinity. And, in the millennium and a half since then, Jesus has remained central to mainstream Christianity, as represented by Orthodox, Catholic, Protestant and, more recently, Pentecostal Churches.

That diversity leads into learning from the riches of the whole Church. Each of those traditions, and their numerous sub-traditions, has things to teach the others about Jesus. I suspect few of us who have been privileged to engage in any depth with the literature, the communities and the faithful members of Christian traditions other than our own would deny that there is much to be learned from them. I myself think back to my time living in Birmingham and two remarkable women, Miss Fisher and Miss Reeve, then in their seventies, who had founded Hockley Pentecostal Church there during the Second World War. They made it a place where, in an open service on Saturday evenings, people came from far and wide to take part in worship where Jesus was Lord, Saviour, healer and giver of the Holy Spirit. And, almost without fail, Miss Reeve at some point would give a prophecy, almost always touching, in a variety of biblical imagery, on the abundance of God's love and gifts. I was intrigued by the fact that, in a tradition that did not put much emphasis on the Lord's Supper, or Holy Communion, the imagery she used was so often that of the meal to which Jesus invites us. 'My children, I have prepared a feast for you, and you have come, but you have only nibbled at the first course. There is so much more I have for you! Come and feast on the abundance I provide!' Her Jesus was the very embodiment of generous and attractive love.

On a more academic note regarding the riches of the whole Church, it has been one of the many delights of my time as a university teacher to see the way in which one whose PhD I was privileged to supervise, the Catholic lay theologian Professor Paul Murray of Durham University, has in recent years pioneered the movement called Receptive Ecumenism. It is an excellent example of generous orthodoxy in practice, encouraging each Christian tradition to be hospitable towards, and learn from, the others, and I hope that it is taken up throughout the worldwide Church, as it deserves to be – and that Paul Murray is a prophet who is heeded in his own country, too.[4]

---

4 See the website of the Centre for Catholic Studies, University of Durham. The essential principle behind Receptive Ecumenism is that the primary ecumenical responsibility is to ask not 'What do the other traditions first need to learn from us?' but 'What do we need to

And, finally, there is the Holy Spirit who makes all things new. Clearly, in the New Testament, Jesus and the Holy Spirit are inseparable, from Mary's conception of Jesus to his resurrection and ascension. It is especially significant that the Gospel of John, which I (along with most scholars) take to be the latest of the four canonical Gospels, and which I (along with some scholars) understand to have been written with knowledge of the other three, Synoptic, Gospels, both has most emphasis on the person of Jesus (most vividly in the series of 'I am' sayings) and also has most to say about the Holy Spirit. This Gospel, which seems to have been written out of eyewitness testimony, and out of reading and rereading the Septuagint (the Greek translation of the Jewish Hebrew Scriptures), the Synoptic Gospels and, I think (along with a few scholars), Paul's letters too, all combined with many years of reflection, prayer and Christian living, unites Jesus and the Spirit as closely and intimately as possible – most clearly in the resurrected Jesus himself breathing the Spirit into his disciples (John 20.19–23).[5]

So, not only are all those marks of generous orthodoxy inseparable from Jesus, but he is utterly vital to each. Having, I hope, established that, in the rest of this chapter I want to do three things.

First, I will recommend the theology of Hans Frei, whom I consider the twentieth-century American theologian who has most generative potential for twenty-first-century Christian theology. He was one of my own teachers, and he had a great influence on numerous others too during his years as a professor at Yale.[6] It is especially appropriate to focus on Frei in this book because it was he who gave fresh currency to

---

learn from them?' The assumption is that if all were asking this question seriously and acting upon it then all would be moving in ways that would both deepen our authentic respective identities and draw us into more intimate relationship.

5 The Spirit is a theme in John from 1.32 onwards, climaxing in the second half of the Gospel beginning with the Farewell Discourses (chapters 13—17) and then in Jesus' death and resurrection (19.30 and 20.19–23). The teaching climax in the Farewell Discourses is about the Spirit as *paraklētos* (advocate, helper, encourager, strengthener, comforter, perhaps best 'the one who cries out alongside'), the key figure along with Jesus and his Father.

6 It is especially encouraging that some of the finest younger theologians in this country and North America have been engaging deeply with Frei. I think especially of Professor Mike Higton at Durham University, whose monograph, *Christ, Providence and History: Hans Frei's Public Theology* (London and New York: T&T Clark, 2004), is in my opinion the best overall account of Frei's thought; and of Dr Ben Fulford at Chester University, who is about to publish a book on Frei (I am grateful for conversations with him while writing this); and, at Yale, Dr Drew Collins, who is also working on a book with Frei as the main conversation partner.

the term 'generous orthodoxy' (he took it from his own teacher at Yale, Robert Calhoun).[7] Frei used it to describe his own position; and many others have found it attractive. But, like other such phrases, it can be taken to mean many things, and can be used as a slogan for very different positions. I will briefly give an account of three key elements in Frei's generously orthodox theology that I would propose as essentials.

Second, I will try to move beyond Frei's largely synoptic focus to a consideration of the Gospel of John as perhaps the best New Testament example of generous orthodoxy in relation to Jesus.

Finally, I will supplement the term 'generous orthodoxy' as applied to Jesus with a phrase that I have deliberately put first ahead of that in my title: 'reliably surprising'.

Frei and generous orthodoxy

So, first, what has Frei to contribute to twenty-first-century generous orthodoxy? Out of many possible points, I will confine myself to three, and even these will be extremely condensed.[8]

The first point is his approach to who Jesus is. His book *The Identity of Jesus Christ* sums this up well. The basic argument is as follows. The Gospels are primarily about Jesus, and they testify to his identity through telling his story in history-like, realistic narrative form. This conveys who he is through his intentional actions, interactions and what happens to him, and inseparable from this story is its conclusion in his resurrection, which is presented as God acting and Jesus appearing. The meaning of the story is found through following its characters and events in their interplay, not, for example, by finding some conceptual or moral sense that happens to be expressed in this narrative form, nor by seeking to reconstruct the history behind it by historical critical methods.

---

7 It is also appropriate to consider Frei now, as the centenary of his birth is coming in 2022, and a group of younger British and American theologians are putting together a conference on him and his twenty-first-century relevance.

8 Frei treats these points in rigorous detail in his writings. The most relevant to what I will say here are: Hans W. Frei, *The Identity of Jesus Christ: The Hermeneutical Bases of Dogmatic Theology*, Foreword by Mike Higton, Introduction by Joshua B. Davis, updated and expanded edn (Eugene, OR: Cascade Books, 2013); Hans W. Frei, *The Eclipse of Biblical Narrative* (New Haven, CT: Yale University Press, 1974); and Hans W. Frei, *Types of Christian Theology*, ed. George Hunsinger and William C. Placher (New Haven, CT: Yale University Press, 1992).

The second point is that all this unavoidably raises simultaneously the questions of historical and of theological truth, and faces readers with a decision, which is sharpest and most significant in relation to the resurrection. As Mike Higton, in his fine Foreword to the updated and expanded edition of Frei's book, puts it:

> Either Jesus really was resurrected – the Gospels are at their central point true, and their world is our world, their God our God – or they are simply a fiction, albeit a fiction that tries and fails to include our real world within itself.[9]

Frei allows that it is conceivable that the resurrection could be falsified, but not that it could be conclusively verified by historical critical methods, which rightly are concerned with 'the kinds of things that happen' and therefore not suited to something qualitatively unique and conceived as the one-off pivot on which history turns. It is true *both* that historical testimony is relevant to this event and person, and therefore critical historical cross-examination is appropriate, *and* that God is essential to the character of this event and person, and therefore, as Higton later says:

> the Gospels do not, at their heart, make a claim that stands firmly within the historical critic's territory, but one that sits awkwardly on that territory's edge. The engagement with historical critics that Frei believes is required is governed not by some general theory of apologetics, nor by some general theory of the independence of Christian truth, but by the logic of the particular Christian claim he has in view.[10]

The careful, thorough case that Frei makes out for this needs to be followed in detail. His remarkable achievement is to have offered the most convincing answer I know to the question of the relationship between what is sometimes called the Jesus of history and the Christ of faith. It is backed up by his major work on hermeneutics, *The Eclipse of Biblical Narrative*, which describes in detail the various ways in which

---

9 Frei, *The Identity of Jesus Christ*, p. xiv.
10 Frei, *The Identity of Jesus Christ*, p. xvi.

historians and theologians, conservatives, liberals and radicals, failed to do justice to the particularity of the Gospel narratives during the eighteenth, nineteenth and twentieth centuries.

The third point is that Frei in his *Types of Christian Theology* offers a map of modern theology that is better than any other I know, including those vague, largely political and generally unhelpful categories: conservative, liberal and radical. (It is one of the virtues of the description 'generous orthodoxy' that its wiser uses also manage to transcend those categories, enabling healthy theology to be conservative in some respects, liberal in others – liberality and generosity go together – and radical in yet others.) The strengths of Frei's five-type continuum are many, but, for my purposes here, two are most important: it pivots around how narrative portrayal of Jesus in the Gospels is understood and so makes central a specifically Christian criterion; and it enables one to identify where generous orthodoxy is on the continuum. Frei gave the Edward Cadbury lectures on the typology in Birmingham University when I was teaching there, and I asked him where he placed his own theology. He replied that he was somewhere in between the fourth type, where he had placed Karl Barth, and the third, where he had placed Friedrich Schleiermacher, but inclining somewhat more towards Barth, and also shaping his theology in dialogue with each of the other three types. I see both Barth and Schleiermacher as generously orthodox, but Barth perhaps as the more orthodox and Schleiermacher as the more generous.

Overall, then, Frei offers the twenty-first century three things: a generously orthodox theology to which Jesus is central; a solution to one of the most complex and important questions in modern Christian theology, the distinction between the Jesus of history and the Christ of faith; and a typology that maps the whole territory of theology in relation to generous orthodoxy.

The Gospel of John and generous orthodoxy

Frei's main concentration in dealing with Jesus was on the Synoptic Gospels.[11] I want to propose the Gospel of John as the main New

---

11 Frei also greatly appreciated the Gospel of John, and it would be fascinating to explore his interpretation of it and its relationship to the Synoptics, but that must await another occasion.

Testament example of a matured generous orthodoxy. As with Frei, I will make three highly condensed points.

First, as already suggested, John's Gospel above all emphasizes the identity of Jesus. 'Who Jesus is' is its core theme; and making the 'who' question primary is essential to mainstream Christian orthodoxy. Orthodoxy tends to go wrong, and to become ungenerous, contentious in inappropriate ways, or to focus on wrong issues, or less important ones, if it fails to give the 'who' question, in relation to both God and Jesus, this priority. One constant temptation of orthodoxy is, for example, to give priority to 'what' questions, such as: 'What is the will of God now?' or, 'What is the meaning of this Scripture now?' Those are, of course, legitimate questions, but it is fatally easy to separate them from the One in whose presence one is asking the questions, and who is himself the Word of God in person. In any doctrinal or ethical discussion it is helpful to think first as profoundly as possible about who Jesus is, who God is. The importance attached to those questions, together of course with the content of the answers, is perhaps more determinative of the generosity or ungenerosity of orthodoxy than anything else.

Second, I have also already reflected on the prominence of the Holy Spirit in the Gospel of John. The Spirit is given 'without measure' (3.34), and this generosity is echoed in the abundance of grace, life, love, truth, glory and joy, symbolized variously by the abundance of light, wine, wind, water, bread, perfume and, finally in the last chapter, fish. Any orthodoxy entering into such generosity is itself challenged to become utterly generous. The conception of life in the Spirit is expansive, attractive and capaciously open to more and more truth, love, joy and glory. Two of the most profound words in John are 'as' and 'in', calling for endless reflection, deepening and expansion. Just try, for example, to fathom the meaning of these two words in the following verses from what I think of as the deepest chapter in the Bible, John 17:

'As you, Father, are in me and I am in you, may they also be in us, so that the world may believe that you have sent me. The glory that you have given me I have given them, so that they may be one, as we are one, I in them and you in me, that they may become completely

one, so that the world may know that you have sent me and have loved them even as you have loved me.'
(17.21–23)

Third, there is the question of ethics in the Gospel of John. Why is there so little direct ethical instruction? The main directions are to imitate the foot-washing of Jesus, 'that you also should do as I have done to you' (13.15), and to love one another, 'just as I have loved you' (13.34). That open 'as' invites mature ethical discernment and continual, loving improvisation in new situations, guided by continual reflection on who Jesus is and the practical implications of his life, teaching, death and resurrection.

There is so much more that could be written on this, but I now turn finally to the other key phrase in my title.

Jesus is reliably surprising

All terms have their limitations. Generous orthodoxy tends to imply a cognitive rather than a practical orientation, a focus on belief and understanding – perhaps, too, if one takes the original Greek behind 'orthodoxy', a relation to right worship as well as right belief. And as regards Jesus, for all its appropriateness, which I have tried to indicate, to call him generously orthodox is somehow not quite adequate. So I have put first in my title a parallel description of him: reliably surprising. This balances the cognitive with the active and the personal, and brings them into the present of the relationship of Jesus with us now.

Jesus is, according to the Bible and Christian tradition, reliable; faithful; the same yesterday, today, and for ever; utterly to be trusted whatever happens. His reliability is that of a love whose dimensions go beyond any understanding and any articulation, even in generously orthodox theology. As the Letter to the Ephesians says, in mind-blowing language:

I pray that you may have the power to comprehend, with all the saints, what is the breadth and length and height and depth, and to know the love of Christ that surpasses knowledge, so that you may be filled with all the fullness of God.
(Ephesians 3.18–19)

But this love is also endlessly surprising. If the Gospels and the rest of the New Testament are to be trusted, Jesus is very surprising – to the crowds, to orthodox religious people and to his followers. He bursts out of the usual categories, titles and expectations that are associated with him. He says, does and suffers surprising, even shocking, things. He has surprising relationships across the deepest divisions of his day, with lepers, tax collectors, prostitutes, freedom fighters, Roman soldiers and a Samaritan woman. He makes the marginal and powerless central, putting a little child in the midst. The supremely shocking surprise is his death by crucifixion. The supremely joyful surprise is his resurrection.

And there are more surprises to come. If anything is clear in the teaching of Jesus about the future, it is that he will surprise us. 'When was it that we saw you hungry . . . or thirsty . . . a stranger . . . naked . . . sick or in prison . . . ?' (Matthew 25.37–39). The master comes on a day when he is not expected (Matthew 24.50). And so on.

I find in the New Testament a development, one might call it a maturing, of the understanding of surprise. If you think of the early letters of Paul to the Thessalonians, there is a vivid picturing of the return of Jesus.

> For the Lord himself, with a cry of command, with the archangel's call and with the sound of God's trumpet, will descend from heaven, and the dead in Christ will rise first. Then we who are alive, who are left, will be caught up in the clouds together with them to meet the Lord in the air; and so we will be with the Lord for ever.
> (1 Thessalonians 4.16–17)

This will happen, he says, suddenly, 'like a thief in the night' (5.2). But in the later Pauline tradition – in, for example, the Letter to the Ephesians (scholars differ about the authorship, but most agree it is later in the same tradition) – such pictures are absent. Instead, the emphasis is on the wisdom and mystery of God's will, realized in Jesus Christ, 'a plan for the fullness of time, to gather up all things in him, things in heaven and things on earth' (Ephesians 1.10), and on the reliable hope this gives (1.12, 18). But the element of surprise is, if anything, intensified and made more fully part of life now. The path to the ultimate future is paved with things that go beyond anything we can think of or even imagine. That prayer in Ephesians 3 culminates:

> Now to him who by the power at work within us is able to accomplish abundantly far more than all we can ask or imagine, to him be glory in the church and in Christ Jesus to all generations, for ever and ever. Amen.
> (Ephesians 3.20–21)

Anyone who prays that should be prepared for a life full of surprises.

Or think of the earliest and latest of the four Gospels on the resurrection of Jesus. Mark, usually considered the earliest, in what is probably the original, shorter ending, has three women fleeing from the empty tomb, 'for terror and amazement had seized them; and they said nothing to anyone, for they were afraid' (Mark 16.8). In John there are fully developed resurrection appearances, with a deepening of the surprise element. There is Mary Magdalene's surprise recognition of Jesus, 'Rabbouni!' in response to his 'Mary!' There are the amazement and joy of the disciples at meeting Jesus, receiving the Holy Spirit and being given a mission comparable to that of Jesus. There is the reconciliation between Jesus and Peter. Finally, there is what Jesus says to Peter about the beloved disciple: 'If it is my will that he should remain until I come, what is that to you?' (John 21.22). That reference to his second coming omits all the spectacular elements of Mark 13, which is akin to 1 Thessalonians, and says what is arguably the main thing: Jesus is the future of the world, and he is free to surprise us.

One might wonder how any Christian orthodoxy could fail to notice and take seriously the capacity of Jesus to continue to surprise us. How can so many Christians appear to think that now Christian doctrine and ethics need not be open to further surprises? How can they imagine that the past is the only guide to the future when Jesus is still alive and active, and has promised not only to lead his followers into all the truth, but also that they will do greater things than he did in his ministry (John 14.12)? This is, of course, dangerous ground, and there are massive fears about irresponsible innovation, questionable claims to inspiration, going beyond Scripture and tradition, and so on. Actually, this is Scripture pointing beyond Scripture, and the fears bear a marked resemblance to the fears of those who opposed or misunderstood Jesus during his ministry. The Church has wisely developed a range of ways to try to discern true innovation from false. But the fear of rejecting surprising and even shocking innovation should, in the light of Jesus and the early Church, be a fear that is taken at least as seriously as a fear of wrong innovation. The primary fear should be of failing to follow where the living Jesus is leading through his Spirit.

The early Church's most vivid experience of this was in the opening up of the Church to non-Jews without them having to fulfill the requirements for entry into the Jewish community. The Acts of the Apostles tells the story of Peter and Cornelius, and the huge shock to Peter when he is told in a dream to go against his scriptures and tradition, transforming the boundaries of the infant Church, by eating with the Gentile Cornelius and then baptizing him and his family.

There are three basic differences mentioned by Paul in his Letter to the Galatians as being relativized by Jesus Christ:

> As many of you as were baptized into Christ have clothed yourselves with Christ. There is no longer Jew or Greek, there is no longer slave or free, there is no longer male and female; for all of you are one in Christ Jesus.
> (Galatians 3.27–28)

One might say that the first, between Jews and Gentiles, was the main preoccupation of the early Church, though it is still very much a live issue. Then, as regards the second, it took many in the Church over eighteen hundred years to follow through consistently the implications of slave and free being both together 'one in Christ Jesus' – and then there was a theologically sophisticated and passionate resistance to it by many orthodox Christians, on strong biblical grounds, which led, for example, to many churches in the USA splitting over the emancipation of slaves. There are lessons to be learned today from such battles in which orthodox Christians are tempted to split, often over matters unrelated to anything Jesus said or did, and not part of the creed. And, third, it took till the last century for some churches to follow through on the 'male and female' difference with regard, for example, to women's ministry.

This all leads back to the Gospel of John in relation to the Synoptic tradition. John's Jesus is the same reliably surprising Jesus testified to in the Synoptics, but with an intensified emphasis on both reliability and tendency to surprise.

The reliability is signalled in a great many ways, among them: the repeated stress on the relationship of Jesus with God his Father; the 'I am' statements of Jesus, and such descriptions of him as the Word of God, Christ/Messiah, king of Israel, the bread of life, the light of the world, the good shepherd, the way, the truth and the life, and many more. The whole Gospel is written to inspire belief, trust, faith, in this utterly reliable one (John 20.31).

As regards surprises, there are several aspects. The main one is who Jesus is, inseparable from the Holy Spirit who continues to generate surprises through his followers, in line with those generated by Jesus. There are many surprises in relation to the other Gospels. Some are omissions – birth stories, Sermon on the Mount, exorcisms, trans-figuration, the institution of the Lord's Supper or Eucharist. Others are additions – turning water into wine, many long teachings (above all the Farewell Discourses), Nicodemus, the Samaritan woman at the well, the raising of Lazarus, and several resurrection stories. And yet others are transformations, very different retellings – of the baptism of Jesus, the calling of disciples, the cleansing of the Temple, the feeding of the five thousand, events around the crucifixion, and more. I think John delib-erately included such intertextual surprises with several overlapping purposes – in order, for example, to make us think afresh, or to reread both the Synoptics and his own Gospel, or to go deeper and broader in our understanding, drawing us more and more fully into a generous orthodoxy that springs from a love that is greater than we can ever take in.

Perhaps the greatest Johannine surprise is the most intimate. This is the place where reliability, ever-new life, deep meaning and generous love come together most fully. It is first introduced at the climax of what has probably been the most influential short piece of theology in Christian history, the Prologue, with the mention of the Son who is 'close to the Father's heart' (1.18, NRSV; literally, 'into the bosom of the Father'). At the Last Supper the anonymous 'disciple whom Jesus loved' is introduced for the first time, lying on the bosom, or breast, of Jesus (13.23, 25 – sadly, the NRSV again misses the vivid imagery of bosom or breast by translating this as 'reclining next to'). Then, at the climax of the Farewell Discourses in John 17, the prayer of Jesus is that the intimacy between himself and his Father is opened up to all those who trust him: 'I in them and you in me, that they may become completely one' (17.23a). The scale of the generosity is hinted at in its orientation to the whole world and in it being measured by the unsurpassable love between the Father and the Son: 'so that the world may know that you have sent me and have loved them even as you have loved me' (17.23b).

Finally, there is that little scene at the very end of the Gospel when Peter asks about the disciple Jesus loved, and we are reminded that 'he was the one who had reclined next to Jesus at the the supper' (21.20, NRSV – literally, 'lay on his breast'). Jesus says that this disciple, who is identified not by a name but by being loved by Jesus (and so seems to stand for all his followers), might possibly remain, abide 'until I come'. But where was he abiding? According to John 19, Jesus had said to him, as he stood at the cross with the mother of Jesus, 'Here is your mother' (after saying to his mother, 'Woman, here is your son'), and then 'from that hour the disciple took her into his own home' (19.26–27). Perhaps we have here the first home of generous orthodoxy.

2

Creeds: Boundaries or paths?[1]

JANE WILLIAMS

In a lecture on generous orthodoxy that took place in 2019, Miroslav Volf argued that 'home' is not just a boundaried space – that is a grave. Instead, home must be described by what goes on inside the boundaries – about sharing and 'resonance'. Although boundaries are often thought of in terms of who or what they keep out, a more interesting question, he suggested, would be to ask what is enabled within boundaries.[2] That is precisely the question I propose to explore in relation to the historic creeds. The creeds are generally taught in theological colleges and faculties in the context of church history and the doctrinal and political debates that led to the formalization of, for example, the Nicene Creed. That is an essential aspect of credal formulae: to be a Christian is to believe and trust in certain things about God and God's relation to the world and to us, to make a commitment to the way of life opened up by this description, and so to lay aside other possible paths. Creeds are, in that sense, boundary markers, outlining the ancient tracks that guide us home. One of the questions to be explored, then, in relation to creeds as enablers of generous orthodoxy is whether, in fact, they have acted ungenerously, in prohibiting other possible pathways. The great christological controversies of the fourth century gradually ruled out a range of descriptions of, in particular, the relationship between Father and

---

1 This essay will be looking at the creeds in general, rather than any particular creed. It will take the Nicene Creed as the 'standard', but will aim to explore the role of boundaries and definitions in relation to 'generous orthodoxy', rather than trace the historical and doctrinal development of creeds. For definitions of the various technical terms used – 'creed', 'confession', 'definition', 'rule' and so on – see Jaroslav Pelikan, *Credo* (New Haven, CT: Yale University Press, 2003), pp. 1–5.

2 Miroslav Volf, 'The Love of God, the Home of God', 2 July 2019, <www.stmellitus.ac.uk/about-us/news/generous-orthodoxy-lecture-series-love-god-home-god-miroslav-volf>.

Son, and between the divinity and humanity of the Son, some of which had to be revisited in the course of subsequent history. Recognition that sometimes misunderstanding rather than significant doctrinal difference lay at the root of different formulations often came too late for the unity of the Christian communities concerned. Parallel hierarchies had already been set up, invested with political and national significance, so that the fragmentation of the Church seemed impossible to undo, even when essential doctrinal agreement was admitted. Although the development of creeds is only one aspect of that sad process of disunity, it may raise the question of whether creeds can truly operate 'generously', or whether suspicion is an essential part of formulating creeds.

Part of the response to this is to explore the other vital place in which creeds are birthed and in which they describe and enable pathways home, and that is in the context of discipleship and worship. It is here that the nature of creeds is most visible: they are a shared expression of the world that Christians commit ourselves to and trust that we are inhabiting. In this setting, too, credal formulae set boundaries – we believe God to be this God, and no other – but in worship it becomes clearer that the purpose of creeds is to enable flourishing in the place the boundaries define, rather than to defend the boundaries from what goes on outside.

This chapter will briefly explore those two functions of creeds – to defend the borders and to enrich participation – and will argue that both are necessary to a generous orthodoxy, though the second function of enabling flourishing is essential to any generosity in the first function, of defending borders. The primary purpose of credal orthodoxy, it is suggested, is to define pathways of a life shaped by the nature of God, rather than to push people off the path and into the wilderness.

The path shaped by the nature of God

Christianity is a 'credal' faith. Self-definition happens in all kinds of settings, not just religious ones, and the markers of self-definition vary considerably. Some kinds of group can only be joined by being born into them, some by shared interests, some by subscription, and all such groups define and defend their boundaries in one way or another. 'The interesting thing about Christianity is why, having broken across national and racial divides, its boundaries and defining marks became principally matters of belief, rather than behaviour, or some other feature.[3]

Some definitions of 'generosity' would suggest that true generosity is marked by lack of interest in boundaries. The philosophical schools of the first few Christian centuries would seem to offer a model of such generosity, in displaying a tolerance of choice and a willingness to accept that reality may be defined in various ways, none of which demonstrates an overwhelming claim to truth. The various schools were called 'haereses', or 'choices', suggesting a free-market, consumerist approach to reality: choose the one that suits best, and that enables the 'good life' as defined by the chooser.[4] That approach becomes, in Christian discourse, a sign of deviance: 'choice', 'haereses', becomes 'heresy', since to choose for ourselves how we will define reality suggests that there is no given reality over against us, no one truth, given and held by one God, and therefore not open to the kind of tolerant scepticism that results from this approach to 'generosity'.

Christians are invited into one reality, which is given by God. Our Scriptures draw us into a world that starts and ends with God, and they show us God's constant, relentless interaction with the world, shaping people according to God's character. The doctrinal statements and the worship practices of Christians are embedded in the response to God, as witnessed to by the Bible. For example, our earliest baptismal liturgies show that declaring faith in the one true God is a necessary part of becoming a Christian.[5] The God in whom Christians believe has a particular character, and since God is defined as the only God, this is the character that shapes all of reality and therefore also shapes how we live. If we are to know how to live, we need to know God. Creeds, then, typically tell us about God and how God is to be known, and what the consequences are for us.

---

3 Frances Young, *The Making of the Creeds* (London: SCM Press, 1993), p. 99.

4 Young, *The Making of the Creeds*, p. 99.

5 There is some debate about whether 'declaratory' creeds exist in the first few Christian centuries, before the earliest known formal liturgies; cf. W. Kinzig and M. Vincent, 'Recent Research on the Origin of the Creed', *Journal of Theological Studies* 50 (1999), pp. 535–59, which argues that creeds develop first in the controversies of the fourth century. But Augustine (*Confessions*, 8.2.5 <www.newadvent.org/fathers/110108.htm>) describes the reception into the Church of Victorinus, and the habit of declaring a commitment 'in a set form of words learned by heart'.

The baptism liturgy of the Church of England requires the candidate or her sponsors to reject 'rebellion against God' by turning to Christ and declaring faith in the one God. This declaration follows the threefold pattern of the Nicene Creed. God is Father Almighty, Creator of everything; God is Son, who becomes incarnate, Jesus Christ; God is Holy Spirit, through whom the Church is given life, today and for eternity. God is as God is seen to be in Scripture, in other words.

A similar pattern can be seen in eucharistic liturgies. Most Eucharistic Prayers are 'credal' in structure, beginning with the acknowledgement of God as Creator and Sustainer, homing in on how God comes to be known and to act in Jesus Christ, and then calling upon the Holy Spirit to enable us to be part of the world so described, so that we are continuing to live in the scriptural narrative.

The scriptural credal structure of these central liturgical works of the Christian Church highlights the essential truth that it matters who we worship. Worship shapes our lives, as individuals and as communities; and this is true whether what we do is acknowledged as 'worship' or not, and whether what we offer ourselves to is seen as 'divine' or not. As Jesus says, 'Where your treasure is, there will your heart be also' (Matthew 6.21). We structure our lives around our values, consciously and unconsciously. Christian worship calls the believer to live in the world made by God, Father, Son and Holy Spirit. Worship is interested in what is happening in the worshipping community; it is not an apologetic or a display but a celebration of who and what we are and do because of who and what God is and does.

Credal language in the context of worship declares that God is the Father and Creator of all things. It rejoices in the fact that there are no alternative realities, no other sources of existence, no other possible descriptions of the world. Furthermore, the source of all that is is *'fatherly'*; the Creator of all reality is not cold and distant but self-giving and loving, bringing into being a universe that is shaped by this particular reality: God is 'Father Almighty' in creating.

This is not abstract knowledge for us, because the 'fatherliness' of God is echoed by the 'filial' response of God to God. God is Father, but also Son; God gives, and God receives and is shaped by gift. The pattern of gift and reception is not an immanent cosmic drama, true only within God's own life, but is the lived reality of the world we inhabit, because God the Son comes to live the reality of our human lives; our world, our human possibilities, are full of the shape of God's activity. God the Son establishes the 'fatherliness' of God as the character of the world, and demonstrates that there is nothing outside that, not even death. The death and resurrection of the Son is the living reality of the assertion that God is 'Father Almighty, maker of heaven and earth': there is no other reality, no shadowy world in which this is not true.[6]

For us as worshippers, the next 'credal' movement is even more signif- icant, because it celebrates the reality that God's movement of gift and reception is not all in one direction. God is Father and Son, but God is also Holy Spirit. God's 'fatherliness', poured out into the Son, is matched by the returning love of the Son in the Holy Spirit. This is where our own worship is located, in this great return of filial love to the Father. Baptism and Eucharist, and all Christian worship, draw us into the wonder of human response made in the image of the Son's love for the Father, gloriously rendered in and through the Holy Spirit.[7] Sacramental worship, in particular, draws us into the reality of the creation that is gift and response, through and through. God, Father, Son and Holy Spirit, shapes all that is, including us. We, too, are enabled to respond to God with the filial love of Jesus Christ, because the Holy Spirit gives us the Son's words and deeds of love. Water, bread and wine, the stuff of creation, are not dead and meaningless matter, but are 'creation', given by God and responding to God. The particularity of the biblical narrative is matched by the particularity of sacrament and worship: real people, physical reality, transfused with the action of God.

The credal pattern of worship, like the narrative pattern of Scripture, is not declaratory but celebratory and participatory. It is creative, because God is Creator; what is created in worship is 'the body of Christ', filled with the Holy Spirit, a constant echo and re-echo of the truth of God,

---

6 For a summary of the theology connecting creation and resurrection, see 'From Creation to Re-creation: Nature and the Naked Ape', in Frances Young, *God's Presence: A Contemporary Recapitulation of Early Christianity* (Cambridge: Cambridge University Press, 2013), pp. 92ff.

7 Thomas Weinandy's book, *The Father's Spirit of Sonship* (Eugene, OR: Wipf & Stock, 2011), helpfully describes the logic of this.

Father, Son and Holy Spirit, the character of all that is. As we worship, this is the world we inhabit, this and no other; it does not cease to exist as the last prayer is said, as the worshippers disperse, as daily life resumes. On the contrary, the worshipping community have affirmed that this is the world we live in, full of God. The pattern of the lives we live is unalterably shaped by the nature of God, Father, Son and Holy Spirit, so that to choose to live otherwise than in this world of gift and response is to choose to live in empty fantasy. All the disciplines of Christian discipleship, nurtured by our daily immersion in Scripture, enable us to flourish more and more as creatures, given our reality by God; as filial beings, given our reality by love; as Spirit-filled beings, given our reality in the joy of responding to the love that shapes the universe.

Credal worship, then, nourishes the Christian community by drawing us deeper and deeper into the reality of who we are because of the reality of who God is. It draws us into the community of all who have shaped and been shaped by the Scriptures, reading them, living them, from all times and all places, unlike each other in every other respect, but with this family likeness in our shared story. Without our affirmation of the nature of God, our choice to give and receive ourselves from God and from one another is anchorless; it becomes a choice of blind optimism, rather than an act of faith and love. Worship shaped by this credal framework has no choice but to be 'generous' because it has uncovered the generosity of reality, grounded in the love of God, Father, Son and Holy Spirit.

This one path, no other

The generosity generated by worshipping the one true God enables but is also defended by some definition of 'orthodoxy'. *Lex orandi, Lex credendi* is not a simplistic formula meaning that only prayer and worship count as belief, but a profound intertwining of the two. We cannot offer joyful worship to what is not God, and the shape of our worship flows from the reality to whom it is offered. Christian worship makes no sense if God is not as it describes; God as described by credal formulae is empty theory unless issuing in lives shaped by worship.

The great christological controversies of the fourth century were, at least in part, affirming the necessary connection between belief and worship-soaked lives. They were, above all, readings of Scripture, provoked by the challenge to live most fully in this narrative and no other. The alternative readings that were ruled out by the increasingly sophisticated and technical creeds and formulae were believed to be those that severed the connection between God and our lived reality, which is why they were so focused on Christology: on the relationship between divine and human.

The archetypal 'heresy', offering a description of reality that must be rejected if the overall coherence of Christian life and witness is to be saved, is Arianism. Arius offered an interpretation of the relationship between Father and Son that was ultimately judged to offer an incoherent account of reality, leaving it without hope of genuine transformation. Arius' reading of Scripture was one that suggested Scripture needed to be corrected in the light of human conceptions and understandings of what is and is not possible. Arius argued that 'fatherliness' is not integral to the eternal being of God, but comes to be as an instrumental adjunct to God's creativity.[8] Arius was determined to defend monotheism, and to defend an understanding of the divine that was current in his world and still exists today: the divine needs to be protected from contamination by the material world. He seems to have theorized that God brings the Son into existence before all other beings and before all time, in order to have the Son as the intermediary necessary for a transcendent divinity to have any interaction with materiality. Creation then comes into being not out of nothing but God, but out of a being who is almost but not quite God. That opens up a disjunction between God and God's self-giving to us that undermines the beautiful logic of worship. Such a transcendent God does not truly give Godself to God and receive Godself again; God is not truly Trinity. Consequently, human worship is not genuinely enabled by entering into the circle of self-gift and reception that we have traced above. Scripture becomes a human misunderstanding of God's passionate commitment to us. Sacraments become merely symbolic, since matter cannot receive the divine, and human worship and life become again an

---

8 There are many expositions of Arius' theology. See, for example, Henry Chadwick, *The Church in Ancient Society: From Galilee to Gregory the Great* (Oxford: Oxford University Press, 2003), pp. 190–200; Basil Studer, *Trinity and Incarnation* (London and New York: T & T Clark, 1994), pp. 101–14; Rowan Williams, *Arius: Heresy and Tradition* (Grand Rapids, MI: Eerdmans, 2002); Young, *The Making of the Creeds*, pp. 45–7.

approximation at obedience and imitation, rather than a Spirit-infused invitation into reality. We try to imitate the Son without the Son's gift of the Spirit, just as the Son tries to image the Father, without the Father's self-gift. Rifts open up all the way between God and worship and so between God and life. We are guessing at the nature of a God who is not given to us in freedom and love. As Athanasius and others argued, in the approach that became orthodoxy after Nicaea, unless the Son is truly God, we are left with 'haereses', options and guesses about the nature of God. And if that is the case, then our worship becomes at best a human system of self-organization, longing for what is good and true and divine, and at worst, idolatry, since we worship what we cannot trust to be the divine reality.

The Council of Nicaea and the creed that emerged from it defends a boundary that must not be crossed. It suggests that there is a necessary path for us to walk along that leads to God. It insists that there is no ontological gap between Father and Son, and that our worship is only truthful if it is caught up in the Father's self-gift in Son and Spirit. Nicaea insists that the Creator of all things is indeed 'fatherly' in all things, and is received in all things 'filially' in the Son and responded to in all things in the loving return of the love of the Spirit. None of this is secondary, coming into being at one remove from the reality of God; and therefore none of this is just an approximation for us: our salvation lies in the reality of God, whose love is eternal, unbreakable, not subject to death, fully able to be gift and response, so that even what is not God is given the gift of the presence of the love of God in the power of the Spirit of Sonship. If this is not who God is, then we are adrift. If the Son is not God 'he could not communicate the divine, because he was himself divine'.[9] The same logic gradually extended to the Holy Spirit: the Holy Spirit, too, must be God, otherwise, again, our discipleship and worship become a human effort, not enabled and filled with the love of God, but only with the best human attempts.[10]

In time, the force of the Nicene Creed's insistence on the unity of Father and Son prevailed. But the victory in this area opened up another

---

9 Young, *The Making of the Creeds*, p. 47.

10 Basil the Great makes the case for the divinity of the Holy Spirit, based on the doxology, baptism and the confession of faith; cf. *De Spiritu Sancti*, 10.26, <www.newadvent.org/fathers/3203.htm>.

fault line through which uncertainty about the foundational truth of Christian life and worship could seep. If the Son is truly God, that would seem to call into question the reality of the humanity of Jesus Christ. If the Son is God, then he cannot also be human, surely? Various combinations were suggested in the century or so after Nicaea, giving more or less space to the divine and the human in Jesus Christ, and thereby suggesting a being who was neither fully human nor fully God, but some strange third category of being.[11] As with the Arian gap between Father and Son, so this non-permeable membrane between divine and human Son has an instant destabilizing effect on worship and life. If humanity and divinity are compartmentalized in Jesus, then that suggests that there cannot be any true self-giving of God to the creature. Human worship becomes again a human activity, rather than a habitation of the Spirit, teaching us to pray and live as daughters and sons. Sonship, filial existence, must always be external to created world, rather than poured into it by the Spirit of the 'fatherliness' of the Creator.

The Chalcedonian Definition, which acts as exegesis on the Nicene Creed's reading of Scripture and on the controversies in the century following, comes to a simple, elegant and technical equilibrium that safeguards God's freedom to be God, Father, Son and Holy Spirit, and to enable human beings to live as ecstatic worshipping beings, giving and receiving themselves from God's self-gift. Chalcedon formulates the 'double homoousion', that the Son is 'of one being with God in divinity, of one being with us in humanity', and that humanity and divinity are held in mutuality in Jesus, 'without confusion, without change, without division and without separation'.[12]

These issues were hard fought because what was at stake was the Christian faith. Is God truly self-giving love, Father, Son and Holy Spirit, and is humanity genuinely enabled to receive the saving gift of God's presence and action? The battles were internal to the Christian Church: the purpose of these statements is not, initially, to defend the faith against outside forces but to state what it is to believe in God as revealed in Jesus

---

11 See Thomas Weinandy, 'The Doctrinal Significance of the Councils of Nicaea, Ephesus and Chalcedon', in Francesca Murray (ed.), *The Oxford Handbook of Christology* (Oxford: Oxford University Press, 2015), pp. 550–65.

12 See <http://anglicansonline.org/basics/chalcedon.html>.

Christ, through the power of the Spirit. The effect of the controversies was undoubtedly to rule out some descriptions of God's interaction with reality, and so to 'anathematize' some who adhered to those descriptions. But, as with credal worship, so with credal statements, the purpose is to form the people of God to live trustfully in the world that God has made, and to walk purposefully towards our fuller and fuller self-discovery in the Holy Spirit.

Orthodoxy and generosity

Christian worship and Christian belief make a claim that the world is this kind of a world and no other because God is God. Creation is the continuing act of the 'fatherliness' of God, whose Spirit gathers us into the Son's response. God gives character to all reality, and to be a Christian is to seek to discern and live from God's character in all things.

The God we worship, whose Spirit is growing in us daily our filial nature as part of the body of Christ, is therefore supremely generous. God's nature is one of constant, eternal, dynamic self-gift and loving response, and everything flows from that generosity and returns to it with joy. Therefore those who are filled with the Spirit of God are growing daily more and more in love and generosity, in response to the reality of God. Our response to God, unlike God's response to God, is not innate to us, not our ontological status, as though our possession independently of God. But that is the glory of grace – we do not need to possess, because we are always being given.

Orthodoxy such as this cannot be optional because if God is not as described by the creeds, then neither is our reality and our calling. The kind of 'generosity' that is actually agnosticism then turns out to undercut the doctrinal basis from which generosity of life and mission flows. Credal orthodoxy requires of Christians a life of gratitude in response to God's self-gift and a willingness to treat others with the loving expectation with which God treats us. Generosity in Christian action flows from our response to the nature of God, as we come more and more to know God. 'Forgive us our sins as we forgive others', 'love your enemy' – these are words ascribed to Jesus Christ, God incarnate, living our human response to the Father. In the power of the Spirit, that becomes our response too.

That is why worship is the driving force of credal orthodoxy. God, as described by the creeds, is known not in abstraction but in response. To know God is to love God. Worship, too, is not a self-referential pastime, where we give an hour or so of our time in order to feel good and then go about our business as usual; worship is to be drawn by the Spirit into the Son's response to the Father; worship is formative, making us into the body of Christ. Just as Jesus is the Son of God in all he is and does, not just in his times of prayer, so that is also the hope and prayer of all Christians: that our lives will become 'filial' in the power of the Spirit.

For the sake of living generously in the world, knowing what kind of a world it is, because of the nature of God, Father, Son and Holy Spirit, the creeds rule out other descriptions and other readings of the Bible. But within this overall framework, there is considerable latitude. The creeds tell us that God is the source of all that is, and that suggests that all of creation is valued and loved. Nothing comes into being outside the creative love and power of God's 'fatherliness'. The creeds therefore require an attentiveness to one another, particularly perhaps to the 'other', who may show us something of God that we could not discover by ourselves. The creeds require us to listen to other kinds of lives, lived in response to Scripture. The creeds tell us that God is not 'transcendent' in a way that leaves God beyond our reality, irrelevant to it. The story God tells about God's own reality is the story of Jesus Christ, a particular human being, at a particular time and place in history, fully carrying the gift of God's 'fatherliness' in created human form. The creeds tell us about ourselves, too, and how we have become alienated from God's 'fatherliness', so that we do not recognize it, or, if we recognize it in part, we hate it. We crucified the human being who carried God's fatherliness in human form. But our sinfulness does not circumscribe or define God, but is used by God to pour out God's ongoing life and never-ending love, flooding even separation and death with presence and life. Nothing that we can do can prevent the Holy Spirit from creating the 'filial', from restoring the Son's response to the Father. The creeds tell us that the Holy Spirit continues to call out the 'filial' response in created beings, in the community that tells again and again the story of God and God's willingness to give Godself in Scripture, water, bread, wine, a human community drawn around the Son. Finally, the creeds tell us that, just as all things come from God, so all things are completed in God: we are not temporary for God; there is room, in the Son, through the power of the Spirit, for creatures in the 'life of the world to come'.

The creeds assume that we know and are embedded in the Bible and the life of the Church. They make no sense on their own, but are a summary of what we live in, day by day. But they do not prescribe what that must look like; their primary interest is God. Once we commit to this description of God, the creeds suggest, we are then capable of, mandated to, live from it and shape our lives accordingly.[13]

The St Mellitus College experiment in 'generous orthodoxy' has been shaped by these intersecting credal concerns for keeping appropriate boundaries about what is said about God because, without these, generosity is an option, a choice, rather than a requisite. Within the life of the college, worship and study are two sides of the same coin: we worship the one whom we are required to attend to. God is not abstract, but particular: this God and no other. But in response to the reality of this God, we are called to worship, to invite the Spirit to draw us into God's filial response of love to God's 'fatherly' self-gift of love.

Credal generous orthodoxy defines a pathway; it does have edges, otherwise it would not be a path; but the point of a path is not its edges but its direction. Isaiah describes the pathway home to God. It is not of our making but it is for our joy:

> A highway shall be there,
>   and it shall be called the Holy Way;
> the unclean shall not travel on it,
>   but it shall be for God's people;
> no traveller, not even fools, shall go astray . . .
> And the ransomed of the Lord shall return,
>   and come to Zion with singing.
> (Isaiah 35.8–10)

---

13 Later confessions, creeds and statements of belief are more prescriptive, less trusting, coming as they do out of a divided Church. See, for example, the Westminster Confession, which clarifies, from a Reformed perspective, what must be believed about Scripture, predestination and the mixed nature of the Church: <www.epcew.org.uk/resources/westminster-confession-of-faith>.

3

The art of hope: Imagining another world in a world that breaks our hearts

JAMES K. A. SMITH

Introduction

The great English novelist Julian Barnes is something of a reluctant agnostic. He admits as much in the very first line of his 2008 memoir, *Nothing to Be Frightened of*: 'I don't believe in God,' he confesses, 'but I miss him.' His *not* believing, he tells us, is at once personal and environmental: an amalgam of his own adolescent conclusions and the cultural assumptions of a secular, post-Christian society in which unbelief is taken to be a default, especially for cultural elites.

I find Barnes's not-believing less interesting than his honesty about its absence – the almost nostalgic pining for a faith he's never had. This absence is most present, he tells us, in the face of art: 'Missing God is focused for me by missing the underlying sense of purpose and belief when confronted with religious art.'[1] Confronted by a beauty that captivates him – whether in a Bach cantata or a Bernini sculpture – Barnes is hounded by a question: 'What if it were true?'

Imagine hearing the Mozart *Requiem* in a great cathedral – or, for that matter, Poulenc's fisherman's mass in a clifftop chapel damp from salt spray – and taking the text as gospel; imagine reading Giotto's holy strip-cartoon in the chapel at Padua as non-fiction;

---

1 Julian Barnes, *Nothing to Be Frightened of* (London: Jonathan Cape, 2008), p. 53.

imagine looking on a Donatello as the actual face of the suffering Christ or the weeping Magdalene.[2]

Julian Barnes in the twenty-first century can't imagine his way back into the belief of a Leipzig parishioner in the seventeenth century. In particular, Barnes anachronistically imposes a binary imagination on those who worshipped with such art. He imagines that the Christian reflecting on Giotto's frescoes during the Mass saw them as true *instead* of beautiful. 'The Christian would, presumably, have been concerned more with truth than aesthetics,' he surmises.[3]

But in fact the Christian can't imagine this supposed dichotomy, as if the believer has to take El Greco's *Resurrection* to be true 'instead of'[4] beautiful – as if one had to choose between truth and beauty, choose between epistemology and aesthetics, choose between God and the world. What if Christianity offered the world a way to refuse such dichotomies and offered a more expansive imagination? What if Christian orthodoxy is like a hidden well of imagination that late modern culture has forgotten and left untapped?

This is the angle from which I want to take up the notion of a 'generous orthodoxy' – not just as an orthodoxy that is capacious, but as an orthodoxy that has something to *give*, something to *offer* the world. A generous orthodoxy is a *generative* orthodoxy because it draws on wells long abandoned by modernity. As we witness the exhaustion of late modern paradigms and the cracks in the secular, the resources of this neglected tradition look more and more like gifts. A generous orthodoxy is a kind of archaic avant-garde whose offerings seem fresh in a world where they've been forgotten.[5] In our secular age, the conceptual resources of Christianity might be *alien* in the best sense of the word: they are almost extraterrestrial, spooky, peculiar, haunting possibilities that feel like they've arrived from another planet. Perhaps our post-Christian societies in the West have reached a point where the peculiarity

---

2 Barnes, *Nothing to Be Frightened of*, pp. 53–4.

3 Barnes, *Nothing to Be Frightened of*, p. 54.

4 Barnes, *Nothing to Be Frightened of*, p. 72.

5 I first encountered this notion of 'avant-garde archaism' in Laurence Cars, *The Pre-Raphaelites: Romance and Realism* (London: Thames & Hudson, 2000), p. 25.

of Christian orthodoxy can be entertained as novel and received afresh as an invitation for another way to be human.

One of the ways Christian orthodoxy is generative – generous in the sense of giving us something we wouldn't otherwise have imagined – is Christianity's refusal of Barnes's dichotomy between truth and beauty, aesthetics and epistemology. One of the reasons why Christianity has generated art that haunts Julian Barnes is because the beating heart of Christian hope is the otherwise unimaginable truth of a God-man, a transpiercing of the frontier between immanence and transcendence, broken humanity and holy divinity. With the incarnate revelation of Jesus comes a revolution of the imagination: the possibility of paradoxically holding together the incommensurate.[6] If Christian orthodoxy is *generous*, that means it has something to offer, something to give: it is generative for humanity. And one of the primary gifts Christian orthodoxy has bequeathed to us, I want to argue, is a capacity for imagining possibilities for art and the imagination that, in turn, invite us to imagine other ways of being human.

I want to explore two aspects of Christianity's aesthetic heritage as an expression of the heart of Christian orthodoxy – and as an enduring gift on offer to our secular age. The first is the *incarnational* impulse of Christian faith which hallows matter as a conduit of grace and revelation, underwriting the Church's long patronage of the arts to begin with, but also in a way that affirms the goodness of finitude, sanctifying the everyday aspects of being human. The second is what I will call Christianity's *prophetic* impulse as an expression of eschatological hope – generating an art of lament that is rooted in the hope of the world being otherwise.

Sensing the invisible

If it seems that I am revisiting 'the basics' of Christianity, veering towards the elementary, that is because I think it is precisely the elemental mystery of the gospel that is both most fecund and most ignored.

---

6 I discuss this christological theme in more detail in the Introduction to *All Things Hold Together in Christ: A Conversation on Faith, Science, and Virtue*, ed. James K. A. Smith and Michael L. Gulker (Grand Rapids, MI: Baker Academic, 2018), pp. xi–xxi.

Christianity is confused with myriad positions and policies and partisan identities, all of which blur the central mystery grappled with in the Nicene Creed: that in God's grace and mercy, God became human, at once sundering and surrendering to time, but without relinquishing eternity or transcendence – that God became flesh and took on the evil we've made of the world precisely in order to overcome it, rising from the dead as a foretaste of what John Owen called 'the death of death in the death of Christ'.

It is this scandalous Nicene orthodoxy that has something to offer – not a moralized religion cut to the measure of our expectations, nor a trite set of comforting rituals that are a panacea for nostalgia, nor the vagueness of a mere 'spirituality' that provides a bit of frisson amid the doldrums of late capitalism. (Those are all forms of religion that take more than they give.) It is a *fantastic* orthodoxy that has something to give, the otherwise-unimaginable reality of a crucified God raised from the dead. To inhabit that reality is to be given the capacity to imagine the world otherwise. And that stretched imagination is what fuels the arts that haunt us and invite us, that penetrate our souls and awaken our deepest longings.

At the very heart of the Christian faith is a kind of aesthetic revolution – a new possibility for seeing and sensing the world.[7] Almost two thousand years before the revolt against representation in art, the Incarnation already challenges the binary distinction between image and prototype, original and copy, the 'picture' and 'the real thing'. When Jesus of Nazareth announces, 'Whoever has seen me has seen the Father' (John 14.9), he simultaneously declares a revolution in the economy of images. For Jesus does not merely say that he is a 'picture' of the Father, a representation of God. Jesus doesn't merely claim that we can see the Father 'in' him, as you might recognize your mother in your daughter's smile, or the way Cézanne's paintings remind you of what it feels like to be in Provence. This is not a relation of mere *resemblance*, a facsimile, a faithful reproduction. Jesus is not a divinely deputized ambassador or

---

7 This revolution is not just visual, but more broadly aesthetic, since Jesus makes similar claims about what is offered to us in bread and wine and the Word. So the Incarnation not only sanctifies sight and images; the incarnate Christ also sanctifies the register of the imagination, meeting us in parables and poetry, story and song.

emissary, a 'stand in' for the God who will never show up. No, according to a generous and generative orthodoxy, to see Jesus is to see the Father – there is a coinherence of divine and human, here of transcendence and immanence, that makes this an immediate encounter with God – while God also overflows and transcends the encounter, irreducible to the measure of my grasping.

What takes place in the incarnate Christ – the *ikon* of the invisible God (Colossians 1.15) – is what Jean-Luc Marion describes as a 'crossing of gazes'. His commentary on John 14.9 is incisive and gets to the aesthetic implications of the hypostatic union. In looking on Christ, Marion comments:

> I look, with my invisible gaze, upon a gaze that envisages me; in the icon . . . it is a matter not so much of seeing a spectacle as of seeing another gaze that sustains mine, confronts it, and eventually overwhelms it. But Christ does not offer only himself to my gaze to see and be seen; if he requires of me a love, it is a love not for him but for his Father; if he demands that I lift my eyes to him, this [is] not at all so I see him, him *only*, but so that I might see *also* and especially the Father.[8]

But if I'm seeing Christ, how can I see the Father? How could I see both? Doesn't it have to be one *or* the other? 'Does not Christ constitute only what can be seen of the Father in place of the Father?', Marion asks. No. 'On that interpretation,' he rightly points out, 'Christ would thus not show the Father but would be a substitute for him, a visible lieutenant of an invisible.'[9] But that is not what Christ claims: his mission, he tells us, is to glorify the Father, and that the person who sees the Son *has seen* the Father. What Christ announces – what Christ embodies – is an entirely different logic of the image, one that refuses the narrow, either-or logic of the image as being 'only' what is seen. Instead, what Christ embodies is a new, paradoxical possibility of the image as *icon* in which we both see and are seen, in which the Father gives himself in the Son, in which the

---

8 Jean-Luc Marion, *The Crossing of the Visible*, trans. James K. A. Smith (Stanford, CA: Stanford University Press, 2004), p. 57.

9 Marion, *The Crossing of the Visible*, p. 57.

visible is the site for an encounter with the invisible.[10] What is given to be encountered in the Son is always more yet never less. That affirmation is at the very heart of Christian orthodoxy.

We need to appreciate how this Christian imagination differs from the flattened possibilities of late modernity, where images are only that – surfaces of pixels that wash over us, that we scroll past, entertained but untouched. The society of the spectacle is, as Baudrillard put it, a society for which images are simulacra without originals – a presenting surface with nothing more, nothing beyond, and no ability to penetrate the depths of our souls. Instead, images are consumed as fuel for distraction, blips of performance, flashes that exist only for the present, without memory or future, ephemeral clusters of light without the power to illuminate. The banal materialism of modernity evacuates the material of significance and instead reduces it to a neo-Gnostic veil that is incessantly rewoven by the next post, the next pic, the next performance.

In contrast, as St John of Damascus articulated in the eighth century, the revolutionary revelation of the Incarnation was, in fact, a realization of the goodness of matter announced with creation itself (Genesis 1.31).[11] The Incarnation was that tipping point in history where there could no longer be any doubt about God's hallowing of the material because God himself became material. The sculptor became the clay. When I revere images, St John says,

> I do not worship matter; I worship the Creator of matter who became matter for my sake, who willed to take his abode in matter; who worked out my salvation through matter . . . God's body is God because it is joined to his person by a union which shall never pass away . . . Because of this I salute all remaining matter with reverence, because God has filled it with his grace and power.[12]

---

10 Marion, *The Crossing of the Visible*, p. 58.

11 See Graham Ward, 'Theological Materialism,' in *God and Reality*, ed. Colin Crowder (London: Mowbray, 1997), pp. 144–59.

12 St John of Damascus, *On the Divine Images*, trans. David Anderson (Crestwood, NY: St Vladimir's Seminary Press, 2000), I.16, p. 23.

Why has Christianity generated such enduring art? Because every painting, every poem, every fresco and film is a salute to all remaining matter that has been hallowed by the Incarnation. But more than that, underwriting Christian investment in the arts is something like this Nicene conviction that the encounter with a work of art is also about *more* than matter – that the material can be an enchanted portal to the immaterial; that an encounter with worked-over matter can activate the *soul* – can remind us we *have* souls. What is mesmerizing and haunting about a Bach cantata is the miraculous way the indentation of airwaves on membranes in our heads can transport us on to a plane of contemplation that feels just barely tethered to the earth, our souls walking a tightrope of elation and longing that feels infinite.[13]

The mystery of the Incarnation is what underwrites the mystery of sacramentality. And something like that conviction – that the grace of God is revealed to us in bread and wine and water – is also underneath the Christian investment in the aesthetic: that the grace of God can be revealed to us in sounds and words and images. The visible is not a barrier to the invisible but a portal. Song can be an antechamber to our silence before the mystery of God's mercy. The craft of speech in poetry and fiction can be stepping stones by which the Word is yet again enfleshed for us.

This, for example, is why Van Gogh continues to captivate us. Van Gogh's sacramental vision, as we might call it, is well captured in Julian Schnabel's marvellous film, *At Eternity's Gate*. As a painter himself, Schnabel treats the film screen like a moving canvas, at once transporting the audience into what it *feels* like to see as Van Gogh sees, while also demurring from trying to do what only Van Gogh's paintings can do with their meaty, almost sculptural tactility.

By dramatizing what we know from Van Gogh's letters, Schnabel gives us a fiction that is true, unveiling, revealing – which is the same impulse that infused Vincent's art. This is narrated in a stark, moving scene in which Willem Dafoe positively becomes the painter (he who has seen Willem Dafoe has seen Vincent):

---

13 For a lovely meditation on this, see Dan Barry, 'Command Performance', *Commonweal* (1 September 2019): <www.commonwealmagazine.org/command-performance>.

What I see no one else sees, and sometimes it frightens me. I think I'm losing my mind. But then I say to myself: I'll show what I see to my human brothers who can't see it. It's a privilege. I can give them hope and consolation.

Pressed as to why he devotes himself to such work, Van Gogh's answer is a matter of conviction, calling, vocation: 'Because my vision is closer to the reality of the world; I can make people feel what it's like to be alive.'

The English painter and writer Julian Bell appreciates just this point in a reflection on the recent Van Gogh exhibit at the Tate. Writing recently in the *London Review of Books*, Bell concludes:

Van Gogh has gained his unique status exactly because he combines the keenest observational practices with an evangelical cast of mind, a missionary intent to which his agonising life story bears witness. This makes him the channel through which the pieties that we associate with a past age have re-emerged and flourished. Loosed from its Christian and Romantic moorings, the thought that the created world might speak to us, as creatures in need of consolation, continues to communicate – thanks in no small part to Van Gogh.[14]

This is an extension of an incarnational conviction, a Chalcedonian imagination: that the material can be at once fully physical and yet more; that an artifact I see can also plumb the depths of the invisible, and can do so at both height and depth, slicing into the invisible corners of my own soul and the invisible heights of a cosmic Creator. Canvas, stone, string can become luminous because they can traffic in the mysterious. Such art is a liberation from the claustrophobia of our unimaginative material*ism*.

Hallowing the everyday

So the Incarnation of God in Christ generates an aesthetic imagination for which the material can be transpierced by the immaterial; matter

---

14 See <www.lrb.co.uk/v41/n15/julian-bell/at-tate-britain>.

becomes a window to God and the soul. We might think of this as the *transcendent* impulse that the Christian imagination gives to the arts, an almost transgressive sense of the possibilities at the border of the seen and unseen.

But this transcendent, even transgressive, impulse is accompanied by an attention to *immanence* that manifests as a sanctification of the ordinary, the hallowing of the everyday, an affirmation of the goodness of finitude that translates into a holy attention to our embodiment. This, perhaps, is the note of the orthodox Christian tradition that was sounded especially by the Protestant Reformation, which is why so many examples of this come to us from the lowlands where this sensibility took hold. In Dutch landscape (and seascape) painting, creation itself is worthy of contemplation. In the work of Vermeer and Rembrandt, the artist's attention illuminates the workaday world of domestic life. As when Jesus stakes the announcement of his resurrection on the testimony of women too often ignored, these painters see the labouring women who have remained invisible – milkmaids and mothers and tables laden with the fruit of the harvest and the spoils of the hunt.

In our own age of market-driven discontentment, an age of materialism in which everything that is solid melts into thin air, this Christian artistic legacy of hallowing the ordinary speaks to a hunger to find joy in the quotidian and receive the quiet delights on offer in front of us. It should remind us that Christianity is the most fulsome *humanism* because it refuses the incessant restlessness of material*ism* by actually affirming the material in a way that we might be *content*.

This life-affirming impulse generates a continuing tradition of art that hallows the everyday, which is so often invisible to us precisely because it is constantly in front of us. One could see works as diverse as Rodin's *The Burghers of Calais* or Alfonso Cuarón's twenty-first-century cinematic masterpiece, *Roma*, as extensions of this aesthetic impulse. Indeed, we see this, too, in *At Eternity's Gate*, when Schnabel takes us not to the enchanted hills drenched in Provençal light but to the intimacy of a hospital bed where Theo climbs into bed with his tormented brother and holds him in an embrace, and the long, enduring shot itself intimates a love that never ends.

Picturing hope

I want to turn to the second generative aspect of Christian orthodoxy that finds expression through the arts.

At the heart of Christian orthodoxy is a confession about time and history: that the Creator of the cosmos has irrupted *in* time and history. Just as the Incarnation, according to John of Damascus, transforms how we relate to matter, so too the mystery of the enfleshed God in Bethlehem is a recalibration of the way we inhabit time. That doesn't mean the Christian imagination is only nostalgic, a backward-looking debt to something that has happened. To the contrary, the Christian inhabits time as the fullness of *kairos*, not just the tick-tock of *chronos*. There is a timeliness of God's presence to the world that is ever ancient, ever new – the long bright shadow cast by the resurrection intersects with the light that reaches us from a kingdom that is to come. The Spirit is present to every age but never reduced to the spirit *of* the age. That Spirit is a gift of the ascension of the Son, and that same Spirit groans for the renewal of all things (Romans 8.22–23).

The proclamation that 'the Word became flesh' underwrites our daily prayer, 'Thy kingdom come'. Christian orthodoxy as articulated in the Nicene Creed is unabashedly calendrical: it is because the incarnate God 'was crucified for us *under Pontius Pilate*' and 'rose again' on 'the *third day*' that 'we look *forward* to resurrection of the dead, and to life in the world to come'. And that revelation of the world to come – the unveiling (apocalypse) – is a vision of a world brought to rights, of how things *ought* to be, of a *shalom* that is now elusive but will then be everlasting.

So what biblical scholar Richard Bauckham says about the book of Revelation might equally be true of art nourished by this Christian orientation in time:

[O]ne of the functions of Revelation was to purge and to refurbish the Christian imagination. It tackles people's imaginative response to the world, which is at least as deep and influential as their intellectual convictions. It recognizes the way a dominant culture, with its images and ideals, constructs the world for us, so that we perceive and respond to the world in its terms. Moreover, it unmasks this dominant construction of the world as an ideology of the powerful which serves to maintain their power. In its place, Revelation offers a different way of perceiving the world which leads people to resist and to challenge the effects of the dominant ideology. Moreover, since this different way of perceiving the world is fundamentally to open it to transcendence it resists any absolutizing power or structures or ideals within this world.[15]

What does the *eschatological* vision of this generous orthodoxy have to offer? What does Christianity offer to the contemporary imagination? Nothing less than the ability to name evil and hope otherwise.

The first moment is crucial. Christian hope refuses both pollyannish optimism and despairing nihilism.[16] 'Optimists', Terry Eagleton points out, 'are as bereft of hope as nihilists because they have no need of it.'[17]

Our inbuilt penchant to name evil lives off borrowed capital. A naturalistic modernism does not offer the intellectual or imaginative resources to either decry evil or generate hope. Naturalism can only aver to the ways things are, the pseudo-sovereignty of randomness and genetic predestination, which precludes the possibility of lament. All that is available to the naturalistic imagination is a description of the way things *are*, and if things just *are*, then one could never protest that something is askew, amiss, out of joint. Evil is a name we reserve for that which should not be; but, in that sense, 'evil' is not a word in the naturalist's lexicon.

In contrast, Christian orthodoxy has the intellectual and imaginative resources to say *that's not the way it's supposed to be*. Thus Christian orthodoxy can name evil as an irruption in the cosmos – one that God himself takes on and overcomes. Which is precisely why Christian orthodoxy can also imagine a world *without* evil, not by denying its

---

15 Richard Bauckham, *The Theology of the Book of Revelation* (Cambridge: Cambridge University Press, 1993), pp. 159–60.

16 As Terry Eagleton points out, 'a professional or card-carrying optimist feels sanguine about specific situations because she tends to feel sanguine in general'. Terry Eagleton, *Hope without Optimism* (Charlottesville: University of Virginia Press, 2015), p. 1. He goes on to rightly point out that, whatever their professed political standpoint, 'Optimists are conservatives because their faith in a benign future is rooted in their trust in the essential soundness of the present' (p. 4).

17 Eagleton, *Hope without Optimism*, p. 4.

existence but because we hope in its overcoming based on the first fruits of the resurrection of Christ, already a sign that death will die. That is the difference between Christian hope and naive optimism.

This, I would wager, speaks to deep-seated human hungers – the hope that the world could be otherwise, that injustices will be rectified, oppression will cease, pain never more. It is hard to imagine a gracious God speaking to a more human and humane desire than the promise at the end of the book of Revelation: that God himself 'will wipe every tear from their eyes. There will be no more death or mourning or crying or pain, for the old order of things has passed away' (Revelation 21.4, NIV). The King who sits on the throne in this kingdom still bears scars on his hands and announces: 'I am making everything new.' There is nothing more scandalous than Christian eschatology, and yet nothing speaks more directly to a hurting, fearful world.

This eschatological orientation fuels art suspended between the already and the not yet. The unique imaginative capacity of the arts speaks to this ineffaceable human hunger for restoration even while honouring the heartbreak of our present pilgrimage. A Christian eschatology nourishes a distinct imagination that refuses to be constrained by the catalogue of the currently available and instead imagines a world to come breaking into this present. Art infused with this eschatological imagination at once laments and hopes. In its lament it honours our experience of brokenness – the heartbreak of the now – and in its hope it gives voice to our longings. It neither wallows in romanticized tragedy nor escapes to sentimental naivety. Such eschatological art is like an embodied form of the Lord's Prayer; each its own Requiem, such that what Jan Swafford says of Mozart's *Requiem* would be true of such eschatological art: it is 'full of death and hope, lacerating sorrow and uncanny beauty'.[18]

Uncanniness is an apt descriptor of such art that paints beauty with ashes, that can walk the soul through the valley of the shadow of death on the way to a feast in the wilderness. Such art stops us short in its uncanny, even paradoxical, ability to embody hurt and hope. Permit me

---

18 Jan Swafford, *Language of the Spirit: An Introduction to Classical Music* (New York: Basic Books, 2017), p. 89.

to consider just a few examples from out-of-the-way works that could be multiplied.

Consider, for example, *The Tomb of Madame Langhans*, created in 1751 by German artist Johann August Nahl for the grave of a pastor's wife lost in childbirth on Holy Saturday, that day – like the long age of the saeculum – suspended between death and resurrection.[19] The grave emblazoned with skulls is a *memento mori*, a reminder of mortality, and the image of lost child and mother together is heartbreaking. But the seeds of hope are pictured for us in a different kind of rupture – not the rupture of loss but restoration as mother and child rise, breaking through the grave, climbing up to new life. We are almost teased by this possibility and it kindles in us a cry of *Maranatha*, come quickly, Lord Jesus, hasten the day when we can meet this child you've known since the womb.

Or consider a public memorial to fallen workers in front of the modernist city hall in Hamilton, Ontario, Canada's steel town. A bronze figure is clinging for his life, his fingers on the edge, shoulders muscles and sinews rippling as he tries to hold on 'for dear life', as we say. We feel the weight of this suspended, precarious body. And we feel the danger that has consumed those who've built our bridges and the skyscrapers we ascend in the safety of ensconced lifts. Confronting us here is the tactile body of those workers who plunged to their deaths, consumed in the dams and the torrents they fought back –these martyrs of 'progress'. But at just the right time of day, a very curious shadow is cast by this figure with arms outstretched. In the negative portrayal of shadow, we see a head bowed under a crown of thorns. The play of light and shadow leads us to wonder: just who is hanging here? Does that shadow suggest another who hung on a tree, mocked with a crown of thorns? Is that the same one who made a mockery of death by rising from the dead? Is that the shadow of hope cast over these lost workers, too?

It is not only death we hope will cease; it is all the death-dealing ways we treat one another, the systems of oppression and painful exclusion that are their own perverted forms of human imagining. Eschatological art laments; it rages against the injustices of might. It is no accident that

---

19 A porcelain reproduction can be seen at the Getty Center in Los Angeles. A print of the work is housed at the British Museum: <www.britishmuseum.org/collection/object/P_1958-0712-2123>.

the Bible's most evocative laments appear in the poetic books – Psalms and Lamentations. Lament is its own slant of light.

Consider, for example, the work called *Sugar and Spice*, part of Letitia Huckaby's 'Suffrage Project'.[20] The print of a young African-American girl looks despondent, her protest sign, 'Enough!', resting on her shoulder its own version of 'How long, O Lord?' The print appears on a vintage cotton-picking sack, and once you realize that, an entire history of oppression and marginalization creeps up from your gut, up your spine, into your heart, halting at a lump in your throat. You don't need it to reach your mind; you now 'know' something you didn't know before. And yet her gentle pastel pink skirt evokes a ballerina's tutu, and the image births in us a longing to see this young girl dance, to see her despondency turn to joy, to trade the now-necessary sign of protest for a banner of praise.

Prophetic art that inhabits this tension of lament and hope does not only communicate a 'message', it enacts what it embodies, it *performs* this turning of mourning into dancing. Lament without hope is merely anger; hope without lament is a lie about the present. Art that is prophetic, that both laments *and* hopes, will be a unique offering to a heartbroken world that has forgotten to sing such songs.

Conclusion

Let me return to Julian Barnes. A little later in his memoir, he makes the mistake of trusting Montaigne's take on Christianity – the mistaken (but common) notion that 'religion's surest foundation is the contempt for life'. Barnes adds his own affirming gloss: 'To have a low opinion of this rented world was logical, indeed essential, for a Christian.'[21] He thus looks to Sir Thomas Browne, 'Montaigne's nearest British equivalent', who imagines that the Christian who laments death is a kind of failure, someone who hasn't sufficiently embraced this 'logical, indeed essential' contempt for life. Such a person would be 'too sensible of this life, or

20 You can see this work in Lawan Glassock's feature essay, 'Living Fabric: Letitia Huckaby Talks to History', *Image* 101 (2019), pp. 34–45, also available at <https://imagejournal.org/article/living-fabric-letitia-huckaby-talks-to-history/>.

21 Barnes, *Nothing to Be Frightened Of*, p. 60.

hopeless of the life to come' – a little too attached to the earth and insufficiently hoping to escape it.

It seems odd to paint such a posture towards pain and death as a Christian failure when it is precisely the agonized posture of Jesus Christ in the garden of Gethsemane, and the canonized longing of Paul for victory over death (1 Corinthians 15.50–57). The common misperception of Montaigne, Browne and Barnes mistakenly assumes that Christianity is a longing to escape, whereas the resurrection is a promise of restoration. Christian hope passes *through* Holy Saturday, and Easter is the proclamation of all things made new, not of a world gladly left behind. There is a both/and-ness to the Christian imagination, and it is just that both/and-ness which infuses art that speaks to human hungers and hopes.

Indeed, it is no accident that God also speaks artfully to us. The poetry of the psalms is a poetry of honesty and hope, a poetry whose artifice and craft we too easily take for granted. Consider, just as one example, this evocative play of darkness and light from Psalm 139:

If I say, 'Surely the darkness shall cover me,
    and the light around me become night,'
even the darkness is not dark to you;
    the night is as bright as the day,
    for darkness is as light to you.

A darkness that could be light is as paradoxical as a man who is God. That both are true is the heart of the Christian imagination, and that alone yields a hope we can offer the world.

4

Christ's mystery

KATHERINE SONDEREGGER

Professor Hans Frei used to say that a faith without orthodoxy was no good for theology; but an orthodoxy without generosity was simply no good at all. I think he is right on both counts, and I hope to pay tribute to the towering shadow cast by Professor Frei upon modern dogmatics by joining together an investigation of the Person of Christ with the complex notion and web of connotation of 'nature.'

Students of Frei will know that in his maturity, Frei wrote a brief Christology for a church publication – even in a more demanding world, this essay was a steep climb for any journal reader – and this remarkable essay was later republished in book form under the title *The Identity of Jesus Christ*. In this essay, Frei combines some complex reflections on personal presence with the idea, familiar to readers of the realistic novel, that the identity of a character is known, and made one, with the events of that character's life. Who a person is is what a person does and suffers: it is, in Frei's words, an 'enacted fit between character and act'. Now, there is much to say about a Christology built along these lines, and I would recommend another contributor to this book, Professor David Ford, for a thorough and insightful examination of this remarkable student of nineteenth- and twentieth-century Protestant dogmatics. But here I will say that it is clear, to my eyes at least, that Frei is making conceptually plain a governing motif in Karl Barth's late work: that the Person of Jesus Christ is *history*, a temporal unfolding in our world of the judging and reconciling work of God. A history of this kind entails the doing and suffering of a life; for Jesus Christ it entailed the relentless movement to the cross. Barth did not shy away from the old conviction, that Jesus Christ came to die, and I will try to defend that idea in my own suggestions for a generous Christology today. But there is a deeper element in Barth's and Frei's Christology that I want to resist: both of them, I believe, feel greater perplexity over the concepts and terms used at Chalcedon than I think necessary or advisable. For these two theological giants, Chalcedon told the truth, but told it slant, to borrow a phrase from the American poet Emily Dickinson. The armature of 'nature' and 'union' and 'substance' needed to be broken open, they said, a breakthrough that would allow the radically fresh winds of history and of event to blow through the whole sacral edifice. Barth compared this fresh movement of the historical to a mighty glacier, once jammed and frozen into massive, inert blocks, suddenly cascading down through a mountain pass, flowing freely, entering the living force of time and current and things taking place.

In this, students of modern theology will know, neither Barth nor Frei innovated. Throughout the nineteenth century we find clarion calls to reinterpret or re-categorize the elements of the Chalcedonian Symbol. Anglican Divines such as Charles Gore and C. E. Raven searched for conceptual tools that belonged, they argued, to the world of persons and of values, not of objects or of things. In German academic theology, post-Kantians such as Wilhelm Herrmann or Rudolf Bultmann sought to anchor the reality of the Incarnation in the mystical presence to the believer of the Son of God, whose Person could not be captured or constrained by empirical tests and modes of thought. In this broad movement of modern Christology we glimpse the underlying axiom that the Person of Jesus Christ though, to be sure, both divine and human, will resist and break through the boundaries of ancient thought, laid down by the bishops at Chalcedon centuries ago. Not 'nature' or 'relation' or 'substance', then, but *event, act, history, narrative*: these are the proper idiom for a Love come down to us at Christmas.

Now I embrace this *instinct* in theology – not everything old must be preserved simply in virtue of its antiquity – but I would like to visit afresh the lingering suspicion that the thought-forms of the ancient world cannot properly express or contain a Christology for our day. I will propose here that the concepts of 'nature', 'substance' and 'relation' or 'Personal Union' are more than ample for a Christology that belongs to our time (and, further, that 'sacrifice', one of the most ancient of ancient thought-forms, can advance our thinking, this today, on the Holy One who came to suffer and to save). The idiom of Chalcedon, joined to the universe of sacrifice: that is my offering for a generous Christology for the present time.

Let me begin, then, with the idiom of Chalcedon. You remember this drill: we are to think on One Person, the Same Son, Lord, Only-Begotten, appearing now in our time and for our sake in two natures, complete in deity, complete in humanity; neither nature mixed nor confused with the other, nor do they stand separated or divided, one against the other. This One Person of the Son we are are to believe on is the Eternally Begotten of the Father, who in our age, became the One born of the God-bearer, Mary Theotokos: the One Christ, the whole Christ, at all earthly times, God and human, the God-man. Now, it may seem to you, and it has to many interpreters of this Chalcedonian definition, that in truth *no one* could think this thing. The claim has been made throughout the modern era that this Symbol does not in fact hold up before us a *concept* or *schema* whereby we think the thought of the Son of God. On the contrary! For these readers of Chalcedon, the Definition is an entirely, or near entirely, negative proposition: this Symbol tells us what not to think, what not to endorse; but leaves entirely unsaid what should be thought and taught and understood. To this end, the Greek alpha privatives are summoned to our attention: not confused, not mixed; not separated, not divided, all expressed in the Greek text by negative or alpha-privative adverbs. We are told to believe in the One Christ, but not, it is thought, just what that term, Person, means. Nor does it appear that we are given much help in understanding how two natures can exist in that One Person, however defined, when governed by these adverbial relations. We know that the whole Christ is born of Mary, and that the term noxious to Nestorius, *Theotokos*, is explicitly endorsed, as if to make the teeth of some Antiochenes set on edge in the very recitation of the Symbol. But just how God is born, and how we are to understand an eternal Person, conceived in and born of a human, virginal mother – that is left sovereignly unexplained, perhaps loftily dismissed altogether. From such reflections is built the modern conviction that Chalcedon does not define or supply concrete teaching and positive doctrine but rather excludes, pares away, prohibits and denies, and in just this way opens out an expansive conceptual space where Christology is to be forged.

Now, there is much truth in this literary or second-order reading of the Chalcedonian text. It does indeed appear to be a 'grammatical rule', to borrow a postliberal phrase, and to show us just how to properly ascribe various states or properties to the one, living Jesus Christ. And, were I to believe that the ancient concepts made use of in this Definition were implausible or inconceivable in our era, I would hope the second-order ruled language would be the most cogent account of this ecumenical creed. Indeed, it may well be that the postliberal impulse towards this Wittgensteinian gesture – grammar and rules, not description and definition – rests upon the earlier conviction in Barth and the nineteenth-century Kenoticists that hellenistic metaphysical terms cannot properly capture the pulsing, saving, earthy and heavenly life of the incarnate Word. Perhaps historically it works like this: a theologian comes to be restive about the metaphysics of ancient Greece and Rome (dry as dust, William James cries!); then she finds these Attic notions too substantialist, too reified for living flesh (Jesus Christ is not a 'thing'); then she becomes convinced that a new way must be forged; and perhaps the negative terms at the heart of the Definition suddenly spring into prominence. Not kataphatic but apophatic teaching can be found there, and the structure of the Definition as a whole will be found to be like 'ruled language', the grammar of faith. Historians of doctrine would know better than I if this is a defensible or plausible trajectory through the material, but it strikes me as a natural way to put together this pronounced hesitancy about the terms and concepts of the Chalcedonian Creed in our modern era.

I would like to propose, perhaps *contra mundum*, that the Chalcedonian Definition, as it stands, is simply good, sturdy, positive teaching; and that its categories are splendidly suited for the task at hand. I am taking up, that is, the 'orthodoxy' side of the happy marriage, generous orthodoxy. It is entirely apposite and plausible, I say, that the Symbol uses the ancient metaphysical terms for objects: natures, relations, substance and properties. That is not because the Attic terms are much to be preferred over modern quantum concepts – though I think a good argument could be made for this preference – but rather because the relation of the incarnate Word to the world is more perfectly expressed through these substantialist terms. Our Lord Christ does not come into this realm an alien, an outsider to our sort and kind. This cannot be said strongly enough. The modern taste for Christ as a *Typus* of the stranger, the outsider and the alien, has slowly seeped back into our Chalcedonian Definition itself. We are prone, in our alienated age, to imagine – perhaps without articulating it plainly – that the incarnate Word is a kind of sacred space voyageur, who must visit a world where he cannot possibly belong. In his incarnate life, he travels through this world as the Great Incognito, the Hidden King and Invading Warrior who will remain always outside, not within the earth he visits in his brief sojourn among us. We might think of this Christology as one built upon the very idea of 'double consciousness', as W. E. B. Du Bois would have it, or of the inner émigré, as historians of interwar-years Germany would express it. In this view, Christ is Lord just because he does not come from here; his kingdom is not from here. This desire to assimilate Jesus Christ to the alienated stranger of much modernist fiction pays tribute, certainly, to the power of Jesus Christ to draw all figures, all concepts, and all flesh to himself. But it does not properly convey or rest upon the full, metaphysical relation of the eternal Word to his cosmos.

Neither does Jesus Christ come simply as human flesh, a divine-human creature, alongside many other human creatures; though he does this, too. This also must be strongly underscored. It is perhaps the obverse, or dialectical pole, of the first worry – the alien Christ – to imagine the incarnate Lord as simply a historical, human life in the midst of his fellows and nation. In this inverted sense, we might say that, in this view, the One Christ belongs *too* fully to his age, blends too neatly in with his historical conditions and constraints, and takes his seat in the human house too comfortably and unremarkably. The proper setting for the eternal Word, now flesh, is not simply humankind! This is far too small an arena for the incarnate Son to inhabit. The rise of higher critical studies of the *Lebens Jesu*, though themselves of great historical value and insight, have tempted theologians to consider the proper stage on which the Lord Christ appears to be only that of the peopled, the human-built and the humane social realm. But this is to confine the incarnate One to only one element of his majestic life. The eternal Word, now flesh, is the

Wisdom of God through which all things are made. He, this very One, come to birth in Mary, is the Architect, the Truth and Logic of the cosmic spheres; he is the very *Ratio* and *Verbum* of everything that is. It is just this insight that prompted Athanasius to affirm that the One Son, while walking this earth, remained heavenly Lord and Ruler of the spheres. In my view, the *extra Calvinisticum*, so called from Calvin's support of this ancient teaching and its detraction by Lutheran scoffers, is vital to a generous Christology today. The One Christ is at home in his universe, not simply as a creature, enfolded within its historical becoming, but rather as its Architect and Lord. The proper measure for the christological environment, I would say, is the realm of the real, *reality itself*, for he, as eternal Son, just is the *Ens Realissimus*.

When Chalcedon uses substantial categories to describe the Word incarnate, then, it does not make a category mistake. It does not overlook, in a blind or naive fashion, the obvious historical and tactile, earth-bound and temporal nature of the life of Jesus Christ. Rather Chalcedon teaches us to assert that this very One, the Same Son, Lord and Only-Begotten, is the grounding Logic of the whole creation. Not simply humankind, as vast and complex as is our species, but rather the entire cosmos is made through the eternal Son, now enfleshed. The broadest possible metaphysical terms should be harnessed to speak of this Son, because everything that is, from the heights to the depths, is anchored and nourished and judged and guided by him. To use idiom of substance, of nature and of property for him is to hallow this use for natural objects, to elevate and consecrate our talk of everyday things. They shadow him, and he is Saviour to them all. When our Lord tells his critics that if his disciples remained silent, the very stones would cry out, he quietly announces his lordship over and his membership within this whole cosmos, animate and inanimate. He belongs here. He comes to his own. The most perfectly general terms of human thought – the logical, the metaphysical, the speculative – convey this fundamental truth: that the Person of Jesus Christ partakes of all that is, just because he is Architect of all. That is the first defence I would make of the positive and ancient categories of this ecumenical Definition.

The second is this: Chalcedon places the emphasis just where it must be, on the proper relation between the deity and humanity in the One

Lord, Jesus Christ. Here the language of 'natures' comes into its own. Our ancestors in the faith were not unaware that 'nature' can bear many senses and connotations. It is not a discovery of today that 'nature' and the 'natural' are complex, loaded and many-sided terms. Thomas Aquinas himself in the Tertium Pars of the *Summa* notes that nature can refer to birth (nativity) to kind or sort (what is natural to a thing) and, to his favourite, a 'principle of operation', and that he borrows from the philosopher Aristotle. Reflection upon the complex range of referent for the term nature, *phusis* in Greek, began with the Presocratics and shows through contrastive terms how supple this ancient notion was. Nature might be contrasted with artifact or *technē*, as in Aristotle; or it might be understood over against metaphysics, again in Aristotle's corpus; nature might just mean a thing or everything, *Natura* in Latin, or as a rough synonym for *ousia*, substance in Greek. Or it might be seen as that which needs no external law, *nomos*, or conventional agreement, as do the social structures of human cities and peoples. Nature could be understood as an inherent pattern or characteristic: what is fitting or expected in a living or organic thing. Or, in its most ancient usage, nature could simply mean 'growth' – the deepest taproot of Thomas's notion of nature as nativity, being born and undergoing change. All this complexity is brought to bear on the term *phusis*, nature, as it appears in our Chalcedonian Creed. So we may well ask: in just what sense does our Lord have a 'nature', indeed two 'natures', in his one, unique Person?

To begin, let me ask one question from this welter of connotation, which touches on some of the most technical, the most beautiful and the most innovative elements in all Christology: is the human nature of Christ a 'thing' at all? One can easily spot how such a question emerges from that earlier survey. If nature can refer to or denote a thing, or perhaps just all things, is the human nature of Christ one such, a thing in the world of things, an object among other objects in the creaturely realm? And if so, does that 'natural thing' become a 'part' of the One Person of the incarnate Son? Are we to think of Jesus Christ as a sort of 'composite' – many philosophical theologians are heading down this road – where the Person of the enfleshed Word is composed of two natures and, perhaps for many, two things. You can see the attraction of such a view: Christ seems, on this rendering, to have a divine part, a divine nature, and a human part, a human nature, and these exist in a relation of composition or constitution in the one reality, Jesus Christ. It's a kind of natural, additive idea. Just as we are built up, in a kind of addition of parts – arms and legs, internal organs and hair follicles, blood coursing through our veins, eyes that gaze out at the world – and all of these seem to compose our person, *mutatis mutandis* we might consider the One Lord, Jesus Christ, to be added up from Divine and human natures, all joined in that elixir we call a living being.

There is much in the tradition in the Latin Church that supports a view like this. Readers of Athanasius will remember how boldly that ancient controversialist used the notion of the Word's 'body' as 'instrument' – a kind of part wielded for our benefit and instruction. Thomas himself, no slouch when reading the tradition, finds a distinct place for what he terms an 'instrumental cause' in the relation of the eternal Son to his ensouled flesh. Modern philosophical theologians might push this analogy of part and whole even further. We might even be tempted, under their influence, to treat the reality of Jesus Christ as a 'mereological sum', as some philosophers put a certain metaphysical account of parts. A mereological sum is simply an object fashioned from its parts, and these might be entirely incongruous: a chair in this room, my arm, and the light post outside – these could be stitched together in a composite, a sum, that makes an object, though to be sure an odd one, with some very odd properties and conditions for persistence or identity. Those of you who have spent time in this philosopher's studies will recognize immediately why such a view attracts theologians of Christology. For does it not allow the radical dissimilarity of the divine and human 'parts' or 'natures' to be joined in one Personal Sum? The Creator–creature distinction seems wonderfully preserved in such an account, and it makes the notion of 'thing' or 'part' even more attractive than was first imagined.

And again, we should not underestimate how urgent is the need to preserve a radical and sharp distinction between Creator and creature. Everywhere in present-day theology are the signs of a collapse of this once untouchable divide. (Here again I am offering a defence of the 'orthodox' side of my remit.) The ancient categories of simplicity, of eternality, of immutability and perfection all subserved a conviction that God could not be identified with anything in the cosmos, however refined and ideal, and surpassed our proper and comprehensive knowledge just because God was his own reality, his own Transcendent Being and Unnameable Glory. Of course as this made the Incarnation all the more mysterious and beyond thought, Christology became the overwhelming battle ground of the early Church. Indeed, as you can see from my strong affirmation of Christ as 'at home' in the world he has built, the careful preservation of a distinction between Christ's deity, as Divine Wisdom, and his humanity, as creaturely nature, is all the more important and delicate to secure. I want to encourage us to see how these classical categories of thought safeguarded a vital terrain for Christian theology: God is not a creature, not even a creature as refined and ideal as extension or temporal sequence, and cannot be properly conveyed through the mechanics of our own inwardness. Whatever we may say about scriptural predicates, or the inwardness of the Divine Aseity, God cannot be passion or empathy or solidarity or vengeance as we know them: he is not a transcendent human-scale person. I will leave to one side the enormous armature of analogy here, as that too must enter into a fully developed Christology, the backdrop to our theme. The desire to import into the Godhead the elements of human inwardness and act, and to do so as a christological imperative, is one of the chief corrosions of the God–world distinction. Beginning a doctrine of God with the incarnate Son, and knowing only him and only him crucified, has dominated modern accounts of the nature and being of God, such that the doctrine of God has become an outworking and expression of Christology, rather than, as was the ancient custom, Christology the dependent of theology, the doctrine of God. My plea here is to return to this ancient reversal: let us begin with a proper doctrine of God, his aseity and triunity, and incorporate within it, and unfold from it, a living and vital Christology, a Christology, if you will have it, from above.

Now, as I said above, the mereological approach to Christology appeared to offer this one great prize: that the radical and sharp distinction between Creator and creature can be properly endorsed and defended. And this is a very great prize indeed! But I want to warn you that dangers also come along in its wake. For, with Chalcedon as our guide, we are now thinking of Jesus Christ as assuming or becoming a full human nature, body and soul, all the while remaining God. This is a very odd use of the word 'part', as it seems to refer to one of the ordinary and most common examples of a 'thing' or 'substance' in the ancient lexicon, a complete human being. Does the incarnate Lord have such as one of his parts: a human being, or perhaps a human nature of body and soul? Students of the tradition will recognize that we are stealing up upon an area that has been given the scare term Nestorianism, and in the more technical side of Thomist Christology, the worrisome *esse secundarium*. If 'nature' is a 'thing', is it just this, a secondary essence or being, that the Son of God assumes or incorporates?

Of course, on the one hand, we seem on scriptural grounds to be firmly nailed down to an account of Jesus Christ that is a human life, a human person, a man and son of Israel. Jesus is recognizable as a human being: his language and act, his hunger and thirst and grief, so prominent in the writings of the Church Fathers, his response to human family and culture, his obedience to or disregard of religious convention – all these are distinctly human and can be seen immediately in the Gospels handed down to us. When in the transcendent stillness that settles down on a once-raging Galilean sea, the disciples cry out, 'What sort of man is this that stills the wind and seas?' we know exactly what they mean.

This is a man of Nazareth and Capernaum, whose mother and sisters we know, who learned carpentry from Joseph, a righteous and devout man, and who learned piety and obedience from his parents at a tender age. The cry wrung from the disciples' lips is not 'How can God still this storm?', but rather, 'How can this man, the one we follow, do this mighty work?' 'What manner of man is he?', to speak in an older and very apt idiom. This Person is the One we recognize from the gospel portraits. It is perhaps along these lines of reflection that Leo the Great, in his Tome, found himself reaching for the otherwise troubling notion of 'natures acting, each in their own way'. He seems to be thinking, in an ordinary and rather commonsensical way, that God acts as he does, and the human Jesus, in turn, acts as he does. Of course, such plain speaking caused many in the East to worry about Leo's Tome – but perhaps from our great distance we might see a deep and familiar instinct at work here: Jesus is a man we know, and his works we record; we know, to borrow a modern phrase, 'what it is like' to be a person such as this. Notice here that I do not think we need to rush headlong into the great mystery of Christ's

Passion to test our instincts about the humanity of the eternal Son. No, the full fleshiness of Jesus Christ is impressed upon us from every page of Holy Writ, and the rounded, human-scale dimension of Christ's life just is the narrative that moves from Bethlehem to Jerusalem. Remarkable moral leaders such as Gandhi are not wrong, we think, to find in Jesus a great-souled man, a teacher in a thousand. Nor in a different register should we overlook the appropriateness of some early second-wave feminists who asked, 'Can a male saviour save women?' Both reactions, in their approval and disapproval, rely upon this common-sense reading of the gospel narrative: this is a human individual, a man among his kind.

Now, because this seems so right to us, it appears to follow that the human nature of Jesus Christ just is a 'thing', a substance or an existent – an *esse* – and that the One Person of the incarnate Word must have two such, a divine and human being. We might even say, as do some defenders of the *esse secundarium*, that it is only in virtue of this secondary existent that we are right to say, 'Behold the Man'. The question for seekers after the Christian way appears to be this: does this mortal individual also have a divine nature, a divine substance? For those who favour a Christology from below – from the earthly path of the Son of Man – it seems that Jesus must be, simply speaking, a human individual, a man from Galilee, who went in and out among us, doing good; and that by gazing upon him and following his ways we see God.

I do not for a moment wish to undermine or jeopardize in any fashion the full historicity of Jesus Christ! But I do think that 'nature', when it applies to the One Christ, cannot mean this; cannot denote an existent, or individual, or instance of the human species. 'Nature', as used in the Chalcedonian Definition cannot mean, 'thing'; just that. For the Word becomes flesh, not a man; or in our modern versions of the Nicene Symbol, the eternal Son becomes fully human. Something much more mysterious is at work in our faith than a human being who happens also to be God; though to be sure, that is mysterious enough. The great mystery of our faith is that the eternal Son of the Most High God became flesh; he was made sinews and flesh and inwardness of the human kind, all the while remaining the beloved Son. God lives a human life; he becomes man; he does not become a man, a human life. Just this is what makes the word 'nature' so powerful, so rich and apposite, in the Church's Christology. The mind and soul of the Son of Man are the human elements or characteristics of the Son of God. The flesh of Christ is the flesh of the Word: that is the central conviction I seek to express here.

I think Thomas is right to twin 'nature' with nativity, with growth, and even, with some reservations, to 'essence or quiddity of a thing'. And I do think that 'property', though very handy in philosophical circles, does not quite carry the proper gravity and reality that the Johannine flesh-making should convey. What we seek here is a sense of the term 'nature' that carries with it the characteristics, identities, patterns, habits and realities that are exemplified by members of a kind. Each of them is 'of that kind', and betrays their membership in the way of life, and sinewy constituents, that mark out this sort in our world.

The eternal Son of God has assumed to his very own this pattern of creaturely being: he has become enfleshed. You can see that I am reaching in my own way for a modification of that favourite connotation of 'nature' which Thomas discusses in the Second Question of the Third Part of the *Summa*: 'nature as principle of motion'. The eternal Son has what I would call a 'mode of being', a human way of life, from Mary, the true Mother of all the living. In the end, what must strike you, as it does me, is that this word 'nature', as it is used in the Chalcedonian Definition, cannot be fully defined in an ordinary way. 'Nature', as it applies to the Son of God in his human life, cannot function or be aligned fully with the way we use this term among mortals and organic life. It must be stretched, elevated, hallowed and consecrated for use in this high calling. The fleshiness of the eternal Word is a full human nature; we know that from Chalcedon. What we cannot know, in any exhaustive fashion, is what that nature entails and expresses when it is predicated of the Son of God. Just this, we might think, is what we mean when we say we use theological terms analogously.

Central to this Christology I am proposing, then, is that the humanity of Jesus Christ finds its identity and definition in the Person of the divine Son. The 'hypostatic reality' of the human nature, to use the older, credal language, is found in the hypostatis, the Person of the Second Person of the Trinity, not in an individuality of a human being. The individuality of Jesus Christ, if I may put it so, is his deity, the Word in its turning toward human matter, our dust and kind. This is a fully Cyrillian Christology, looking upon the eternal Son as the true acting subject of the human nature, dwelling among us, full of grace and truth. Just this, I think, is the force of Cyril's manifold and sometimes shifting reference to a personal or hypostatic or real or even natural union, the intimate union of Deity with human soul and body. God in the Person of Son now has this 'mode of operation', this 'way of life': he the Son nows lives a fully human life.

It is this 'modal reality' of the enfleshed Son that makes Jesus Christ so impervious to our control, so stately and so humble, so commanding and so deeply attractive. He is Lord in just this rich and sovereign sense. I think this is why we cannot seem to prise out of the Gospel accounts an ordinary and recognizable human individual. In an odd way, Jesus Christ seems to slip out of our grasp just when we imagine we should be able to seize him. I think it is most difficult to say just 'what kind of a person he is', what his likes and preferences might be, his most prominent personality traits, his sense of humour. I do not think we could ever describe him, in shorthand or in personality type, as we do our friends, when we characterize and sum them up for a new member of our circle. It is not simply because the Gospels are the kind of texts they are; though to be sure they mirror faithfully the transcendent mystery of their subject. And it is not in the end because we have four Gospels rather than a single canonical portrait. No, I think rather we have these four, and they exhibit the particular form they do, just because the human nature we are shown in this complex, folded and angular narrative is the human way of life of the Son of God. We are watching God living humanly; and that exceeds all telling.

I think too this Cyrillian-style Christology might go some way to explain why the One Jesus Christ seems at once particular and universal, belonging in some way to a distinct place and kind, yet bursting forth from that sacred nation to all corners of the earth, inhabiting every tongue and nation, claiming all humankind, indeed all creation, for his very own. In his own historicity, his own native tongue and people and place on earth, Jesus Christ is also the Lord of all, the Everyman, the true cosmopolitan and world citizen. We properly assign these lofty titles to the risen and ascended Lord; but we do that because they belong first to the mysterious mode of the eternal Son, his personal self-expression as human living. It is real flesh and blood, real becoming, real death – but all that as enfleshed Word, the Divine Sophia leading and inhabiting and giving reality to a human way of life. It may well be that the Jesus who stares out at us from the pages of Holy Scripture cannot be fully recognized – categorized or contained or known, even as a first-century Judean Son of the Commandment. He walks through our earth at his own sovereign angle, and as he turns his face like flint towards Jerusalem, all of us, his disciples, are terrified. Karl Barth aimed to capture just this in his telling phrase, Jesus Christ as Lord; and what I believe Cyril intended in his very firm insistence that the whole human nature of Christ inheres in and receives definition, personhood, in the royal Person of the eternal Son. What I would say, in my own more modern idiom, is that when the Word of God took human flesh, he instantiates a very odd human life – that is, a sinless, holy and perfect one. It would be his life, his flesh; and we have only the poor terms of nature and relation and person and substance to capture such a revolutionary truth.

A generous Christology takes up the language of Chalcedon, most especially the language of nature, and places it in in our empty, uplifted hands, to praise this beloved Son, the very Impress and Character of the Father of Lights, become flesh, in these last days, for our sake and our salvation. It is a small gesture, but I hope one that honours everything generous and everything orthodox; a very happy marriage indeed, a banquet to which all flesh is invited and in which it will receive its richest blessing.

5

By the word worked: How a speaking God tells us who he is

FLEMING RUTLEDGE

If the eternal Word of God is what Christian doctrine – Christian orthodoxy, if you will – says it is, it is the Word of God demanding our allegiance in season and out of season, a Word from everlasting but also a Word on target. I therefore make no apology for beginning by bringing you the news – as if you didn't know – that the USA is in crisis, and for Christians this is a time to speak. On my side of the pond, when the Word in the Person of Jesus Christ becomes captive to a tribal political agenda that marginalizes and even demonizes one's fellow human beings, it is a time to speak.

It is perplexing to me that there has been so little effective resistance, from the churches in particular. Of course one might say that the American churches are in crisis too. As is well known, membership has plummeted in the traditional Protestant denominations. At the same time, in the USA, we see that many 'evangelical' megachurches of varying theological persuasions, often with little relationship to any historically recognizable Christian doctrine, are thriving, and these two American church factions – the 'mainlines' and the 'Christian Right' – have almost no conversation or even contact with one another. I and many others have agonized about this. It does not seem sufficient simply to say (as many do), 'Just preach the gospel', when there is so little agreement about what the gospel actually is.

It is on that particular front that I have worked all my life. It is extraordinary that Christians in America who have declared for decades that they don't think politics has any place in the Church are the very ones who have become conspicuously hyper-partisan in recent times. If I have any cause to be proud of my work, it is that I have staked my turf on the fault line between so-called 'liberals' and 'conservatives'. At all points of the spectrum the very nature of the gospel is at stake, as indeed it always has been. The Epistles of Paul document that fact, in detail, from the very earliest days of the Church. Rereading Galatians and the Corinthian correspondence reminds one of that fact in no uncertain terms.

With what weapons, figuratively speaking, does the Church wage her battles against lies? Paul said to the Galatians, 'If anyone preaches to you a gospel other than what you received [from himself], let that one be anathema' (Galatians 1.9, author's translation). This overheated language does not go down well in our tender-minded times. But it bears remembering that the Word of God is a two-edged sword. The one who wields it does well to remember that it cuts in both directions.

Now I propose to talk about the very nature of the gospel as we find it in the christological doctrine of the Word of God. I am not an academic theologian, or indeed an academic at all, and I don't pretend that this will be an academic chapter. It will be more like a Bible study combined with a sermon. I don't know how many of my readers are preachers, but I presume that most of you listen to preaching, and that means that you have high stakes in what the Church preaches.

The destiny of the transformed Saul of Tarsus, the 'Hebrew of the Hebrews', was to proclaim the gospel to those who would come to know Christ through his apostolic preaching. It would be a good thing for the Church if we could recover that word 'apostolic' to define ourselves. The word 'apostolic' does not refer primarily to the consecration of bishops. It refers most of all to the apostolic *preaching*. 'To know Christ and to make him known' has surely been the goal of that preaching. Yet it is worthy of special note that Paul, the apostle to the Gentiles, was like us, in that he never met Jesus in person during his human lifetime. And yet he knew him.

He knew his Lord, his *Kurios*. To those who heard Paul's preaching, the apostle said, you are meeting 'not I, but Christ in me'. It is the will of God that his Son should be transmitted person to person. Jesus himself, at the climax of the Fourth Gospel, says to you and to me, 'Blessed are those who have not seen but yet believe.' This is the Lord's own stamp of approval upon the apostolic witness, for this Gospel is not at second hand. It begins with the definitive declaration that Jesus himself is the living, incarnate Word of God, present at all times and in all places to those who confess him as Lord.

This should give preachers a courage and a confidence that they often do not seem to have. I've always cherished a story told by Donald Coggan, who was Archbishop of Canterbury in the 1970s. He was a man of towering faith and holiness who has been, I think, much underrated. He made a powerful impression on me as a young ordinand when he visited the USA. He cared deeply about preaching. He told a story about one of his episcopal visitations. The church had been newly renovated with an altar in the round, and the vicar was very proud of it. When His Grace entered the church, he saw that there was no pulpit. He enquired about this, and the vicar said, 'Oh, that's all right, we'll bring you something when the time comes.' When the time came, Dr Coggan said, with undisguised disgust, 'He brought out this miserable little *stahnd* from which to proclaim the everlasting gospel!' My educated guess is that this vicar did not know what the everlasting gospel was.

Decades later, in the late 1990s, I was visiting in Edinburgh on a Sunday morning. I decided to go on foot to the High Kirk (St Giles), for the pleasure of a long walk in one of my favourite cities. On the way, I passed a small, unpretentious church. There was a little sign out front with three words printed on it: 'Jesus is alive.' I forgot St Giles and turned into the little church. I was not disappointed. The preacher was elderly (probably about the same age I am now!) and somewhat enfeebled in his delivery, but he bore something precious. He knew the Lord. It was very obvious. He knew him as a living and life-giving presence. He knew him, and he conveyed his presence in his preaching. Long ago I learned that once in a while I would meet someone who obviously knew the Lord. Unfortunately, that's not true of everyone in church leadership. And I think that if people don't know the living Lord, then the clergy and lay people who preach and teach the Christian faith, however sincere and well meaning they may be, are falling short.

This is what I'd like to try to convey. All too many sermons set forth Jesus as a peerless teacher and lover of humanity who was admirable and worthy of following but is also – not to put too fine a point on it – *dead*. The well-known American preacher Will Willimon is fond of saying that the Jesus Seminar and its acolytes always operated on the premise that Jesus is dead. I'm afraid that this has widely taken hold in the churches. I do not often hear sermons in which Jesus is alive. There are many sophisticated people who seem to think that Jesus as we have him in Scripture is largely a literary creation. I'm a devoted Sherlock Holmes fan and I have made my trek to Baker Street to see where he supposedly lived. You can go to Norway and take a Kristin Lavransdatter tour to all the places that this fictional character inhabited. Sometimes I get the feeling that for many people, the Jesus of the New Testament is like that – a beloved literary figure who has such a hold on some people's imagination that he *seems* alive.

Other preachers and interpreters in the Church preach Jesus as a moral exemplar. The Queen sometimes does this. I thank God for her as a witness to Jesus – she is obviously a woman of faith (Lord Coggan told me that 50 years ago), and in view of her difficult position she can hardly be expected to say more – but the biblical portrait of Jesus, which in the end is all we have to go by, cannot simply be lined up with that of a moral teacher and exemplar.[1] People have been sold a bill of goods on this. We should all be deeply aware of the Christology of the four Gospels – the way in which the Evangelists shape their stories to reveal who he is. I am not sure this is well taught in our seminaries in the USA. If it was, we would not have the situation we have in our parishes. In the USA, after 40 years of our new lectionary, many churches have removed their special lectern Bibles – the big, heavy, leatherbound ones – because people have grown accustomed to thinking of the Gospels as little pieces of text printed on little sheets of paper that the readers bring with them to the lectern. They are 'stories about Jesus', detached from their christological matrix. God knows, we need to hear the stories about Jesus! But when they are not read and understood in their context, they lose much of their significance. Speaking of generous orthodoxy, we need better doctrine – specifically, a more robust Christology.

---

1 About a month after the lecture on which this chapter was based was delivered in London, the coronavirus pandemic of 2020 swept Europe. The Queen delivered an Easter message almost unique in her reign, in which she was more explicit about the divine status of Jesus Christ.

Jesus is alive. That is the testimony of all four Evangelists and all of the apostolic witness. But how, exactly, is he alive? That question has vexed the Church over the years. I think immediately of a certain type of nineteenth-century hymn, one that proclaims, 'You ask me how I know he lives: He lives within my heart!' That's not *wrong*, exactly; Paul says that Christ lives 'in me', and the New Testament clearly proclaims the presence of the Holy Spirit with and in believers. But any hyper-individualized way of demonstrating that Christ is alive is neither biblical nor doctrinal. This is a book on 'generous orthodoxy', and orthodoxy is about doctrine (that dread word!) so I propose to say a few things about the christological doctrine of the Jesus who lives – and in the end, there is nothing in the world equivalent to the *generosity* of God in the living Jesus Christ.

How is Jesus alive? He is alive and present in the sacraments: in baptism he is present as the Spirit, and in the Eucharist he is present in the gathering of the saints who receive his body and blood. He is alive and present in works of mercy and acts of deliverance. He is alive and present in our midst 'when two or three are gathered together' in prayer, as he himself promised.[2] And yes, he is indeed alive in the hearts of individual believers. But most of all he is alive in the Word, because he himself *is* the Word.

There's an erroneous notion, which I hear about once a week. It is supposedly a saying of St Francis: 'Preach the gospel at all times; if necessary, use words.' I heard it just a few weeks ago in a sermon at an Episcopal funeral. Francis never said that, but it is quoted as if it were Holy Writ. We can all understand the well-meaning thought behind it – a gospel preached without the fruits of the Spirit (Galatians 6.22–26) would not be the gospel – but this airy dismissal of words as unimportant or secondary needs to be struck down whenever it pops up, because it leads to a wholesale abandonment of the crucial biblical identification of God with his Word. Our God is a God of words, a God who names and lavishly communicates God's own self to us precisely *through speech*. In a doctrine-free religious tradition, a burning bush in and of itself would be a revelation – one that would be open to interpretation by a 'spiritually' sensitive person. That is not our Exodus story. Moses is actually

---

2 One of the great sayings among African-American Christians is, 'God got in the midst.'

a spiritually *insensitive* person. He sees only 'a great sight'—a bush that does not burn. It does not become anything other than a remarkable vision until God speaks: 'I AM WHO I AM'. And furthermore God says, 'I am the God of Abraham, Isaac, and Jacob: this is my name forever' (paraphrasing Exodus 3.14–15). What kind of name for God is that? Is that something that human beings would ever make up for a god?

The unique God of the Bible is One who speaks to us, in order to identify himself and to establish his purpose for us. The ultimate expression of God's Word is the Son of God himself. Jesus *is* the Word of God. If we are so fortunate as to be in church on Christmas morning, that is the message we hear on that day, the feast of the Incarnation: 'the Word was with God, and the Word was God . . . and the Word . . . dwelt among us, and we have seen his glory . . . full of grace and truth' (John 1.1, 14, ESV).

I am repeating myself, but perhaps it needs repeating, since the habit of preaching Jesus as a moral exemplar is so deeply entrenched among us. As I observe the preaching of the church, there is insufficient evidence that we know Jesus as the living Word. So much teaching and preaching about Jesus calls upon us to do what Jesus did and act as he acted, with no emphasis on the way he marshalled *words* as living weapons of eschatological warfare. In Revelation 1, the word of God issues from his mouth as a sword. Of course it's true that Jesus revealed God in his actions also; John calls them his 'signs'. But it's important to note that his signs don't speak for themselves. In and of themselves they are mute, and many who see them do not believe. The signs are never simply visual; they always come with *words of revelation*, words that reveal who Jesus is and why he is doing what he does. In Mark's Gospel, his first action in beginning his public mission is to exorcise a demon, *through language*. He doesn't just wave his hands around; he speaks: 'Be silent, and come out!' and the bystanders say, 'What is this? A new teaching – with authority! He commands even the unclean spirits, and they obey him!' (Mark 1.27)

This reaction of onlookers to Jesus' 'new teaching' needs to be proclaimed in all its revelatory force. In an often-read passage from Luke, Jesus inaugurates his ministry in the synagogue at Capernaum, reading from the book of Isaiah where the prophet defines the signs of the kingdom of God (captives are released, the blind recover their sight, those who are oppressed are delivered). So far so good. But Jesus does not stop there. He then says – and when this is read aloud in the church, it should be read with great solemnity – 'Today this Scripture has been fulfilled in your hearing' (Luke 4.16–21). With these words he announces himself as the long-awaited Messiah, the one who will inaugurate the reign of God in his own person. The crowd, recognizing that this man whom they knew as a local boy, the son of the carpenter, is now claiming too much for himself. His words, first appearing gracious, become offensive to them as they realize what power he has. Further along in Luke, we read that 'They were all amazed and kept saying to one another, "What kind of utterance is this? For with authority and power he commands the unclean spirits, and out they come!"' (Luke 4.36). And as we know, there was a double reaction to his words. Many rejoiced to receive deliverance but many others who heard him read from Isaiah were ready to shove him off a cliff (Luke 4.28–29), not because he took up the cause of the poor but because he designated himself as the promised Messiah. It's fundamentally important to recognize that Luke is calling attention to the active agency of the word as spoken by this man Jesus of Nazareth. It is not enough simply to take the introductory words from Isaiah and make them into a template for the purpose of the Church without recognizing that this chapter presents us with a full-blown theology of the word of God.

Listen to the beginning of the book of Genesis, the first words of the Bible:

In the beginning God created the heavens and the earth. The earth was without form and void, and darkness was upon the face of the deep; and the Spirit of God was moving over the face of the waters. And God said, 'Let there be light'; and there was light.
(Genesis 1.1–3, RSV)

Will Willimon writes: 'Preaching is always a reenactment of the primal miracle "And God said . . ."[3] Everything we believe about God is predi-

---

3 William H. Willimon, *Conversations with Barth about Preaching* (Nashville, TN: Abingdon, 2006), p. 120.

cated on three words: 'And God said . . .'. Without that, there is no story and no gospel. God created the universe through speaking. God called a people into existence by speaking to Moses. God commissioned the prophets to speak, to be God's voice. And in the opening words of Hebrews (such a wonderful book!) we read:

> In many and various ways God spoke of old to our fathers by the prophets; but in these last days *he has spoken to us by a Son*, whom he appointed the heir of all things, through whom also he created the world. [The Son] reflects the glory of God and bears the very stamp of his nature, upholding the universe *by his word of power*. (Hebrews 1.1–3, RSV)

Listen to this: the Church's apostolic preaching declares not only that 'Jesus is alive' but what's more, Jesus is alive and powerful. Jesus Christ upholds the universe by his word of power – not just his power, but his *word* of power. I think many good churchgoers today have not entirely taken that in. The unique feature of the God of the Bible, a feature found nowhere else in religion, is the centrality of the word of God. The word of God, the 'word of power', is the foundation of everything else. The story of our redemption after the Fall in the garden of Eden begins with these words: 'And God spoke to Abra[ha]m' (Genesis 12.1, author's translation). Let us not hear any more about this gospel of works with words tacked on as a mere option. Hebrews again: 'See that you do not refuse *the one who is speaking*' (Hebrews 1.25). Notice that: God is identified precisely as the one who is *speaking*.

My own ministry of preaching takes me to pulpits in many different denominations, and I also hear sermons every Sunday in a wide variety of churches. I will just say that as I travel around in the USA, I get the impression that many congregations don't seem to have a sense of the biblical doctrine of the word of God. They don't expect anything life-changing from the sermon. There is no excitement about the sermon, no anticipation. In The Episcopal Church in the USA, it's the liturgy and the communion service that keep people coming, if they come at all. It hasn't always been that way. For 14 years I preached at Grace Church in New York, in Greenwich Village. People – largely young – came because they expected a powerful event of the word of God. As they found that happening, they found each other as well. Once you've preached in an atmosphere with this sort of synergy, you aren't satisfied with anything less. This kind of expectation keeps us preachers fresh. This expectation is the work of the congregation, and it should create excitement from Sunday to Sunday. For the preacher, it is always a sobering, even scary, responsibility – but you are carried and borne up by the promise of God that you are to be used as a vessel for God's living Word.[4]

The title of this chapter is 'By the word worked'. This is a borrowing from classical theological teaching. You will no doubt recognize the Latin phrase *ex opere operato*: 'by the work worked'. This refers to a dispute about the fitness of clergy to perform the sacraments of baptism and the Lord's Supper. Suppose the presiding minister has engaged in 'notorious sin'? Would that negate the effect of the service performed? Would a baptism by such a person be invalid? The Roman Catholic Church, at the Counter-Reformation Council of Trent, decided that it would be valid. The sacrament itself was of God, and therefore had power to override the unworthiness of the person presiding. It was *ex opere operato*, 'by the work worked'. Taking off from that I devised the theme 'By the word worked'. It isn't any good in Latin, but in English I find it a snappy way to recall the true author of the Scriptures and, by gracious extension, the words spoken by those who inherit the mantle of the apostolic preaching, The effective agent in the true gospel sermon is not the preacher, or the listener, or even the synergistic energy produced when preacher and listeners are interacting at the level of the gospel. It is God who is the animating agency inhabiting the written text as the preacher is led by the Holy Spirit, speaking words that effect what God intends. The most precious gift that God gives to preachers is listeners with an ear to hear what the Spirit says to the churches (Revelation 2.11). Blessed are those who find themselves in congregations where this is understood and where the eagerness for the Word each Lord's Day is a sign that God is on the move.

The story from Mark of the healing of the paralytic gives us a picture of the power of the word of Jesus. All he has to do is say, 'Take up your

---

4 For the record, the Episcopal church of Calvary-St George's has now taken over the role of gospel preaching to a youthful and truly diverse congregation in Manhattan – but why aren't all the churches like that?

pallet and go home.' The action follows instantly upon the command. This story from the early days of Jesus' ministry describes an intricate display of authority on several levels. First, Jesus pronounces the man's sins forgiven, without his even asking. No one can tell whether this takes effect or not, and besides, the scribes are thinking, 'Who can forgive sins but God alone?' Jesus knows what they're thinking. They require a visible demonstration. Therefore, he utters a word of command: 'Take up your pallet and go home.' This instantly heals the paralysed man *but also* operates as a kind of sop, a fillip tossed in the direction of his antagonists. As Calvin says, the Lord confirms and seals his authority by a visible sign, adjusting his approach to their shallow level. The implication is clear. Although only one result is visible – the man is healed – the Evangelist is showing us that by the mere word of Jesus *both* things are accomplished, both the visible healing and the invisible forgiveness of sins. By the word worked. Everyone is astonished to see the man get up 'immediately' and go out on his own two feet. 'We never saw anything like this!' they exclaim. Little did they know. The full implications are yet to be revealed.

Karl Barth writes that the Bible is 'a word of command . . . It effects decisions.'[5] Not 'affects', 'effects'. (I'm not able to get behind that to the German, but it sure works in English!) The Word of God does not 'affect' us as if it were a moving incident in a film, or an unusual experience we've had. It is 'effective': it calls forth, it engenders, it brings into being. 'We must speak of its *power*,' Barth writes, 'of its might, of its operations, of the changes it produces.'[6] J. Louis Martyn calls the gospel of Jesus Christ a 'performative announcement'.[7] It calls forth what it declares. God declares that the Word of God 'shall not return to me empty, but it shall accomplish that which I purpose, and prosper in the thing for which I sent it' (Isaiah 55.11, RSV).

Without this fundamental doctrine of the word of God, there is no preaching. I've never forgotten a visit from a clergyman at our home in New York shortly after I entered seminary. He was the rector of our former parish in Virginia, and a very effective leader in the civic struggles

---

5 Karl Barth, *CD* II/2, p. 708.

6 Barth, *CD* I/1, p. 173.

7 J. Louis Martyn, *Theological Issues in the Letters of Paul* (Nashville, TN: Abingdon, 1997), p. 110.

of the late 1960s. He asked about my studies at Union, and I told him I was taking homiletics. He asked me some questions, which led to my broaching the subject of the word of God. He drew himself up to his considerable height and said, 'I would never dare to claim that I spoke the word of God! What presumption!' We revered him for his courage during the late 1960s, but on that day I learned that there was something missing at the centre. He was like a man I knew from my days at Union in New York, in the 1970s. He was pastoring a congregation in a rough section of New York City during that tumultuous decade. He was interviewed by *The New York Times*. He said rather smugly, 'I don't write sermons. I don't have the time. Inner-city preachers don't preach . . . Preaching is feeding the poor.' I have never heard any African-American pastor say anything like that. In fact, what I hear is more like what Johnny Ray Youngblood said to another *New York Times* reporter. Reverend Youngblood was the celebrated pastor of a large African-American church in Brooklyn, where he initiated a whole host of social programmes. Yet he said, 'There's no substitute for preaching. I don't care what else a preacher does in the community or what causes he promotes, the people want to know on Sunday morning whether there's a word from the Lord.'

There have been many powerful words from the realm of geopolitics: Pericles, the Gettysburg Address, Frederick Douglass's Fourth of July oration, the words of John Paul II during the Solidarity struggle in Poland, 'Do not be afraid!' The words themselves evoked something of the strength they urged. The most famous example is probably that of Winston Churchill during the Battle of Britain. Edward R. Murrow said that Churchill had mobilized the English language and sent it into war.[8] The erstwhile Mayor of New York, in his brief but consequential finest hour during the days after the attacks on the World Trade Center, used Churchill as his exemplar.[9] He had heard that Churchill admitted later that he was not sure the English people could do what he said they would do. The Mayor was not sure about the American people either, but he trusted the words themselves to communicate the strength that was needed. But even these world-historical examples, powerful as they

---

8 John F. Kennedy famously borrowed this line from Murrow.
9 Alas, this was Rudy Giuliani. His finest hour was all too short.

are, fail us when we speak of the word of God, for one fundamental reason. Jesus' words, and the words of Scripture concerning him, are different. He himself *is* the Word. He is the Word spoken at the beginning (Hebrews 1.2 again) and by him nothing was made that was made (John 1.3). As I write these things it comes over me with new force – there is nothing else in world religion equivalent to this. In our important work of compassion and fellow feeling towards those of other faiths, we must not allow our distinctive doctrines to be adulterated. We must expect the word of God to be present and powerful even in our own feeble efforts, taken in faith that the Lord himself is at work in them.

One of the unique features of the gospel that we preach is that it is defined solely by the One who is himself the Word, *ho logos*. 'Preaching is always a reenactment of the primal miracle, "*And God said . . .*"'[10] The speaking of God is Jesus Christ himself, and the Holy Spirit is the breath of the speaking of God in Jesus Christ. Therefore the preacher's confidence is not in human words (plural). Rather, our confidence is in the Word that inhabits and gives life to our words. Barth writes, 'The Word of God is uncreated reality, *identical with God himself.*'[11] And further, the Word of God is also *an action*; as the prophet Joel proclaims, 'The LORD utters his voice . . . he that executes his word is powerful' (Joel 2.11, RSV).

It is my experience, as one who listens to other preachers almost every Sunday all over my country and beyond, that many preachers do not understand any of this. I know that many of my readers probably do not preach regularly, but perhaps you teach – or influence – those who will. The Church needs nothing more than a host of new young preachers who believe that God has spoken, that he has spoken in his Son, that his purpose for his word is that it be spoken by human beings—cracked, defective, human voices, but commissioned by him nevertheless to be conduits of the living, breathing, active, perpetually explosive word. Therefore Paul can write to the Thessalonians:

> And we also thank God constantly for this, that when you received the word of God which you heard from us, you accepted it not as

---

10 Willimon, *Conversations with Barth about Preaching*, p. 120.
11 Barth, *Church Dogmatics* I/1, p. 180.

the word of [human beings] but as what it really is, the word of God, *which is at work* in you believers.
(1 Thessalonians 2.13, ESV)

Every preacher gets tired and discouraged from time to time. Preachers understandably get angry when people don't respond – and these days in our Western culture, they fail to respond more often than not. But the seed of the Spirit of the Lord is growing secretly. The example to recall and live by is that of Elijah, when the order went out from Queen Jezebel that he should be murdered. This is from the most political section of the Old Testament, by the way – the first and second books of Kings:

Elijah was afraid, and he arose and went for his life, and came to Beer-sheba, which belongs to Judah, and left his servant there.
But he himself went a day's journey into the wilderness . . .
And there he came to a cave, and lodged there; and behold, the word of the LORD came to him, and he said to him, 'What are you doing here, Elijah?' He said, 'I have been very jealous for the LORD, the God of hosts; for the people of Israel have forsaken thy covenant, thrown down thy altars, and slain thy prophets with the sword; and I, even I only, am left; and they seek my life, to take it away.'
(1 Kings 19.3–4, 9–10, RSV)

And the 'still, small voice' of God came to Elijah and said:

'Go, return on your way . . . Yet I will leave seven thousand in Israel, all the knees that have not bowed to Ba'al, and every mouth that has not kissed him.'
So [Elijah] departed from there, and found Elisha the son of Shaphat, who was ploughing, with twelve yoke of oxen before him . . . Elijah passed by him and cast his mantle upon him. And he left the oxen, and ran after Elijah . . . and ministered to him.
(1 Kings 19.15, 18–21, RSV)

The word of the Lord came to Elijah and rebuked him even as he was about to re-empower him, as if to say, 'Elijah, you thought you were so important? You thought my power resided in you alone? You thought you were the only preacher? I've preserved seven thousand believers out there, so get going and stop feeling sorry for yourself. I've got a disciple ready and waiting for you, someone who will exceed even you in declaring my word.' God will not leave himself without a witness. The word that raised Elijah from his despair can raise a despairing church. He *can* and he *will*: 'Fear not, little flock, for it is your Father's good pleasure to give you the kingdom' (Luke 12.32, ESV).

There is nothing more needful for the preacher of the gospel than confidence in the hidden power of the Word. Barth writes: 'Whether our witness is authentic or not can be determined only by the Giver of the commission.'[12] There is great freedom and confidence in knowing that. And of course there is authentic witness to be seen outside the Church. There is an alternative mode of power that Jesus demonstrated on earth, that he exercises in heaven, and gives to his servants and witnesses in our own time whether they know it or not, the kind of power that the Englishwoman Fiona Hill displayed in the United States Congress during the recent impeachment hearings. In the short term, her truth-telling has met with defeat. In the long term, it will be seen as a thread in the tapestry of redemption by the power of the word of God.

There is nothing more needful for the preacher of the gospel than confidence in the hidden power of the word. Success as we might define it cannot be defined by human measurements. It can be determined only by the Giver of the commission.[13] There is great freedom and confidence in knowing that. Faithfulness to the word means throwing ourselves upon Jesus Christ, who is the Word, and leaving the results up to him.

'Jesus is alive.' He is alive with the power that brought the creation into being, the power in which Abraham placed his trust: the One who calls into existence the things that do not exist (Romans 4.17). He lives. Not I, but Christ in me, and Christ in you. May it be so.

---

12 Barth, *Church Dogmatics* I/1, p. 63.
13 Barth, *Church Dogmatics* I/1, p. 63.

6

Cosmic reconciliation in Christ as the basis for generous orthodoxy

STEVE SMITH

The focus of the Epistle to the Ephesians on unity makes it a helpful text for exploring themes relevant to generous orthodoxy. What is notable about the ecclesiology of Ephesians is its focus on the universal Church, with its picture of the Church painted on a cosmic canvas where Christ has a role of central importance as the redeeming and uniting head of the Church. What Ephesians discusses on a cosmic scale it then applies to the actions of the local church, and as such it helps frame generous orthodoxy's basis in Christology and eschatology. This chapter will examine the Epistle's central role for Christ in the eschatological plan for the Church, then go on to argue that church practice is informed by the eschatological tension opened up between the goal for the Church and the Church's contemporary reality. The final section evaluates how the writer takes this eschatological tension and christological focus and uses it to inform a practical ecclesiology focused on unity; in the conclusion this is brought into dialogue with generous orthodoxy.

Christ and the plan for the fullness of time

Ephesians begins with a eulogy (1.3–14) with the writer blessing God because he is the one who has blessed us in Christ (1.3); these blessings are then detailed throughout the first chapter where there is an emphasis on being 'in Christ', with 'in Christ', 'in him' or similar expressions occurring multiple times. As part of this eulogy, in 1.9–10 the writer refers to the mystery of God's will which is revealed to us. This mystery

76

is an important theme recurring in Ephesians 3.3, 4, 9 and 6.19, and the content of this mystery is given in 1.10: 'as a plan for the fullness of time, to gather up all things in him, things in heaven and things on earth' (NRSV). This statement is pivotal in the eulogy, climactic even, and as such exerts great influence on the ecclesiology of the letter. The verb here (ἀνακεφαλαιόω, rendered 'to gather up' in NRSV) is uncommon and only occurs in Romans 13.9 elsewhere in the New Testament, and is unusual in the Greek literature; typically the word contains ideas of summing up, often as a conclusion or summary of an argument.[1] That is not a precise fit with the thought of Ephesians 1.10, so the specific meaning of the verb here is a source of scholarly discussion: some scholars argue it contains ideas of repetition or recapitulation, so that it refers to bringing things *back* to a state of overall unity in Christ, a form of reconciliation;[2] other scholars incorporate ideas of headship to the meaning of the word, such that it refers to gathering under the headship of Christ.[3] But neither

---

1 For 1.10 as climactic, see Chrys C. Caragounis, *The Ephesian 'Mysterion': Meaning and Content*, ConBNT 8 (Lund: CWK Gleerup, 1977), p. 143; and the structure of the passage in John Paul Heil, *Ephesians: Empowerment to Walk in Love for the Unity of All in Christ* (Leiden: Brill, 2007), pp. 55–75. There are four main uses of ἀνακεφαλαιόω in the literature, and these include summing things up with a quotation from a prior work. None of these clearly apply to Ephesians. See J. B. Maclean, 'Ephesians and the Problem of Colossians: Interpretation of Texts and Traditions in Ephesians 1:1—2:10' (unpublished PhD thesis, Harvard), summarized and discussed in Peter T. O'Brien, 'The Summing Up of All Things (Ephesians 1:10)', in *The New Testament in Its First Century Setting: Essays on Context and Background in Honour of B. W. Winter on His 65th Birthday*, ed. P. J. Williams et al. (Grand Rapids, MI: Eerdmans, 2004). For details of translating ἀνακεφαλαιόω, see Stig Hanson, *The Unity of the Church in the New Testament: Colossians and Ephesians* (Uppsala: Almquist, 1946), pp. 124–5; O'Brien, 'Summing Up'.

2 Max Turner argues that the verb's ἀνα- prefix needs to be given full force, adding the element of repetition or recapitulation such that it refers to 'God's bringing of them back into harmonious unity in and through Christ', expressing a thought similar to Colossians 1.15–20: Max Turner, 'Mission and Meaning in Terms of "Unity" in Ephesians', in *Mission and Meaning: Essays Presented to Peter Cotterell*, ed. A. N. S. Lane, Antony Billington and Max Turner (Carlisle: Paternoster Press, 1995), pp. 139–40, quotation p. 40. He is not alone in this position, Andrew T. Lincoln, *Ephesians*, Word Bible Commentary 42 (Dallas, TX: Word Books, 1990), p. 33. But the preposition does not add its full force to the compound verb, as argued correctly by Ernest Best, *A Critical and Exegetical Commentary on Ephesians*, International Critical Commentary (Edinburgh: T&T Clark, 1998), pp. 140–1. Having said that, Turner is correct that the argument in Ephesians is ultimately about reconciliation, just like Colossians.

3 In terms of etymology, the verb is derived from κεφάλαιον 'sum, sum total' (BDAG, p. 65), rather than from κεφαλή, meaning head, but the interest in Christ as head in Ephesians 1.22 leads some to argue that ideas of headship are included. So for Harold Hoehner the term means 'to unite under one head', Hoehner, *Ephesians*, p. 221. While it may be that Ephesians 1.22 adds Christ's headship to the developing thought of the Epistle, headship is not part of the semantic range of the verb itself, and until the argument develops at the end of the chapter, ideas of headship are not apparent to the reader at Ephesians 1.10.

repetition nor headship is contained in the verb itself, so it is likely that the meaning in Ephesians 1.10 just concerns summing up or drawing things to a climactic point, a gathering together and unification of all things in eschatological conclusion.

There are two things that need to be said about this unification. First, this unification has an essential christological character. The repeated 'in Christ' language of chapter 1 reaches a climax in 1.10 where Christ is shown to be the sphere in which unification happens. Christ is not just the means for unity, he is the one in whom cosmic unity is restored. As such, Christ is the 'centerpoint toward whom all things are drawn – they are together *in him*'.[4] Second, this gathering together in Christ includes the sort of reconciliation discussed elsewhere in the New Testament. While the verb itself in 1.10 may not denote the element of repetition that *re*-unification involves, neither does it exclude it –1.10 is entirely consistent with a biblical concept of restoration. The biblical narrative of reconciliation is familiar, and does not require rehearsal here, but Ephesians enlarges the canvas on which this narrative is written: this is a reconciliation of *all things*, something Ephesians defines as things in heaven and things on earth (1.10), giving a truly cosmic dimension. As such, this means that a 'universal synchronization' has begun in Christ.[5] This reunification is detailed in Ephesians 2—3, and it is to these chapters that we now turn.

The unity of Jew and Gentile in Ephesians 2—3

Ephesians 2.11–22 adds detail to the imagery of gathering in 1.10 in two ways. First, in the restoration of relationship with God. The Gentiles, those who were separated from the blessings of Israel (2.12) and once 'far off', are now 'brought near' (2.13) through the blood of Christ. This near

---

4 Constantine R. Campbell, *Paul and Union with Christ: An Exegetical and Theological Study* (Grand Rapids, MI: Zondervan, 2012), p. 146. Campbell argues that 'In Christ' here has this locative sense rather than an instrumental one, and this finds widespread agreement elsewhere; see the discussion in Grant Macaskill, 'Union(s) with Christ: Colossians 1:15–20', *ExAud* 34 (2017). This is also how the phrases in Ephesians 1.3–7, 9 are understood. See O'Brien, 'Summing Up', p. 214; Hoehner, *Ephesians*, pp. 221–2.

5 Jody A. Barnard, 'Unity in Christ: The Purpose of Ephesians', *ExpTim* 120, no. 4 (2009), p. 168. For the theme of restoration in the New Testament, see Hanson, *Unity*, pp. 5–23; Max Turner, 'Human Reconciliation in the New Testament with Special Reference to Philemon, Colossians and Ephesians', *EuroJTh* 16, no. 1 (2007).

and far language is likely drawn from Isaiah 57.19, a text which receives a clearer allusion in Ephesians 2.17, where the Ephesian writer makes the point that both the Gentiles (those far) *and the Jews* (those near) have been drawn to God in a Christian group.[6]

Second, Christ also restores the horizontal relationship between Jew and Gentile (2.14–16), making both one, achieving this through the cross, by the abolition of the division contained in the Mosaic laws. This restoration is illustrated in the metaphor of breaking down the 'dividing wall, that is, the hostility between us' (2.14) – this wall is most likely a metaphor for division rather than a reference to a specific wall (such as one in the Jerusalem Temple). The resulting peace is christologically defined: the Greek text of Ephesians 2.14 contains an emphatically fronted pronoun which emphasizes that this peace is about Christ ('for *he* is our peace'), as Hoehner states, 'Peace is an abstract idea that is personified in Christ.'[7] Therefore the Church consists of a unified humanity which is the beginning of the cosmic reconciliation, a reconciliation grounded and defined by Christ.

In 3.6 there are three terms used to describe the Gentiles, all compound words that include the term 'fellow', and these give more detail of this process of reconciliation: the Gentiles are fellow heirs, fellow members of the body, and fellow sharers in the promise (3.6); these actions are all accomplished 'in Christ Jesus'. This Jew/Gentile unity in Christ forms part of the content of the mystery that is revealed to the 'rulers and authorities in the heavenly places' (3.10), but the revelation is more than this. The language of 3.9–10 bears considerable similarity to the promised unity of all things under Christ in Ephesians 1.10 (where *all* of heaven and earth were involved), so the revelation of 3.9–10 must include this eschatological cosmic unity as well. This means that the Church is an act of

---

6 Frank S. Thielman, 'Ephesians', in *Commentary on the New Testament Use of the Old Testament*, ed. G. K. Beale and D. A. Carson (Grand Rapids, MI: Baker Academic, 2007), pp. 817–18. This contrasts with the view of Markus Barth who thought it was the reconciliation of Gentiles with all Jews, Christian or not. See Markus Barth, *The Broken Wall: A Study of the Epistle to the Ephesians* (London: Collins, 1959), and more recently, Tet-Lim N. Yee, *Jews, Gentiles and Ethnic Reconciliation: Paul's Jewish Identity and Ephesians*, SNTSMS 130 (Cambridge: Cambridge University Press, 2005). Paul's echoes and subversion of the views of a Jewish faction ('so-called circumcision') in 2.11 tells against this, see Turner, 'Mission', p. 144; Barnard, 'Unity', pp. 169–70; Michael D. Goulder, 'The Visionaries of Laodicea', *JSNT* 43 (1991), p. 16.

7 Hoehner, *Ephesians*, p. 366. For the wall as a metaphor, see pp. 368–70; Yee, *Jews*, pp. 144–54.

revelation of the cosmic plan of God to reconcile all things in Christ, and this revelation is to all the heavenly realm. The Church that reveals this is not just the Church universal, but it is expressed through the unity of the local church too. This unity itself serves as a reminder to all heavenly beings that they will be subject to this coming unity under Christ; as such the power of evil angelic beings is broken.[8]

This present revelation of future cosmic unity is part of an eschatological tension, and it is important to explore this further before noting how Ephesians demonstrates the outworking of it in the local church.

The Church and eschatology

The church age is a time of partial fulfilment, and Ephesians contains what appear to be some potentially contradictory statements to describe the Church in this time: the Church is seated in heavenly places with Christ (2.4–6), yet this has a future aspect (2.7); Christ is the head of the Church and has filled everything (1.23), yet the Church prays for fullness (3.19); the Church has been built on foundations with a cornerstone in place (2.20), but is growing into a holy temple (2.21–22). The details of Ephesian eschatology do not need to be explored here; what is important to note is that Ephesians maintains an eschatological tension between the state of the Church now and its future, and this is reflected in its description of the unity of the Church in the present age where the Church is a witness to eschatological cosmic unity. This eschatological tension is explored through a series of metaphors to describe the Church, and through a series of ethical injunctions that guide the Church. It is to these that we need to turn to define the Ephesian view of church unity in the present age.

---

8 Caragounis, *Mysterion*, p. 139; Ernest Best, *A Critical and Exegetical Commentary on Ephesians*, International Critical Commentary (Edinburgh: T&T Clark, 1998), pp. 325–6; Hoehner, *Ephesians*, p. 448. For the relationship of 3.10 to 1.10, see Heil, *Ephesians: Empowerment*, p. 144; Hoehner, *Ephesians*, p. 448. The terms Ephesians 3.10 uses for heavenly beings are used in 6.12 for evil beings only, and 1.21 for all heavenly beings. For arguments in favour of a reference to all beings in 3.10, see Hoehner, *Ephesians*, p. 448; Turner, 'Mission', p. 146. For a broader discussion on the powers in Ephesians, see Carey C. Newman, 'Narrative Apocalyptic in Ephesians', *PRSt* 44, no. 3 (2017), pp. 323–8.

Metaphors for the Church in Ephesians

The first significant metaphor is the Church as the *body of Christ* (Ephesians 1.22–23). In the Ephesian development of the Pauline metaphor, Christ is the head of the Church, and the Church is filled by Christ as Christ is filled by God. This means that the Church receives the fullness of Christ: whatever Christ has from God is given to the Church so it can grow toward its eschatological goal united under his headship.[9] This concept of Christ as the head, the empowering source ruling over the Church, expands the understanding of his role in the verb as the one in whom all is summed up in 1.10. The role of Christ as empowering head gets developed later in Ephesians (see below).

The second metaphor is that of a *temple*. As part of the discussion of Jew/Gentile unity in 2.11–22 the writer goes on to describe their growing together into a holy temple whose foundations are the prophets and apostles, and whose cornerstone or capstone is Christ (2.20–21). Whether this stone is part of the foundations or the final stone at the peak of the building is disputed, but the latter is more likely because Christ is described separately to the rest of the foundations, and a headship image is more consistent with the ideas of Christ as head elsewhere in Ephesians (1.23; 4.15–16, etc.). If this is the case, then the Church is built on a foundation but it is still growing on to the place where the capstone fits (2.20–22). This temple imagery is important because it draws on the concept of the temple as the meeting point of heaven and earth, and as the place of sacrifice, with Jews and Gentiles becoming unified through Christ's sacrificial death. In addition, the metaphor may also be illustrating the relationship of the Church and the cosmos: just as the Temple was understood as a microcosm of the cosmos (the cosmic imagery on the Temple curtain is significant in this regard), the fate of the Church in unity has a key role in revealing the fate of the wider cosmos.[10] However,

---

9 John Paul Heil, 'Ephesians 5:18b: "But Be Filled in the Spirit"', *CBQ* 69, no. 3 (2007), p. 509; see also Andrew Perriman, '"His Body, Which Is the Church . . ." Coming to Terms with Metaphor', *EvQ* 2, no. 2 (1990). This approach understands πλήρωμα as a passive. For fuller discussion, see Hoehner, *Ephesians*, pp. 295–301, and Hanson, *Unity*, pp. 127–9. This is a similar thought to Colossians 2.9–10.

10 See the discussion in Gregory K. Beale, *The Temple and the Church's Mission: A Biblical Theology of the Dwelling Place of God*, New Studies in Biblical Theology 17 (Leicester: Apollos; Downers Grove, IL: InterVarsity Press, 2004).

more importantly for our purposes, this temple metaphor is a dynamic image: the universal Church is growing in Christ (2.21), as it grows in holiness – this is an image picked up later in the Epistle.[11]

In the third metaphor, the Church is described as a *soldier dressed for battle*. Ephesians 6.10–18 is not a text about the resistance of individual Christians, despite the text usually being read as instructions to individual believers. In continuing the theme of the common life of the Church, which is threaded throughout the whole of the paraenetic section (see below), it is more likely that the emphasis in Ephesians 6.13–18 is on corporate life, detailing the response that the whole Church is to make as it metaphorically takes up the armour together.[12]

These three metaphors then find a fundamental place in the articulation of the paraenesis in the second part of Ephesians, where the activity of the Church in the present age is presented; it is important to conclude the overview of unity in Ephesians with this paraenetic teaching.

The life of unity in the Church

While the division of the chapters of Ephesians into doctrine and paraenesis is not absolute, chapters 4—6 have a greater focus on the practical outworking of the theology discussed in chapters 1—3; much of this is focused on matters relevant to unity of the Church in Christ, concerning living in community together. Overall there are three themes that concern cosmic unity.

1 The focus on mutual blessing

What is notable about the beginning of the paraenetic section is its focus on unity. Ephesians 4 is the only place in the New Testament which uses the word for unity (ἑνότης is only in 4.3, 13), and it contains the rich sevenfold formula repetition that focuses on 'one' in 4.4–6. The readers

---

11 For a discussion of this imagery and the arguments for the significance of the stone, see Hanson, *Unity*, pp. 131–2; Lincoln, *Ephesians*, pp. 154–6. For the Temple and its significance, see David Peterson, 'The New Temple: Christology and Ecclesiology in Ephesians and 1 Peter', in *Heaven on Earth*, ed. T. Desmond Alexander and Simon J. Gathercole (Carlisle: Paternoster Press, 2004), pp. 164–72.

12 Martin Kitchen, *Ephesians* (London: Routledge, 1994), pp. 116–19; Stephen E. Fowl, *Ephesians: A Commentary*, NTL (Louisville, KY: Westminster John Knox Press, 2012), pp. 200–1.

are called to 'maintain the unity of the Spirit in the bond of peace' (4.3), not to create a unity that does not exist, but to pursue actively the unity that is already true. Then throughout the paraenetic section the writer urges the readers, in specific terms, to refuse all of the things that threaten their unity, whether pride, lack of love or selfishness. As Max Turner argues, in calling on the readers to 'clothe yourselves with the new self, created according to the likeness of God' (4.24), the writer is looking for people to be orientated towards belonging together in love, and building towards unity together in the eschaton. This concern with building community is seen in the ethical injunctions in 4.25–32, where references to anger, falsehood and wrongful speech are matched with calls for generosity (4.28), kindness and forgiveness (4.32). What is notable for Turner is that these ethical injunctions are directed at relations within the Church, not with the world, and therefore 'flow from the Christo-soteriology and ecclesiology' of earlier in the letter, where the Church is the demonstration of cosmic reconciliation in Christ. It is these relationships within the Church, and the relation of the Church to Christ its head – and not local pastoral concerns – that lie behind the household codes and discussion of marriage in chapter 5, especially the mutual submission of 5.21.[13]

All of this means that the ethics of the Epistle is focused on growth in unity as an outworking of the unity produced by relation with Christ; in this way it enables an effective demonstration of the unity on a horizontal plane that is detailed in Ephesians 2.11–22, and it builds on the metaphor of church as temple.

2 The gifts of the risen Lord

Immediately after the discussion of the priority of unity the writer uses a quotation from Psalm 68.18 (Ephesians 4.8) to draw attention to two significant themes from the first part of the Epistle; these themes are then developed in the life of the Church from the unity it already possesses in Christ (2.11–22) towards its eschatological goal of cosmic reunification in Christ (1.10). The dominant theme is the giving of gifts from the risen

---

13 Turner, 'Mission', pp. 152–5, quotation p. 153. This whole section is indebted to Turner's work, but see also Heil, *Ephesians: Empowerment*, pp. 187–203. For the ethics of the Epistle as an outworking of the theology, see the helpful discussion in Kitchen, *Ephesians*, pp. 70–82.

Christ. The gifts are different types of leadership to direct the growth of the Church (4.11–16). Several things can be said about this. First, the psalm was used in Judaism to refer to Pentecost and the ascent of Moses to give the gift of the law, and its role in Ephesians draws attention to the giving of the Pentecostal Spirit by Christ; the ministries therefore have both a christological and a pneumatological focus, shedding an important pneumatological insight on to the prophetic and apostolic foundation for the Church as temple in Ephesians 2.20. Second, these gifts are for use 'until all of us come to the unity of the faith and of the knowledge of the Son of God, to maturity, to the measure of the full stature of Christ' (4.13), a reference to the eschatological age. What is notable is the state of the Church at this time: the maturity mentioned (literally, 'mature man', ἄνδρα τέλειον) is singular, meaning that it is not describing individuals each attaining maturity, rather it is a corporate unity of one body, the Church,[14] a unity the Church already participates in (4.2). This is not simply the temporal terminus of the leadership gifts, it is also their goal, as 4.15–16 clarifies with the reference to growing into the head who is Christ. So the leaders in the church age work towards the eschatological cosmic unity in Christ that 1.10 promises and 2.11–22 states is already inaugurated.[15] Third, John Paul Heil has noted the significance of the language of 'Christ filling all things' in 4.10. This language is present elsewhere in Ephesians: it is in Ephesians 1.23 as a present reality, and it is part of the inauguration of the cosmic reconciliation of 1.10; in 3.18–19 the writer prays for the filling of the Church so they can understand the cosmic unity and fullness towards which they are going. So, in the context of these other uses, its use in 4.10 emphasizes the role of the gifts of Christ in the bringing about of this very cosmic fullness and cosmic reconciliation.[16] As this develops the Christ-as-head metaphor, it demonstrates the role of Christ filling the Church towards a goal of cosmic reunification.

---

14 This gift imagery is discussed in Lincoln, *Ephesians*; see p. 244 for the psalm and Pentecost, and the wider discussion in pp. 254–55. See also Hoehner, *Ephesians*, pp. 554–5.

15 Turner, 'Mission', p. 150.

16 There are several other lexical links between 1.23 and 4.10–16: Mark D. Owens, 'Spiritual Warfare and the Church's Mission According to Ephesians 6.10–17', *TynBul* 67, no. 1 (2016), pp. 94–5. For the significance of πλήρωμα, see Heil, 'Ephesians 5:18b: "But Be Filled in the Spirit"', pp. 509–10.

Second, the psalm quotation introduces the related theme of defeating enemies ('made captivity itself a captive', 4.8). In the psalm these captives are the enemies of Israel; in Ephesians the emphasis is on Christ overcoming his enemies.[17] This theme of victory over the enemies is central to cosmic reconciliation, and forms the topic of 6.10–20, to which we must finally turn.

3 Standing against opposition

The final section of the letter (6.10–20) serves as a summary of the Epistle,[18] and in doing so it picks up on significant themes concerning church relationships in a cosmic setting, with 6.12 listing cosmic forces (translated by NRSV as 'rulers . . . authorities . . . cosmic powers of this present darkness . . . spiritual forces of evil in the heavenly places'). While this is the fullest list in Ephesians, these powers have been referred to before: they are the beings Christ is exalted above (1.21–23), the forces under which people once lived (2.2), and the heavenly beings who receive revelation of the mystery through the Church (3.10); and 6.10–20 adds that they stand opposed to the Church. There are three aspects of this opposition that are directly relevant to discussions of church unity in a cosmic setting.

First, as discussed above, the soldier metaphor concerns the church community prepared for battle together, not individuals standing alone. Second, 6.15 refers to putting on to the feet the readiness of the gospel of peace. This is an enigmatic phrase that is often understood as referring to preparation for proclamation of the gospel, but this is not what the verse says explicitly, and it makes the 'feet' about preparation for offence rather than standing firm defensively (which is a more natural understanding of preparing the feet). Better to understand the verse as a defensive action where the 'gospel of peace' is understood as the good news of reconciliation between God and humanity, and between Jew and Gentile (see

---

17 This is true whether the captives are the enemies or those previously held captive by the enemies; in both cases it requires Christ defeating enemies: Hoehner, *Ephesians*, pp. 531–2. Here, see Clinton E. Arnold, *Ephesians: Power and Magic: The Concept of Power in Ephesians in Light of Its Historical Setting* (Grand Rapids, MI: Baker, 1989), pp. 56–7; Thielman, 'Ephesians', pp. 823–4.

18 Lincoln, *Ephesians*, pp. 432–3; Kitchen, *Ephesians*, p. 112; Donna R. Reinhard, 'Ephesians 6:10–18: A Call to Personal Piety or Another Way of Describing Union with Christ?', *JETS* 48, no. 3 (2005); Owens, 'Spiritual Warfare'.

2.11–18). Understood this way, it describes either the firm footing that Christ's peace brings, or being prepared for battle by *living out* the unity that Christ has won.[19] In either case this echoes the ideas contained in 3.10 where the unity of the Church is a testimony to the powers.

Third, the 'sword of the Spirit' (6.17) is a more offensive weapon. This sword is defined as the word (ῥῆμα) of God, and the only other time this word occurs in Ephesians is 5.26, where it refers to the gospel message; so it is likely that 6.17 also refers to the proclamation of the gospel. As Mark Owens writes, seen in the context of the entire Epistle, this proclamation of the gospel 'serves to extend Christ's victory':[20] the proclamation of the achievement of Christ, his great bringing of peace, and his restoration of those far and near (Ephesians 2.13–14) invites still more people to respond to it. As such, it becomes both a message pointing to the great cosmic reconciliation in Christ and acts as a testimony against the heavenly powers who oppose this restoration.

Cosmic reconciliation and generous orthodoxy

Within the book of Ephesians the reconciliation of all things together in Christ is a major driving force for its theology of the Church. This action of God in Christ redraws the constitution of the people of God, with radically different groups of people drawn into relationship: those who were far off (the Gentiles) and those who were near (the Jews) both receive a new relationship together in which there is no dividing wall. Christ is the head of this cosmic body, a Church that is described as dwelling in the heavenlies. However, this inaugurated unity seen in the Church is not complete, that completion only happens in the eschaton; the church age is therefore a period of eschatological tension within

---

19 For shoes as the firm footing brought by Christ's peace, see Hoehner, *Ephesians*, pp. 842–4; for preparation by living out unity, see Owens, 'Spiritual Warfare', pp. 98–9. See also the informative discussion in Thomas R. Yoder Neufeld, *Put on the Armour of God: The Divine Warrior from Isaiah to Ephesians*, JSNTSup 140 (Sheffield: Sheffield Academic, 1997), pp. 136–9; Best, *Ephesians*, pp. 599–600. For a wider discussion of the spiritual powers in 6.10–20, see Hoehner, *Ephesians*, pp. 824–30; Arnold, *Power*, pp. 66–8 .

20 Owens, 'Spiritual Warfare', pp. 101–2. See also Lincoln, *Ephesians*, pp. 376, 451. For a discussion on ῥῆμα, see Hoehner, *Ephesians*, pp. 824–30.

which the Church serves as a revelation of the eschatological unity of all things.

Much space is devoted in Ephesians to exploring how the Church functions in this eschatological tension. It does this partly by exploring the nature of the Church, using a series of metaphors (the Church as a body equipped by the head; the Church as a temple, growing into Christ; and as a soldier, standing against opposition), but also through a call on the Church to grow this unity found in Christ (chapters 4—6). This growth happens through Christ, who is the head of the Church, the one who through his pneumatic gifts equips the Church to know his fullness. The writer commands believers to act in a way that prioritizes human interaction; he describes Christ giving gifts that draw the Church together as one new human; and finishes by describing the Church as constituted as one body taking up eschatological armour in its resistance of the forces that would seek to undermine the work of Christ.

This picture painted in Ephesians is of the universal Church and is drawn on a wide and long canvas. Generous orthodoxy – the mutual loving, serving and prioritizing of the needs of those of other traditions among those who worship the one Christ – can be seen in its light. Generous orthodoxy and church unity are not *exactly* the same thing (generous orthodoxy, as framed here, is addressing a question directed primarily at the Anglican Church, although its implications are obviously far more widely applicable), but with all expressions of church unity it shares two fundamental questions: how is the Church defined (orthodoxy), and how are differences within that Church held together (generosity)? Ephesians has an answer to them both, and it is the same answer: Christ. Any conception of unity consistent with Ephesians has to be drawn primarily in christological terms. The unity of the Church is initiated in Christ, who draws diverse groups of people together to constitute his people; the eschatological unity of all things is located in Christ and finds its goal in Christ; and it is Christ who is the head of the Church, such that church membership is defined in relation to the head, and life in the diverse body is facilitated by the head. So, church unity cannot be driven by concern for church politics, programmes, forms of government, or a concern for a common purpose, even if that purpose is the mission of God. Ultimately, it is driven by mutual allegiance to

Christ, and a common dependence on Christ as the head and equipper of the Church as all things are gathered to him. This means that generous orthodoxy has to be focused on a commitment to put Christ first, with a generosity arising towards others seen in the light of his redemptive work; in practical terms, it is a commitment among those who worship Christ, to relate *especially* to those with whom they differ, to seek the blessing of others, and to build together with them into a united temple for the Lord.

But Ephesians also paints this unity on a cosmic scale: the unity of the Church is a central part of the cosmic plan for the reconciliation of the entire creation. Examining the role of the unity of the Church in this cosmological and eschatological setting permits restored relationships between very different people to be seen as part of the same process as the restored divine and human relationship, and the unification of all things. A cosmic perspective also keeps the eschatological goal of reconciliation in view, reminding the Church that while restoration may have been inaugurated, it is in the process of realization, and it requires practical attention from all believers. Finally, a cosmic perspective also emphasizes the role of the Church at the vanguard of God's restorative activity in their expression of the eschatological new humanity, and it permits Ephesians to explore opposition to the unity of the Church as it describes the role of the cosmic powers (in Ephesians 6). How the Church acts matters because creation is watching, and unity needs to be defended by standing firm. In these ways, the cosmic perspective drives the Church to maintain and develop unity and mutual care. The differences in doxology, praxis and theology discussed by generous orthodoxy are matters arising within a community of believers, and such things cannot be allowed to divide the people of God when God himself brings together such different groups of peoples as Jews and Gentiles into one Church; so restoring and maintaining relationships must be regarded as of critical importance for all who name the name of Christ. For the Church lives, as the metaphor of the soldier illustrates, standing firm in its unity, in a commitment to a missional unity that declares the cosmic redemptive plan of Christ, where the very act of living in unity serves to proclaim the eschatological message of reconciliation, both in this world and to cosmic forces.

7

For God and for the world: A generously orthodox Church

TOM GREGGS

It is difficult to be generous when one is fighting for one's survival. Generosity might seem best to belong to those who have surplus from which to give. To speak of a generous (and generously orthodox) Church at a time in Europe and elsewhere in the Western world when churches are crumbling, roofs falling down, congregations declining, denominations close to closure, number of vocations ever smaller, and influences on society waning, may seem to be an unwise approach to a theology of the Church in the twenty-first century. Survival of the remnant at all costs might seem wisest. And yet, churches orientated on their own survival tend to be far less attractive, far less likely to thrive, far less likely, therefore, to survive. There is profound truth to Michael Jinkins's observation: 'Ironically the church is most attractive when it pursues its vocation unconcerned with its own survival.'[1] Our God, after all, is the God of the widow's mite, of the jar of nard, of the one lost sheep – the God who values the small, the generous and the one for whom the many are risked.

In an age when we are so focused on survival, we must calmly remember that the Church is made alive as the body of Christ by an event of the Holy Spirit; and God is faithful and constant; and God's mercy endures for ever. An attitude of generosity in accounts of ecclesiology should protect us from any propensity to a knee-jerk reaction to the situation of decline, involving all kinds of degrees of the 'hyperactivity of panic' evidenced by church leaders, overseers and administrators

---

1 Michael Jinkins, *Church Faces Death: Ecclesiology in a Postmodern Context* (Oxford: Oxford University Press, 1999), p. 32.

across ecclesial and theological divides: 'This manifests itself in clutching for any and every programmatic solution and structural reorganization in the desperate hope that survival is just another project or organizational chart away.'[2] A generously orthodox ecclesiology needs, instead, to ask what the operation and activity of *God* is in creating a people for God's own Self: *what* the Church *is*, and what the Church's role is in the *economy of God* and what *God's role* in the Church is.[3] Rather than becoming a self-referential community orientated towards its own constitution and continuation, the Church must be a community which exists only for the sake of God and the world.[4]

In this chapter, it will be argued that the Church is a creation of the Spirit unlike any other community. As such, the internal life of the churches must be one of generous orthodoxy towards each other in a context of ecumenical openness. Instead of endless debates about polity and structure (issues that are *adiaphora*, matters of doctrinal indifference), there is need for a generous catholicity towards one another in order that the focus of the Church's existence for the world might come more to the fore. Ungenerous, internal focus takes the focus away from the true purpose of the Church as a community that exists for the sake of God and for the sake of the world. The first section of this chapter considers, therefore, the internal generosity of the Church – the ecumenical call to unity. It considers these internally generous dynamics in order to move ecclesiological discussions away from self-referential arguments to a united witness and life for the world. The second section outlines briefly what this generous ecclesiology might mean for the Church's relationship to the world.

1 Generous to each other: the internal dynamics of ecclesiological generosity

The vast majority of ecclesiological discussions take place on the level of internal debate over the structure, polity and ordering of the Church.

---

2 Jinkins, *Church Faces Death*, p. 9.

3 Tom Greggs, *Dogmatic Ecclesiology Vol. 1: The Priestly Catholicity of the Church* (Grand Rapids, MI: Baker, 2019).

4 Cf. Jinkins, *Church Faces Death*, pp. 32, 83.

So often, the discourse happens at a level little more advanced than a theological (or, more accurately, ecclesiological polity) version of the kinds of arguments between flower arrangers over where the flowers should be placed in relation to the communion table. Most attempts at identifying the presence of the Church do so by locating particular forms of practice, structures of polity. This can happen in multiple ways. On the one hand, there can be an approach that focuses on ministerial orders. Despite the fact that throughout history there have been manifold structural forms in patterns of ministry, there is an ever-present propensity to focus on the threefold order of deacon-priest-bishop as the condition for identifying the Church. This might be especially the case ecumenically following the World Council of Churches' publication of *Baptism, Eucharist and Ministry*, and it has also been ever more significant in episcopally structured Reformation churches following the Caroline and nineteenth-century movements.

However, the Church has in the past practised ordination to a variety of orders (as Orthodox Churches do in the present) – sub-deacon, acolyte, exorcist, lector, porter, taper-bearer and chanter. At the same time, Reformation Churches have mitigated on the number of orders, and certainly questioned the extent to which any can be understood as a condition of the presence of the Church. Even Richard Hooker, whose *Of the Laws of Ecclesiastical Polity* is perhaps the most influential legal and theological text for the Church of England, leaves open the question of the number of orders, and – while arguing for the pragmatic and scriptural benefits of an episcopacy – does not deem such an order divinely appointed, or necessary to the Church's essence: Hooker recognizes from the European Reformation a variety of possible polities expressed in different localities, though he himself prefers and argues for episcopacy (and either a threefold order of deacon-priest-bishop or twofold order of deacon-priest with the bishop existing as an office from within the order of the presbyter).[5] His account, indeed, is a generously orthodox one. He never unchurches any other Reformation Church: the account of polity offered is for the *bene essentia* and not the *essentia* of the Church.

---

5 Richard Hooker, *Of the Laws of Ecclesiastical Polity*, ed. Arthur McGrade (Oxford: Oxford University Press, 2013), book 7.

However, Kenneth Kirk's rather scathing maxim often proves true in contemporary settings: 'Catholics [and the Orthodox] believe that their orders are valid because they belong to the true Church; Anglicans believe they belong to the true church because their orders are valid.'[6] The resultant lack of generosity often flows forth from such perspectives.

But it is not just churches with a threefold order that display this kind of behaviour. Non-episcopal churches can equally claim their own structures to be the condition of the presence of the Word of God, with nineteenth-century Baptist preachers famously offering sums of money to anyone who could claim a more ancient lineage for their church than they did – as a church founded on the shores of the Jordan, by John the Baptist! There is a capacity for a form of restorationism in dissenting and non-conforming churches which sees the formation of polities other than their own (which are considered 'biblical') to be a deviation from the Bible, such that those with episcopal or priestly structures are also effectively rendered unchurched. In so many quarters, from all ecclesiological perspectives, our internal capacity to unchurch or claim superiority on the basis of polity over and against one another is an ungenerous failing to do all we can to uphold the plea of Jesus to the Father that we may all be one (John 17.21).

This kind of internal discussion of polity has also replicated itself in ecclesiology in terms of disputation of theological issues. By this, I do not mean the central dogmatic issues that we find in the first seven councils of the Church – that God is Trinity; that Christ is true God, true human and ontologically one. Rather I mean that often the truthfulness of a church is seen in practice by its members as the result of some minor doctrinal, liturgical or moral issue. We divide over the significance of the *genus majestaticum*, or the significance of free will, or even single matters of biblical morality (usually ignoring plenty of others – such as the use we make of our money). I am a theologian who makes his living from knowledge of such issues and I hardly think them unimportant. But these are matters that are not central to the apostolic deposit of the Christian faith and yet often become the basis for disagreement among friends – brothers and sisters who love the same Lord. Historically,

---

6 Kenneth E. Kirk, *The Apostolic Ministry: Essays on the History and the Doctrine of the Episcopacy* (London: Hodder & Stoughton, 1946), p. 189.

they have been the condition for vilifying the other. Indeed, it is worth considering the extent to which members of most churches could give any catechetical account of these issues of doctrine even though they are used as a basis for division. Such matters are often flashes in the pan of history, and many historical issues seem to lack the same divisive importance today that they once did in many quarters. There is, indeed, a fabled story relating to my own tradition of a Calvinistic Methodist who was on horseback and came to a narrow part of the road where only one horse could pass. Another rider approached, and the Calvinist Methodist realized it was none other than the Arminian John Wesley. Realizing that one of them would need to dismount, the Calvinist said to Wesley: 'Only one horse can pass here. You, Mr Wesley, are an Arminian, and I will not get off my horse for a fool!' To which Mr Wesley is reputed to have replied, as he dismounted: 'Aye, sir; but I will.' I doubt many of us would be rehearsing these same eighteenth-century arguments today. But what are the ones that are the Shibboleths of our own ecclesial prejudices? What are the things today over which we divide which future generations will find as strange as we do when we read about divisions over whether Christ carried a purse, or the fierce debates in the nineteenth century over whether a widow could marry her brother-in-law?

More fierce still is the kind of internal division we see in relation to modes of liturgy and worship – whether we unerringly follow the Book of Common Prayer, a sober 'low and slow' extemporary but ordered pattern, or a charismatic 'waiting on the Lord' with particular use of music and worship songs, which culminates in prayer and praise in tongues, or whatever distinctive feature. These not only set up rival denominations, but rival congregations and seminaries within denominations. Indeed, they can go so far as to make one group consider the other's faith not only diminished but potentially missing or heretical. This kind of lack of generosity towards the other is far from a generous account of the Church, and a locus for the works of evil. C. S. Lewis makes this point powerfully in his *Screwtape Letters*, in which the senior devil addresses his nephew with the following point:

I warned you before that if your patient can't be kept out of the Church, he ought at least to be violently attached to some party within it. I don't mean on really doctrinal issues; about those, the more lukewarm he is the better. And it isn't the doctrines on which we chiefly depend for producing malice. The real fun is working up hatred between those who say 'mass' and those who say 'holy communion' . . . And all the purely indifferent things – candles and clothes and what not – are an admirable ground for our activities. We have quite removed from men's minds what that pestilent fellow Paul used to teach about food and other unessentials – namely, that the human without scruples should always give in to the human with scruples. You would think they could not fail to see the application. You would expect to find the 'low' churchman genuflecting and crossing himself lest the weak conscience of his 'high' brother should be moved to irreverence, and the 'high' one refraining from these exercises lest he should betray his 'low' brother into idolatry. And so it would have been but for our ceaseless labour.[7]

What works does the devil perform to make us ungenerous today, I wonder?

While we might cite the ecumenical movement in the last century as a wonderful movement towards the good, even in ecumenical discourse, so often the real desire is for uniformity rather than unity; it is for conformity rather than communion. The logic and mode of engagement is often inwards, defensive, factionalizing and related to issues of power – usually in relation to which man (and it is almost always a man) can do what to whom on which other man's authority. Rather than grasping the hope for *oikoumene* (the whole world), too often on the basis of polity and liturgy, the focus (at least in multilateral engagement) is on the kind of theologizing that says, 'Only me and thee are saved, and I am not so sure about thee.' Too often the call to be *one* comes to be understood as the call to be the *same*, despite there being differences in the very earliest communities – between Paul and Peter, between a council of elders (Acts 15; 1 Peter 5) and a more episcopal structure (Philippians 1.1; 1 Timothy 3.1–2), between a polity relating to what we now know to be orders and one based on evangelists, prophets, pastors and so forth (Ephesians 4.11).

---

7 C. S. Lewis, *The Screwtape Letters* (London: Geoffrey Bles, 1942), pp. 84–5.

I have written at length in other places about why I believe this to be the case, and space does not allow this to be rehearsed now.[8] But there is tremendous worth and wisdom in the words of Gordon Rupp:

> At a time when all the stress seems to be on objectivity, the emphasis on inwardness and fellowship in experience deserves consideration as something more than old-fashioned. In the first place, because it thinks of unity rather as a ray of light than as a box, it unchurches fewer Christians . . . It answers the convictions of Christian men [and women] in contact with their separated brethren that there is a unity deeper and wider than we can define. It stands for that unity which exists now, amid all division and separation, without which none of us could Christianly exist for a moment, to which scriptures, creeds, experience, worship, behaviour can only point, since it is a unity hid with Christ in God. And it is dynamic, for it must be incomplete until all nations and races, and indeed all things in heaven and earth, are reconciled in him.[9]

Such a perspective, indeed, can be found paralleled in figures from episcopal traditions as well. Bishop J. A. T. Robinson in 1954 in relation to what is described as 'the South India problem', relating to episcopacy, stated:

> What we are concerned to deny (as unbiblical, unhistorical and un-Anglican) is a particular interpretation of the episcopate which would automatically unchurch any part of the Body that for historical reasons has failed to preserve it. For that is to exalt it as a precondition of the Church, whereas the only precondition of the Church is the Kingdom of God. We affirm that the episcopate is dependent on the Church, and not the Church on the episcopate.[10]

---

8 See my *Dogmatic Ecclesiology* and 'The Priesthood of No Believer: On the Priesthood of Christ and His Church', *IJST* 17, no. 4 (2015), pp. 374–98.

9 Gordon Rupp, *Protestant Catholicity* (London: Epworth, 1960), pp. 35–6.

10 J. A. T. Robinson, 'Kingdom, Church and Ministry', in Kenneth M. Carey (ed.), *The Historic Epsicopate in the Fullness of the Church* (Westminster: Dacre, 1960), p. 22.

Robinson does go on to see the threefold order of ministry as the *bene essentia* of the Church, but does not engage ungenerously towards other ecclesial expressions as if such a mark were the *essentia* of the Church, the *sine qua non* without which the Church would not exist.

The matter here in our internal orderings and identities is an issue of order. To argue the objectivity of orders preserves the objective bounds of the revelation and the gospel, or that the confessional claim of one group is the only way the gospel could be understood, or that holding a particular view of a particular moral issue or a particular mode of worship is what puts one inside the walls of the Church, is simply false. How could they? The Lord is the Lord and the gospel is free! The objective bounds of revelation and the gospel are the bases for our polity, orders, structure, theology, ethics and liturgy. This point is also made by the former Archbishop of Canterbury Michael Ramsey from an episcopal Reformation tradition:

> Catholicism, *created by the gospel, finds its power in terms of the gospel alone.* Neither the massive polity of the Church, nor its tradition in order and worship, can in themselves seem to define Catholicism; for all these things have their meaning in the gospel, wherein the true doctrine of Catholicism can be found.[11]

This is the account of unity that we find in the call to unity in Ephesians (notably with an account of ministries in terms of apostles, prophets, evangelists, pastors and teachers): 'There is one body and one Spirit, just as you were called to the one hope of your calling, one Lord, one faith, one baptism, one God and Father of all, who is above all and through all and in all' (Ephesians 4.5–6). It is the objective unity of Christ that is the basis for our unity together. John Calvin makes this point wonderfully: 'The church is called "catholic" or "universal," because there could not be two or three churches unless Christ be torn asunder – which cannot happen!'[12] Or else, in the words of the Congregationalist New Testament scholar T. W. Manson: 'We talk glibly about "our unhappy divisions";

---

11 Michael Ramsey, *The Gospel and the Catholic Church* (London: SPCK, 1990), p. 179.
12 John Calvin, *Inst*, 4.1.2.

but, in truth, so long as we are under one supreme Head, our divisions must remain essentially unreal.'[13] This means that our catholicity (our universal unity) rests within Christ and Christ's revelation; it is not that our catholicity determines the truth of the gospel. Christoph Schwöbel makes this point helpfully with regard to the Reformation Churches and their understandings of catholicity: 'The catholicity of the church does not guarantee the universality of the truth of revelation. The universality of the truth of revelation is the foundation for the catholicity of the church.'[14] The ecumenical call to full visible unity is a call for the Church in its lived and present catholicity to move towards the unity and catholicity *it objectively already has in Christ.*[15] Ecumenism cannot be a call to a single form of institutional uniformity (however much it is argued for on the grounds of Scripture and tradition) as the basis by which to adjudicate the Church's catholicity and apostolicity –its universality and authentic continuity with the deposit if faith given to the apostles – as to do so would itself fail to witness to the breadth of the biblical testimony on this matter.

Of course, there is a need for some degree of boundedness (or centredness) for the Church, and this has been expressed in various ways within the Reformation traditions. The Anglican Church's *39 Articles* summarizes the point well in the nineteenth article:

> The visible Church of Christ is a congregation of faithful [people], in which the pure Word of God is preached, and the Sacraments be duly ministered according to Christ's ordinance, in all those things that of necessity are requisite to the same.

There will inevitably always be debates about what is meant by 'pure Word of God' which might lead to a degree of ever-narrow 'purism' of the Word, just as there are going to be debates about what it is to ensure the sacraments are 'duly administered'. But at this point, one does well

---

13 T. W. Manson, *The Church's Ministry* (London: Hodder & Stoughton, 1956), p. 89.

14 Christoph Schwöbel, 'The Creature of the Word: Recovering the Ecclesiology of the Reformers', in Colin E. Gunton and Daniel W. Hardy (eds), *Essays on Christian Community* (Edinburgh: T & T Clark, 1989), p. 128.

15 Manson, *The Church's Ministry*, p. 89.

to remember the Reformation's key concern (perhaps *the* key concern) to reject any doctrine of the Keys – the idea that the Church itself (in its particular polity and practice) possesses the keys to the kingdom of God as the successor of Peter such that what it decides on earth is true in heaven (cf. Matthew 16.19). The Reformation teaches us that the empirical, visible, particular Church is a body that is simultaneously justified and sinful, and that our visible churches subsist within the hidden church which is known only to God and is (as the creed tells us) one, holy, catholic and apostolic. There are no lines of certain continuity between the bounds of the visible Church and the invisible Church, such that the visible Church formally controls membership of the invisible Church. Polity, liturgy, and even theology cannot be the condition for membership of this invisible Church, and (from this side of the eschaton) there can be no absolute sense of the visible Church's bounds and members corresponding to the boundaries and members of the kingdom of God. The visible Church always subsists within the invisible or hidden Church in Protestant theologies (at least), and drawing our lines too tightly and ungenerously is likely, indeed, to put us – with the pharisees and lawyers – outwith the kingdom's bounds.

John Wesley offers a wise approach to these issues of boundedness in his sermon 'A Catholic Spirit', which is effectively an account of generous catholicity. As I have described in more detail elsewhere,[16] Wesley argues that Christians of different congregations and denominations should come together (based on an account of the creed understood in relation to the affective belief not only in the head but in the heart and life) in an attitude of brotherly and sisterly love across the differences they have. Our concern should not be focused on what are (to his mind) the relatively minor differences that exist between denominations that assent to the (Nicene) creed. He meditates on the verse, 'If thine heart be right, as mine with thy heart, give me thy hand' (2 Kings. 10.15), as a basis for relationships across theological and ecclesial differences. Rather than be divided, we should seek (within our different polities and theologies) a unity that is found in the love of God and of humankind. Wesley writes

---

16 See my *Dogmatic Ecclesiology*, ch. 13; and 'The Catholic Spirit of Protestantism: A Very Methodist Take on the Third Article, Visible Unity, and Ecumenism', *ProEccl* 26, no. 4 (2017), pp. 353–72.

that Christians should come together in special love for each other, in which there is effectively spiritual attraction to one another across denominational differences. Through this, relationships are generated as we move closer to each other and to God simultaneously:

> 'If thine heart be right, as mine with thy heart,' then love me with a very tender affection, as a friend that is closer than a brother; as a brother in Christ, a fellow-citizen of the New Jerusalem, a fellow-soldier engaged in the same warfare, under the same Captain of our salvation. Love me as a companion in the kingdom and patience of Jesus, and a joint heir of his glory.[17]

There are practical forms to this love. Christians across denominations should pray for members of other denominations and for those denominations themselves: rather than debate and contest across denominations, Wesley suggests we wrestle with God on the other's behalf so that *God* would correct what we consider to be wrong about a given other, or what the other finds wrong in us. Accompanying these prayers should be good works directed towards members of other denominations. These should provoke the other also to love and good works, creating a virtuous cycle in which we outstrip one another in love. Such behaviours should lead us all to a more faithful and active form of discipleship. We should join together (within the differences that remain between us) in the work of God and in supporting the other in the other's work for the kingdom and for mission. To this end, we should witness well of each other and support each other pastorally.[18] Christians across denominations should seek, therefore, to come together even in their differences *for the sake of the one God whom we worship and who alone is the God of our salvation, for mutual support and for the sake of mission to the world.* Rather than focus on our internal divisions, we should focus less on those and more on the God and mission of the Church. Karl Barth puts this matter helpfully when he writes: 'No polity can create renewal or reformation. But this it can and must do . . . The polity of the Church can and must

---

17 John Wesley, 'A Catholic Spirit', *WJW* 2:90.
18 Wesley, 'A Catholic Spirit', *WJW* 2:91–2.

give a form to the Church which expresses the conviction that Jesus Christ alone is its hope.'[19]

2 The external dynamics of the Church: for God and for the world

The principal reason not to focus on the relatively minor internal divisions of the Church and not to seek uniformity rather than unity is because the Church is called not to concentrate on itself, but to focus on the One it worships and to whom it witnesses in a life of service. The Church is a creation of the Holy Spirit in a given time and place to witness to the reality of Christ's once-for-all and singular act. The Church came into being on the day of Pentecost by the Holy Spirit's coming. The Spirit who came at Pentecost is the same Spirit by whom Christ was incarnate, and who rested fully upon Christ in his baptism. There is, therefore, no distinction between the message of Christ and the message of the Spirit: the Spirit declares whatever the Son speaks. As St John writes:

> When the Spirit of truth comes, he will guide you into all the truth; for he will not speak on his own, but will speak whatever he hears, and he will declare to you the things that are to come. He will glorify me, because he will take what is mine and declare it to you. All that the Father has is mine. For this reason I said that he will take what is mine and declare it to you.
> (John 16.13–15)

The presence of the Spirit who relates the 'there and then' of Christ's work to the 'here and now' of our life is the condition of our hearing and receiving the Word of God, and of the Church's life, therefore, as the *creatura verbi*. The Spirit speaks in our present the words of Christ and enables us to receive, in our present, the activity and action of Christ. So often, our ungenerous ecclesiologies focus on human conditions for the Church's existence, rather than the epicletic call for the Spirit's presence as the community gathers. Indeed, it is worth noting that in

---

19 Karl Barth, *God Here and Now* (London: Routledge & Kegan Paul, 1968), p. 76.

Acts 1 (before the foundation of the church), we have what appears to be a church or that which the Reformers call 'a semblance of a church': there is worship, a polity in the election of officers, a sermon, a pastoral role even in the opening chapter of Acts. But this body still is not the Church, since the Spirit has yet to come: and the Holy Spirit is the *sine qua non* of the Church. The effect of the coming of the Spirit is that the disciples go from being orientated inwards, locked away in an upper room, to being orientated outwards upon the world: they become, by an event of the Spirit, active participants in the once-for-all completed act of Christ for the world. The Spirit comes and the Church is created; and the evidence of the creation of the Church by this event is that the disciples move from being orientated (ungenerously) on themselves to being orientated (generously) on the world. The reason that this is evidence of the Church's existence is that, through the coming of the Spirit, the Church is able to be formed into the body of Christ in a metonymous manner – that is, the closest possible association between Christ and the Church but not the identity of one thing and another. The Church cannot replace or continue the unique work of Christ, but it can be formed into the likeness of him who is our head. That likeness is the likeness of him who lives not for himself but entirely for God and for the world. For the Church to be, by the Spirit's gracious work, the body of Christ, it must – like the disciples in Acts 2 – move from being orientated on its own existence and survival to being orientated on the God who loves all the world enough to send His Son, and on the world that is so beloved of God that God sent his Son to die for it. The Church's existence is one that actively participates by the Spirit in that which it has passively received in Christ.

The Church, therefore, shares certain forms of the life of Christ in its own contingent existence in the here and now. Like Christ, in the Church there is no competitive relationship between a life ordered towards God in worship, prayer, liturgy and service, and a life ordered towards the world. Indeed, like Christ, the Church does not exist for its own sake but by the Spirit for the sake of the world as the Father desires. This is a crucial point. Ungenerous ecclesiologies tend to suggest that the world exists for the sake of the Church: those outside of active participation in grace exist so that the Church might know that it receives the benefits of salvation graciously; the world is a reminder to the Church of the damnation it deserves. But that ordering is completely the wrong way around: the Church exists for the world. It is because God desires the salvation and redemption of the whole of creation that God creates the Church through the Spirit to be a witness and active participant proleptically in the 'here and now' of the salvation to which it witnesses to the rest of creation. Like the form of Christ on Calvary – the one who could call down angels to save him if he chose, but who follows the Father's will for the sake of creation – our form is never to be one of self-preservation, but one of self-offering, witness and service for the world.

It is in this sense of being for God and for creation (and not for ourselves) which should help us to describe and unpack the marks of the Church that are found in the creed – one, holy, catholic and apostolic. There *is* objectively only one Church and that Church is one because God is One and, in the life of the Church, we witness to the one saving event of God once and for all in Jesus Christ. Our unity is not a uniformity, but a unity created by God. Indeed, Manson makes this point nicely. He states that rather than giving us a single policy or form, 'Our Lord did better than that: He gave the Church Himself. His real and abiding presence in the Church is the supreme "means of grace" and the supreme "ministry of grace."'[20] We are united in being the presence of Christ, sharing in his eternal worship and intercession, and witnessing to the world of the God of our salvation effected by the Lord Jesus.

Our catholicity, furthermore, is an expression of the universality of the Church throughout the world and for the world. The boundaries of the Church's life exist not so we can cordon ourselves off in a cloistered manner from the world, but so that these boundaries can be crossed into the world in mission, witness and service. Cardinal Dulles makes this observation perhaps more powerfully than any other and is worthy of detailed quotation:

The Church, according to this statement, possesses catholicity as a gift it can never lose because, thanks to the messianic outpouring of Pentecost, it inalienably bears the mystery of Christ, in whom all

---

20 Manson, *The Church's Ministry*, p. 21.

things have been summed up. The Church, however, lives and effectively achieves its catholicity inasmuch as it expresses in its actual conduct the integral truth and unbounded charity of Christ and his divine Spirit. The full consummation of this universal communion in the truth will never occur on earth, but is an eschatological gift reserved for the day of Christ's return in glory. Through missionary endeavour the Church continually strives for a fuller realization of its catholicity.[21]

Similarly, the holiness of the Church cannot simply be understood to be a separation from the world. The holiness of our God is never a holiness from creation, but a holiness *for creation*. As the perfect, spotless lamb of God, Christ does not separate himself from sinners, prostitutes and tax collectors, but invites them to be his honoured guests: he is not contaminated by their sin, but contaminates them with his holiness. Our holiness as the Church is also a holiness for the world, crossing the boundaries between the world and the Church for the sake of the world.

And the apostolicity of the Church is a deposit of faith that is given to the Church in order that it might be sent into the world for the world. The faith we are given apostolically to proclaim is a faith which is good news to the world of its reconciliation and the redemption that awaits. To be apostolic is to engage in that mission to the world: it is to be orientated out beyond its own internal life and inwards orientation.

Conclusion

So what is a generous ecclesiology? It is an ecclesiology based on the generosity of our God in Jesus Christ by the Spirit. The Church cannot focus on its own survival. On one level, it cannot because it cannot in the present time ever cease to exist: Christ is alive and his body of the Church exists because the Spirit of God is constant and faithful. On another level, the Church ultimately is never going to survive. The images, indeed, we are given of the eschaton are not ones in which there is an eternal church,

---

21 Avery Dulles, *The Catholicity of the Church* (Oxford: Clarendon Press, 1989), p. 25; cf. Karl Barth, *The Church and the Churches* (Grand Rapids, MI: Eerdmans, 2005), pp. 13–15.

but they are images of a city with no temple, since God alone is our temple (Revelation 21.22). The Church's purpose is not for its own form, existence or life. The Church exists for the God who loves the world and for the world which is beloved of God. We need never fear generosity in the Church and in our ecclesiology. We have the unfailing hope of the God of our salvation, who, in the riches of divine generosity, gave to us the greatest gift of all – the gift of God's own life in the Son who lived, died and was raised for us:

> and hope does not disappoint us, because God's love has been poured into our hearts through the Holy Spirit that has been given to us. For while we were still weak, at the right time Christ died for the ungodly.
>
> (Romans 5.5–6)

We tell of the greatest and most freely given gift of all. What have we to be ungenerous about in relation to each other and in relation to the world?

8

Lessons from the mechanics of early orthodoxy

SIMON CUFF

For Nev

It is a strange and persistent feature of Christian thought that it tends to overemphasize the unity of Christianity past while at the same time overemphasizing the diversity of the contemporary Church. As the contemporary Church seeks to discern whether apparently diverse voices are really following the blueprint set down by Christian orthodoxy, previous generations are mined as allies if they are useful in present struggles amid divergent voices, or they are all too easily ignored.

Only when a voice from a previous generation regarded as orthodox seems so antithetical to the orthodoxy of the present are they vociferously rejected or their witness strictly qualified and contextualized. More often than not they are passed over with silence if their witness does not serve the interest of whatever side this or that Christian happens to be on in the latest episode in the history of intra-Christian dispute and debate. Silence is usually preferable to articulated opposition so as to avoid the risk of unwittingly providing ammunition to your fellow Christian on the opposite side of whatever the debate might be.

In the midst of all this, episodes in the history of the earliest Church are sometimes recast as confirmation of the prejudices of the present and almost always taken as demonstrations of the unity and uniformity of the first followers of Christ.

The Council of Jerusalem, recounted in Acts 15 (and possibly Galatians 2), appears to settle debates around the necessity of circumcision for male salvation and is a prime of example of this tendency.

It is regularly taken as an example of unity and uniformity with which more current debates are implicitly or explicitly condemned. Verses that underscore this hermeneutic of uniformity are highlighted. The Council's decision is taken 'with the consent of the whole church' (Acts 15.22). Likewise, the decision to choose representatives of the apostles to travel with Barnabas and Paul is a unanimous one (Acts 15.25).

However, reading the Council of Jerusalem as a witness to early uniformity of orthodox belief is to miss the lack of uniformity to which the episode attests. Acts 15 includes at least one, possibly two, groups within early Christian practice and belief who do not represent the newly arrived-at orthodoxy which removes the requirement of circumcision *for male Gentiles*: the brothers from Judea and the Pharisaic believers in Jerusalem.

It is usually quietly assumed that the brothers from Judea teaching the necessity of circumcision (Acts 15.1) and the Pharisaic believers in Jerusalem who likewise insist on the necessity of circumcision simply fall into line after the apostles and elders make clear that circumcision is not required *for those Gentiles* turning to God (Acts 15.19).

However, this is an argument from silence. The circumcision of Timothy in Acts 16 might itself suggest that the Council's edict was not uniformly accepted. While ordinarily traced through the father in this period (see the genealogies in Matthew and Luke's Gospel), Timothy's racial background may have been disputed, as he is born of a Jewish mother and Greek father.

Even if it is the case that those referred to in Acts 15.2 and 15.19 are converted to the orthodox view that circumcision is not needed for males of Gentile origin, it is not the case that this decision removes the requirement of circumcision from those males of Jewish origin. If Timothy's background is disputed and his Jewishness suspected, this might itself be evidence that the Council envisaged the *necessity* of circumcision for those males of Jewish origin.

At most, the Council is evidence of at least two approaches to the issue of circumcision *within* Christian orthodoxy dependent on whether the male believer is Jewish or Gentile by background.

Again, it is usually assumed that the early Church quickly and universally dropped the requirement that male believers of Jewish origin be circumcised. It seems more likely that this was a result of an evolution in practice rather than a revolution in the discovery of orthodoxy at the Council of Jerusalem. Indeed, there are some indications that the requirement for circumcision for male believers of Jewish origin in Christ continued to be recognized as a way of being validly Christian for some time into the second century CE.

Within our canonical Gospels, passages that envisage the continuing validity of the Jewish law are difficult to assimilate to the prevailing reading of early and uniform rejection of law in the light of the gospel. The Jesus of Matthew's Gospel seems, at least *prima facie*, to reckon on the ongoing and perhaps permanent validity of the law (Matthew 5.17–19) and may be evidence that at least some Christians of Jewish background continued to be law-observant and encourage others to be so. It is famously difficult to establish a coherent attitude towards the law in the writings of Paul. At least some passages suggest some sort of continuing validity for those attempting to keep the entirety of the law.

Even if Paul thought that belief in Christ rendered law observance unnecessary at best and a sign of infidelity at worst, there is also the evidence of Paul's own law observance for the sake of convincing others of the saving power of the gospel.[1] This is not only evidence for Paul's willingness to practise the demands of the law (and so evidence that he regarded being a Christian of Jewish background not entirely antithetical to the law's precepts), it may also be evidence for the persistent law observance of Jewish believers in Christ.

We can go further than speculate that such believers existed. Writing some time after Paul, in the mid-second century, Justin Martyr is aware of believers in Christ apparently of Jewish background who persist in observing the precepts of the law.

In chapter 47 of his *Dialogue with Trypho*, he discusses with his Jewish interlocutor the salvation of those who believe in Christ yet follow the precepts of the law. Trypho asks whether those who recognize Christ

---

1 Cf. 1 Corinthians 9.20. See Martin Goodman, 'The Persecution of Paul by Diaspora Jews', in Jack Pastor and Menachem Mor (eds), *The Beginnings of Christianity: A Collection of Articles* (Jerusalem: Yad Ben Zvi Press, 2005), pp. 379–87, for the view that Paul's persecution could represent a voluntary subjection to the demands of the law. See further Paula Fredriksen, 'Why Should a "Law-Free" Mission Mean a "Law-Free" Apostle?', *JBL* 134.3 (2015), pp. 637–50.

and yet wish to obey the law will be saved. Justin responds that they will, unless they try to convince Gentiles of the necessity of circumcision. In a follow-up question, Trypho elicits from Justin that there are those who disagree with him on this matter. Justin repeats his condemnation of those law-observant Christians who try to incite Gentile believers to follow the law.

That there was disagreement among the early Church over whether the circumcision of Jewish believers was a matter of indifference or something to be argued against is attested to in another source which slightly pre-dates Justin but goes further in its rejection of the precepts of the law. The *Epistle of Barnabas*, written at some time towards the end of the first century or the beginning of the second century, takes a much firmer line against the circumcision of *any* male believer, even those of Jewish background. It adopts the unusual position of believing that God had in fact always taught the Jewish people that circumcision was not to be practised: 'circumcision is not a matter of the flesh. But they violated his law, because an evil angel instructed them' (*Barnabas* 9.4).[2]

For our purposes, we have here at least three divergent positions within the early Church. There are those believers in Christ who do not regard male circumcision or following the law as necessary for salvation, and do not engage with any of those Jewish believers who do. This group is referred to by Justin as those who 'do not venture to have any intercourse or extend hospitality' with such law-observant Christians (*Dialogue* 47). This group shares the view of the author of the *Epistle of Barnabas*.

There is another group within the early Church that adopts Justin's position of indifference towards those of Jewish background who continue to practise male circumcision and obey the precepts of the law, as long as they do not encourage Gentile believers to do likewise.

Finally, there are those apparently of Jewish background who are believers in Christ, recognized by the Church to be such, and yet continue

---

2 See James Nicholas Carleton Paget, 'Barnabas 9.4: A Peculiar Verse on Circumcision', in *Vigiliae Christianae* 45.3 (September 1991), pp. 242–54. Quotation from *Epistle of Barnabas*, in Bart Ehrman (ed. and trans.), *The Apostolic Fathers, Vol. 2* (Cambridge, MA: Harvard University Press, 2003), pp. 1–84. Carleton Paget notes that this might be reflective of the debate preserved in Philo's *On the Migration of Abraham*, pp. 89–93, between those who follow a strictly allegorical interpretation of the law and those, like Philo, who permit an allegorical interpretation but not at the expense of a literal observance of the demands of the law.

to practise the requirements of the Jewish law, including male circumcision. This group may well believe they are acting in accordance with the edict of the Council of Jerusalem in Acts 15, which we saw removed the necessity of circumcision for male Gentiles but says nothing of the requirement for male Jewish believers in Christ. There may be traces of such a view in some of our New Testament witness that envisages a continuing validity to the precepts of the law. Justin's rejection of those of Jewish background who persuade Gentiles to live likewise may suggest the existence of another group of Christians of Jewish background who regard the precepts of the law as valid not only for Jewish believers but all believers in Christ.

While it is clear this latter group is rejected both by the edict of the Council of Jerusalem and by Justin a century later, it is by no means clear that the beliefs of the former – that Christ is the messiah, and that as Jews they are required to follow the precepts of the law – places them outside the label of orthodoxy at this point. Justin's recognition of their view as a legitimate, if somewhat eccentric, manner of following Christ suggests that for at least one orthodox Christian this group could command the label of orthodoxy.

As so often in the history of ideas, we are reliant on sources that are handed down to us as products of, or amenable to, the ultimately dominant point of view. Our view of our Christian past is clouded by the view of the party that became dominant and upon whom we depend for our image of the orthodoxy of the early Church. We stand in the ultimately dominant tradition of Christianity that sees belief in Christ as antithetical to observing the precepts of the law. That this view was ultimately dominant is not in doubt.

However, our own debt to this ultimately dominant tradition can blind us to the continuing persistence of divergent views around the status of the Jewish background from which Christianity arose and the continuing validity for some Christians of the precepts of the Jewish law for a considerable period at the beginning of the history of the Church. At the end of the fourth century, John Chrysostom is so perturbed by members of his congregation who continue to find some kind of value in the various feasts and fasts of the Jewish year and other observances of the law that he sees fit to rip up his planned sermon series. He preaches instead against those who 'will join the Jews in keeping their feasts and observing their fasts . . . if they hear no word from me today, they will then join the Jews in their fasts; once they have committed this sin it will be useless for me to apply the remedy.'[3]

These sermons are more properly written against those Christians who have begun, or would persist in, some elements of Jewish practice. Whether these Judaizing Christians are doing so in an unbroken chain of practice inherited from earlier Christian groups, or whether this is a new-found form of false piety isn't clear. For our purposes, it is worth noting that John Chrysostom does not question their being Christians, even if it's probably true to say at this point in the fourth century they are regarded as 'bad' rather than 'eccentric' Christians from the perspective of the majority view.

The material we have surveyed above, however, shows that there is a period in which such Christians of a Jewish background were regarded neither as 'bad' nor 'eccentric' but as a legitimate form of orthodox Christianity. Even when such law-observant Christians were being regarded as eccentric by those such as Justin, their orthodoxy was not in doubt (as long as they did not persuade Gentiles to follow them in their observance of the law). The image we have of an early orthodoxy that is uniform does not stand up to the divergent Christian witness of proto-orthodoxy.

Writing as Western Christians in the twenty-first century, we stand in traditions of Christianity that have undergone the turbulent events of the Reformation. Whether Catholic or Protestant, no tradition has escaped the antithesis of law and gospel through which many Reformed theologies, both Catholic and Protestant, have constructed the orthodoxy of post-Reformation Christianities and of which all modern theologies are forced to take note.

This twin perspective leads to the potential for a particularly large blindspot when it comes to how we view the earliest Church. The ultimate victory of the view that saw obedience to the law as unnecessary for salvation at best and as an obstacle at worst leads us to silence or

---

3 John Chrysostom, *Discourses against Judaizing Christians* 1.5, trans. Paul W. Harkins, Washington: Catholic University of America Press, 1979, p. 4.

to overlook those Christians who diverge from this view, and yet are regarded as fellow Christians by those we regard as unimpeachably orthodox. This silence is magnified to the point of rejection by our debt to Reformation debates, which encourage us to regard as antithetical to orthodox Christianity any group that would countenance the need to follow the precepts of the law while believing in the saving power of Christ.

We are ever-tempted to read our history according to the tradition of victory in which we stand – both in terms of debates within the early Church and debates stemming from the Reformation. Due to the nature of surviving source material the effect of this is felt more strongly in our reconstructions of early Christianity.

The analysis of Robert Kraft remains true with regards to the temptation for both Jews and Christians to view the early history of their respective confessions from the perspective of the dominant parties that ultimately won out. It is worth citing in full:

> The temptation to use such terms as 'Judaism' and 'Christianity' primarily in connection with what has *survived* in one's own tradition as 'Judaism' or 'Christianity' is understandable. It is also extremely misleading. That which resulted when a certain type of Christianity achieved official status in the Roman Empire of the fourth century, and standardized for itself certain doctrinal and liturgical norms, should not be used to judge the earlier centuries ... For Christianity, the reign of Constantine became a major turning-point; for Judaism, the catastrophes of 66–73 [the war with Rome and the destruction of the Temple] and 132–135 [the Bar Kochba revolt] were equally pivotal. We must be careful in any attempt to move behind these major developments that we do not simply read later Christian and Jewish history back into the earlier periods.[4]

Kraft also makes another observation which is of importance for the divergent forms of Christianity that we have been surveying in this

---

4 See Robert A. Kraft, 'The Multiform Jewish Heritage of Early Christianity', in Jacob Neusner (ed.), *Christianity, Judaism and Other Greco-Roman Cults: Studies for Morton Smith at Sixty, Vol. 3* (Leiden: Brill, 1975), pp. 174–99, p. 176.

chapter. He notes how indebted we are to Christian sources for the nature of Jewish thought at this time, again with a clarity that bears quoting at length:

> It is truly amazing how little we would know about pre- and non-rabbinic Judaism if we were solely dependent on the literature and traditions preserved by Judaism itself . . . It is from Christian transcribers, and not from Judaism, that we have inherited the well known works of such persons as Philo, the Greek speaking Jewish philosopher-apologete of Alexandria who was a contemporary of Jesus and Paul, or of the Palestinian apologetic-historian Josephus . . . Any attempt to distinguish clearly between 'Jewish' material and its Christian use in this literature is subject to serious difficulties. After all, it is preserved as Christian literature even when what we consider to be characteristically Christian interests and ideas are not obvious. Apparently the orientation of the various Christian users was flexible enough to allow some sort of positive status to these materials without it causing serious conflict with 'Christian' ideas. Many early Christian groups seem to have developed directly out of Jewish backgrounds and settings ('Christianity began as a sect of Judaism' is the oversimplified slogan), reacting to some things and modifying others, but also preserving a large part of the Jewish heritage, with which positive contacts were sometimes maintained for long periods of time.[5]

A more complex picture emerges of the earliest *centuries* of the Church with respect to the continuing validity to some elements of Jewish thought and practice than we would have come to expect, or likely been able to see, given our indebtedness to the ultimately dominant tradition of Christian thought and the Reformation lenses we bring to our earliest history.

We have spent some time setting out this diversity because I believe it teaches us something of the capacity of early orthodoxy to tolerate a diversity rather larger than our dominant interpretative traditions and lens might have led us to believe. What on earth, you may well ask, has

---

5 Kraft, 'Multiform'.

this to do with generous orthodoxy? I have attempted to refocus our sights on the perceivable diversity of recognized ways of being Christian in the earliest period of our faith. In contrast to the silence with which the various groups we discovered in Acts 15 and Justin's *Dialogue* are usually met, early Christianity was content to discern real Christian commitment in those who held divergent views on the question of the necessity of law observance. In doing so they provide an early witness to something of the phenomenon of generous orthodoxy this volume explores.

This is not to paint too rosy a picture of the early Church. Just as in ours, there were always those who found such diversity difficult and would rather more uniformity in practice and belief to continue to follow Christ from the cosy security of their tribe. The entire basis of Acts 15 is the preaching of those who insist that the precepts of the law must be universally followed. Conversely, we saw too in the *Epistle of Barnabas* those for whom the literal application of the law was severely misguided, and by implication those believers in Christ of Jewish origin who desired to maintain their observance of the law.

The irony here of course is that insistence of both groups on uniformity of practice is itself evidence of the diversity of early Christian belief. Not only, as we have seen, are their opposing views contained within the proto-orthodox tent, but so too the view of Justin Martyr that law-observant Jewish Christians have a place in the kingdom.

For those Christians in Acts 15 who insisted on the necessity of circumcision for Gentile believers in Christ the irony runs rather deeper. Their insistence on the uniformity of practice is precisely that which alerts some members of the wider Church of the presence of Christ in those they had previously discounted. The apostles and elders are alerted to the work of the Spirit in those Gentiles who, as Jews, they had previously regarded as outside the bounds of holiness.

As Matthew Thiessen notes: 'The earliest Christians, however, were astounded at the manifestation of the Holy Spirit among those formerly deemed to exist outside of the realm of holiness.' He notes 'the surprise elicited by the movement of the Spirit across genealogical boundaries.'[6]

---

6 Matthew Thiessen, *Contesting Conversion: Genealogy, Circumcision, and Identity in Ancient Judaism and Christianity* (Oxford: Oxford University Press, 2011), p. 148.

This begs the question among which groups the Spirit is at work today whom we may have previously deemed outside the realm of holiness or beyond the boundaries of where we have been taught that the Spirit is at work. This realization is at the heart of generous orthodoxy – the Spirit blows where it wills and beyond the boundaries of our particular tribe.

At this point, we might be tempted to limit this diversity solely to the question of law observance of Jewish believers in Christ in the early Church, and assign an end date to such diversity that coincides with that time when there ceased to be a significant number of such believers. There are, however, reasons to think that there is some amount of diversity that is an irreducible part of the body of Christ. St Paul reminds us that 'there are varieties of gifts but the same Spirit' (1 Corinthians 12.4).

In his *Catholicity and Heresy in the Early Church*, Mark Edwards has demonstrated the diversity of Christian thought during perhaps the key formative period of Christian orthodoxy up to and including the Council of Chalcedon in 451 CE. He attempts 'to dismantle the antithetical constructions which obscure the diversity of Christian in thought in our modern patrologies'.[7]

There is not space here to describe the intricacies of Edwards's argument in any detail. For our purposes, he notes the close relationship between heresy and orthodoxy in this period of the Church. He demonstrates the role of 'heretical' constructions in the formation of later orthodoxy – either constructions that were later deemed heretical being drawn upon as source material of later orthodoxy, or the way in which present orthodoxy is shaped by its rejection of what are deemed heresies of the day. He sets out, for example, how the arguments of heretics such as those termed 'Gnostics' forced the early Church to argue in a certain way that in turn shaped the subject matter of Christian orthodoxy.

With respect to the role of prior heretical constructions shaping later orthodoxy, Edwards set outs the 'extraordinary assimilative capacity of early catholic doctrine'.[8] He further describes the capacity for heretical ideas to continue to influence the contours of Christian orthodoxy, noting: 'even a body that has been eclipsed will not cease to exert the

---

7 Mark Edwards, *Catholicity and Heresy in the Early Church* (Farnham: Ashgate, 2009), p. 142.
8 Edwards, *Catholicity*, p. 175.

force of gravity on the one that is interposed.'[9] We have seen something of the truth of this dictum above. We saw how the teaching of those who required male Gentile believers in Christ to be circumcised forced the Church to make a decision in favour of Gentile inclusion without the necessity of circumcision – a stance that continues to this day.

Perhaps, more importantly, Edwards reflects on the role of the Scriptures in the Christian life and the implications for continued divergence of views even within Christian orthodoxy. He notes that the primary mode of theology for most of the great theologians of the early Church was not great works of systematic theology or even treatises of credal defence but homilies and commentaries:

> Decrees and formulations of great councils could lay down a canon of interpretation and eke out the vocabulary of the scriptures where they required elucidation, but to treat the creeds themselves and not the scriptures as the matter of theology would be to study the constellations without the stars.[10]

Just as now, so then. Theology arises out of the life of the Church of which they and we are a part. Theology is the result of a living and life-giving engagement with the written word in whatever circumstances we as the Church find ourselves.

At this point some will assert that this engagement with Scripture naturally leads to uniformity. However, the testimony of Scripture itself tells against this. As we have been tracing in just one case, Scripture itself hints at a divergence of views within Christian orthodoxy which it did not feel the need to iron out into uniformity in the formation and closing of the scriptural canon.

More crucially, the existence of four Gospels within the canon stands as a persistent reminder that following Christ has never been susceptible of collapse into one Christian experience, one way of following Christ, one path of discipleship. All Christians believe that Jesus is the Way, but the testimony of the four Gospels themselves, by their sheer existence,

---

9 Edwards, *Catholicity*, p. 176.
10 Edwards, *Catholicity*, p. 163.

points to inherent diversity in that Way, the irreducible multiplicity of callings given to us in Christ.

Some caution is needed here. Perhaps unfortunately for those of us who have to live alongside others who do not share our calling or particular way of heeding Christ's call in our lives, this irreducible multiplicity of callings does not lead to a multiplicity of Christianities that have nothing to say to each other. The witness of the diversity of the early Church and the existence of divergent views within the umbrella of proto-orthodoxy does not allow us the luxury today of resting easy in our particular Christianity and spending our days in splendid isolation.

Edwards helps us underline this point:

> Most believers have in fact found it possible to suppose that all the canonical evangelists held one gospel; whether their intent supplementary or polemical, it is certain that all four evangelists wrote ostensibly for the world, and not for one conventicle. The same is true of catholics in the next century who were openly polemical: to Ignatius and Irenaeus the church which they defended was not one denomination, but the saving ark.[11]

As we are reminded in the letter to the Church in Ephesus: 'There is one body and one Spirit . . . one Lord, one faith, one baptism' (Ephesians 4.4–5). This does not, as we have seen, lead to complete uniformity within the one saving ark. Instead, amid the diversity of Christian callings, we are to suffer the pain of other Christians diverging from our own practice and calling, 'with all humility and gentleness, with patience, bearing with one another in love' (Ephesians 4.2). It is precisely because of the pain that can come from the reality of living with a multiplicity of Christian callings that we are reminded of the need for humility and forbearance when faced with those Christians whose discipleship seems alien to us and who traverse a different path from that which has been given to us to follow on the Way.

The human tendency to tribalism and to erect boundaries is so strong that we should always be aware of its power to lead us astray as we follow

---

11 Edwards, *Catholicity*, p. 174.

the path set down for us. This is especially the case as we seek to follow the one who in his pre-resurrection life persistently questioned not merely the legitimacy of one tribe but the very process of tribalism from which we human beings find it almost impossible to escape.[12]

Aware of this, we should be cautious in erecting too firm a boundary around what constitutes a legitimate Christian calling within the limits of orthodoxy, lest we fall foul of a human tendency to seek the security of a tribe and misstep in following the call of Christ outside the boundaries of our tribe. This being said, how are definitions of legitimate diversity and divergence of views within the Church, as we have been tracing it from the earliest days of its existence, arrived at and by whom.

Perhaps not surprisingly, the four Gospels help us here. By the simple fact of their existence as *four* testimonies to *the* gospel, Rowan Williams notes:

> That the Jesus-tradition never finally systematised itself into a single coherent body of instruction in a single narrative framework is itself an important fact. The *way* in which the telling of the story of Jesus (especially of his death) functioned in producing conversion or enlightenment was clearly not readily assimilable to the transmission of a picture of the world or a model for behaviour.[13]

Instead, Williams notes that the key to understanding this earliest period of the history of the Church and the formation of orthodoxy 'is not the *experience* of hearing the Christian kerygma but the record and image of Jesus himself'.[14]

Williams remind us that it is Jesus himself who decides upon the limits of Christian orthodoxy and those to whom we are to exercise generosity perhaps despite ourselves. The Church permits divergent views within it, as we have been tracing, because Jesus calls divergent people and peoples to himself. What unites those believers in Acts 15 who taught

---

12 See Rowan Williams, 'The Finality of Christ', in *On Christian Theology* (Oxford: Blackwell, 2000), pp. 93–106.

13 Rowan Williams, 'Does It Make Sense to Speak of Pre-Nicene Orthodoxy?', in Rowan Williams (ed.), *The Making of Orthodoxy: Essays in Honour of Henry Chadwick* (Cambridge: Cambridge University Press, 1989), pp. 1–23, p. 15.

14 Williams, 'Pre-Nicene Orthodoxy?', p. 17.

circumcision was necessary for all males, those who it taught it was necessary for only Jewish males, and perhaps ultimately our forebears who taught it was necessary for no males, is not a common confession, set of beliefs or way of life but a positive response to Jesus' call in their lives.

This does *not* mean that there are not better, worse and ultimately wrong ways of speaking about Jesus, God, the Trinity and so on by those who respond positively to Jesus' call in their lives. The deposit of later orthodoxy is the gift of speaking well or better about these fundamentals of the Christian faith. It *does* however mean that the cornerstone of that orthodoxy is not a fully worked-out system of ideas or manner of life. Indeed, as Williams notes:

> In so far as certain features of the development of the canon and orthodoxy paradoxically worked *against* the absorption of Jesus into a thematised religious subjectivity and system of ideas, they preserved the possibility of preaching Jesus as a questioning and converting presence in ever more diverse cultures and periods, and the possibility of intelligent debate and self-criticism within Christianity.[15]

The centre of all orthodoxy, and thus of generous orthodoxy, is none other than Christ himself: the whetstone of all Christian faith and life. This witness of early orthodoxy is the reminder that Christ surpasses all earthly systems and formulations, and is not reducible to any one particular ecclesial position or tribe. Indeed, the witness of the four Gospels seems to indicate that Christ not merely condones a multiplicity of response but is himself the cause, through the imparting of the variety of gifts and the calling of the variety of people on which he continues to found and build his Church.

I want to conclude by summarizing the lessons of generous orthodoxy that might be traced in our above exploration of the various paths stemming from those first encounters with Christ that we can trace out of the New Testament witness and within the life of the earliest Church.

---

15 Williams, 'Pre-Nicene Orthodoxy?', p. 17.

First, as Christians who inevitably stand in particular traditions of belief, we need to know in which tradition we stand as we engage and are confronted by others whose tradition appears not to be our own. We need to put aside the impulse to focus our criticism on those traditions that are not our own, and to focus our interrogation on the tradition in which we stand, as we seek to follow the ever-questioning presence of Christ. What have those who have passed the faith on to us highlighted, and what have they have overlooked? What sources of Christian wisdom and witness have they entrusted to us? What have they passed over, and do we agree they were right to do so? How are their decisions and the heated debates of previous generations shaping our own? Are those debates, to use Edwards's metaphor, continuing to exercise a gravitational pull on us that might blind us to Christ's presence in those outside the tradition that is our own?

Second, Thiessen reminded us of the surprise of the early Christians to see the work of the Spirit in those they had already rejected as outside the bounds of holiness. Instead of the uniformity of Christian witness we usually expect from our earliest forebears, we have seen that diversity of response to Christ and divergence even within orthodoxy have been persistent features of Christian life. From attitudes to the law, to the existence of four Gospels, to the variety of Christian callings and gifts, an element of diversity is to be expected as the Spirit works outside the bounds of our own tribes and expectations of what constitute legitimate responses to Christ. Generosity here is required because of the discomfort of being confronted with ways of following Christ that are not merely our own, but challenge the comfort and security of our particular tribe of Christian community.

Finally, all of this has something rather profound to say about the unity of the Church. Christian unity is not so much to do with uniformity of practice or way of life but unity of response. The seeds of lived unity lie in focusing our attention ever more closely on the one who died and rose for us, and allowing ourselves ever to be questioned by him. This requires that we put the whole of ourselves, our lives, our thoughts, our denominations, our ways of being Christian, at the service of, and under the scrutiny of, the one who is ever calling his Church into being. If we do so, we begin to be the kind of Church whose very earliest witness we have traced in this essay and whose particular witness to unity remains ever relevant to the Christian life.

For Williams this process is ever-constitutive of what it means to be church:

> 'normative' Christianity [remains] an interwoven plurality of perspectives on what was transacted in Jerusalem. And the notion of a church whose unity lies primarily, if not absolutely and simply, in a shared attention to the questioning story of a crucified and resurrected Lord, *and* an attention to how that story is being assimilated in diverse and distant communities, culturally and historically strange, is not without relevance to our own day.[16]

Nor, we might add, to the business of living the Christian life and the project of generous orthodoxy to which this volume attests.

---

16 Williams, 'Pre-Nicene Orthodoxy?', p. 18.

9

Liturgy, generosity and the mystery of worship in the Spirit: Towards a theology of worship

MICHAEL J. LEYDEN

Introduction

In this chapter I argue that a commitment to generous orthodoxy liberates the Church *from* anxiety over differing worship styles and localized practices *for* mutual enjoyment of and participation in the Spirit's work across global Christian traditions. I treat generous orthodoxy as a theological rule that shapes our posture towards others by emphasizing spiritual substance over liturgical style, in the light of which we are called to worship the Lord wherever he may be found in the Church.

Some theological foundations

Worship is Godward facing. Its rationale is encounter, taking the posture of adoration and thanksgiving. In worship we proclaim the worthiness of the triune-God revealed in the gospel. We do so by rehearsing the particular story wherein this God is wholly revealed, without remainder and without speculation: the story of the birth, life, death, resurrection, ascension and second coming of Jesus Christ (cf. Isaiah 55.6). Worship is thus part of our response to this particular, identifiable and narratable God. To ensure it remains faithful, worship requires continual immersion in this narrative; ceaseless attention to the particular story wherein all other stories make sense. This, after all, is what is declared in the sacrament of baptism (Romans 6.3–4).

The Church has long believed that as we worship in this Christ-centred fashion, we are transformed by the Holy Spirit. The Spirit comes from Christ (John 20.22) and is given to those who are his (Galatians 4.6; 1 John 4.13); the Spirit gathers us to Christ, compelling the Church to confess, 'Jesus is Lord' (1 Corinthians 12.3) and to call upon his Father as our Father (Romans 8.15–17). The Spirit enables the preaching of Christ's gospel (1 Corinthians 2.4) and gives gifts for the building up of Christ's body (1 Corinthians 12.4–11). The same Spirit enlivens our worship (John 4.24), eliciting our collective astonishment, gratitude and joy at the substance of the gospel. As we rehearse Christ's story in word and sacrament, the Spirit alerts us to its radical implications for our lives: we are moved to become more fully ourselves in Christ (Matthew 22.37; Romans 12.1–5), bringing glory to God the Father. Such is the Trinitarian metaphysics that underpins any theological account of worship.

Every worshipping community does *liturgy* (from the Greek word meaning 'the work of the people'), that is, it orders its gathering in ways that are theologically and practically coherent, enabling corporate participation. Each, therefore, engages in a series of concrete practices which, though not intrinsically worshipful, when done in the context of the gathered community turning its attention to Jesus Christ, constitute worship.[1] That is to say that worship happens as and when the community's acts of singing, lifting hands, preaching, listening, bowing, robing, prostrating, kneeling, processing, eating, holding vigil, drinking, declaring, speaking in tongues, anointing, laying on hands, sharing, reciting and so on are commandeered and enlivened by the Holy Spirit to become actions that move us Godward. In this way, these actions interrupt the self-absorption and patterns of control and self-determination according to which we try to live the rest of our lives.[2] Instead, absolute contingency confronts us both as individuals and as the Church, as, by the Holy Spirit, the One who gives meaning, purpose

---

1 On this point, see Gregory Dix, *The Shape of the Liturgy* (London: A & C Black, 1982), pp. 12–15.

2 In some instances that is made explicit with the *epiclēsis* – the 'calling down' of the Holy Spirit – during sacraments. The scriptural significance of ritual actions is considered in Dru Johnson, *Knowledge by Ritual: A Biblical Prolegomenon to Sacramental Theology* (Winona Lake, IN: Eisenbrauns, 2016).

and direction to all things is present claiming our attention.[3] Like Isaiah, worshippers are undone and reassembled by God (Isaiah 6.1–5) as we confess and celebrate the lordship of the risen Jesus (Philippians 2.9–11). It is the Christ-focused, Spirit-empowered nature of what is done that makes each gathering worshipful.

Naming tensions

So far, so good . . . perhaps. But, in practice, the worshipping life of the Church is not without its complexities and indeed its tensions. What one person regards as Christ-centred and Spirit-filled, another might consider to be little more than a ritualistic distraction or an artistic performance. There are many such tensions we could name, but two are especially important in exploring generous orthodoxy.

The first tension I want to consider is theological. One side emphasizes the immediacy of responses to the work of the Holy Spirit, who is understood to be *directly* operative in the moment of the community's gathering, leading people Christ-ward and orchestrating worship. From this perspective, planning and preparation might be minimal, other than perhaps bringing useful tools (instruments, Bibles, communion vessels), as worship is understood as an event laden with anticipation. Participants might feel prompted by the Spirit to sing a song, read from Scripture, pray the liturgy, dance, pray in tongues, share a word of knowledge and so on. The Spirit will lead. On the other side of this tension is concern for human responsibility and responsiveness to God. Emphasis might be on the production and curation of liturgy (whatever form it takes), since what is important is the *offering* of something that is sacrificial, carefully considered and theologically coherent – utilizing the best of our skills and talents and resources – with all the planning and preparation that such coherence requires. Songs, prayers and ritual actions might be selected to reflect the Bible reading or liturgical season; the whole service might be constructed around a theme or significant event. Worship is

---

3 On the interruptive power of worship, see Alexander Schmemann's magisterial book, *For the Life of the World: Sacraments and Orthodoxy* (Crestwood, NY: St Vladimir's Seminary Press, 1973). A longer discussion can be found in his, *The Eucharist: Sacrament of the Kingdom* (Crestwood, NY: St Vladimir's Seminary Press, 1987).

the people's work, and at stake is the principle of quality: our Lord and Saviour is worthy of our very best effort, and that usually takes planning.

Overall, this tension is about subjectivity: is worship something we humans do *for* God and in which he is the object of our efforts, or something that God does in us and through us? Many want to argue for both: worship is something Christians offer to God as a sacrificial response to the gospel of Christ, and so we plan and prepare, bringing the best of who we are in what we do (Psalm 116.17; Hebrews 13.15); but it is also something the Holy Spirit inspires and enlivens, without whom the liturgy is dry and continually redirects to idolatry. I tend to agree. But far from solving the tension over subjectivity, a simple affirmation of the both/and approach can be frustrating. That's because worship is often deeply felt by participants, as *what* we do is understood as the vehicle for our theological understanding of what *ought* to be done. Our liturgy has implicit meaning.

Thus, questions of subjectivity give rise to a related but distinct second tension: the theological substance of worship produces concern for preference and style. One end of the tension emphasizes liturgical order, habitual formation, obedience and service of God. Proponents often take their cue from scripted worship in the Bible (for example, in Exodus 35—40). Now, while the claim is that, usually, personal preference is less important than obedience to God, in practice many people (me included!) often like liturgical structure and written orders of service because of their familiarity, coherence, biblical literacy and sense of occasion. We shouldn't pretend otherwise. On the other hand are those who argue that charismatic freedom necessitates liberation from bondage to scripted or formal liturgy (me included!) and who thus regard extemporariness and spontaneity as central to genuine Spirit-filled worship. After all, the Spirit is free and brings freedom as a gift (2 Corinthians 3.17). Various iterations of this tension exist, but the structure of the divide is basically the same, oscillating between specific accounts of order and freedom.[4]

---

4 See Ronald Byars, *The Future of Protestant Worship: Beyond the Worship Wars* (Louisville, KY: Westminster John Knox Press, 2002). Also helpful are John Leach, *Liturgy and Liberty: Combining the Best of the Old with the Best of the New in Worship* (Eastbourne: Monarch, 1989), and his *Living Liturgy: A Practical Guide to Using Liturgy in Spirit-led Worship* (Eastbourne: Kingsway, 1997); Mark Earey, *Beyond Common Worship: Anglican Identity and Liturgical*

It is sometimes said that these tensions are healthy, preventing stagnation. But increasingly theologians recognize that more often than not in the history of the Church they reduce to a series of sharp disagreements, caricatures and stereotypes. Many of us have heard contemporary versions: for example, that liturgical worship constrains God, or is culturally irrelevant, or is Spirit-less; or that non-liturgical contemporary worship is chaotic, disordered, exclusory or without due reverence; or that traditional liturgical worship is best for good order, is more God-centred, and more obviously scriptural; or that contemporary non-liturgical worship is a more 'real' experience of freedom and hospitality in the Holy Spirit. The sharpness is a result of deep connection to local preferences and styles of worship. Our past experiences get preserved and repeated as, like Peter, we mark the places of meaningful encounter with God (Matthew 17.4). Preferences get traditioned through repetition, setting a community's horizons and expectations and shaping its sense of identity. Over time one worshipping community can lose sight of its familial relation to another: indeed, another's traditions represent a challenge to local knowledge and experience. Differences divide and caricatures abound – 'happy-clappy', 'bells and smells', 'restricted', 'chaotic', 'high', 'low', 'reverent', 'free'. Familial bonds weaken, and suspicions strengthen.[5] Not only is this tragic, but the worst cases of these tensions have given rise to a phenomenon that scholars have named *the worship wars*.

The worship wars

There is general agreement that the worship wars develop in a context of theological anxiety.[6] Specifically, anxiety about ecclesiology and how

---

Diversity (London: SCM Press, 2013); and Graham Hunter, *Discipline and Desire: Embracing Charismatic Liturgical Worship* (Cambridge: Grove, 2017).

5 Todd Hunter candidly notes some of these tensions in passing in his *The Accidental Anglican: The Surprising Appeal of the Liturgical Church* (Leicester: IVP, 2010). See also Andrew Wilson, *Spirit and Sacrament: An Invitation to Eucharismatic Worship* (Grand Rapids, MI: Zondervan, 2018).

6 Along with those already cited, see Thomas G. Long, *Beyond the Worship Wars: Building Vital and Faithful Worship* (Lanham, MD: Alban Institute/Rowman & Littlefield, 2001); Lyndon Stratton, *Beyond Worship Wars: A Call to Dialogue and Honesty* (Winnipeg: WA Press, 2012); and Robb Redman, 'Worship Wars or Worship Awakening? Paradigms, Perceptions, and Worship Innovation', *Liturgy* 19.4 (2004), pp. 39–44. In 2019 the *Christian Resources Exhibition* in the UK held a plenary panel discussion, 'A Call for an End to the Worship Wars', chaired by

localized worship traditions with their particular styles and practices relate to the Church universal in a way that is theologically coherent. What's at stake is the identity and unity of the body of Christ. To ignore one another (as much as we may wish to!) does not solve this problem. What is done elsewhere by another community claiming also to be church impacts the community of which I am part: *What do the differences between us and them mean? What does God desire? Who is correct?* Such questions, left unanswered, make people anxious:

> it's hard to look the other way, particularly when we find ourselves dismayed by the way our neighbour is doing it. It is easy to say, 'live and let live', but the fact is that biblically and practically we know that the church is one body... we challenge each other, sometimes politely and carefully, sometimes in ways that stir up mutual antagonism. Everyone gets defensive, and then we have something like a worship war.[7]

As even a glance at the history of the Church illustrates, anxiety-fuelled antagonism is never good: it results in 'bitter disagreements, angry arguments, political machinations . . . conflicts . . . and combat'.[8] Schism and separation quickly follow.[9] But since the topic of disagreement is central to the life of the whole Church, we remain interested and challenged by others' traditions. In several instances, the 'live and let live' model equates to establishing a vantage point to take a position *against* others (even if it is largely encumbered by ignorance and misunderstanding). Indeed, some local churches articulate their identity in the light of these disagreements, 'we are not like those others over *there*'. Of course, in certain circumstances this is necessary, allowing

---

Worship Academy International founder Chris Bowater, <www.keepthefaith.co.uk/2019/10/04/call-for-end-to-worship-wars-at-cre-national-2019/> (accessed October 2019). See also Pete Ward, *Selling Worship: How What We Sing Changed the Church* (Milton Keynes: Paternoster, 2005); and Tim Lomax, *Creating Missional Worship: Fusing Context and Tradition* (London: Church House Publishing, 2017).

7 Byars, *The Future of Protestant Worship*, p. 10.

8 Lester Ruth, 'The Explosion of Worship Wars: The Coming of Conflict', *Liturgy* 32.1 (2017), pp. 3–6.

9 Marva J. Dawn, *How Shall We Worship? Biblical Guidelines for the Worship Wars* (Eugene, OR: Wipf & Stock, 2003), pp. 10–13.

for appropriate awareness of context. Contextualization promotes 'adaptation [of] liturgy to local culture' to improve connection and cultivate accessibility, participation and relevance with those who may be on the margins of church, or totally unchurched.[10] The driving force is mission, with the idea that familiarity in worship is more attractive to potential converts. Such adaptation enables seeker friendliness. But in the worship wars, anxiety feeds off an unspoken, lurking suspicion that contextualization involves dilution, even distortion, of the gospel. Worry about the relationship between the universal and the particular abounds: is what's done *locally* really faithful to what the Church is *universally*? With this in mind, proposed solutions to the problem of theological anxiety have emphasized renewed attention to ecclesiology – the doctrine of the Church.

An ecclesiological solution?

Since worshipping God is the hallmark of the people of God this solution suggests that a ceasefire may be called on the worship wars if we re-examine our collective ecclesiology.[11] For this to happen, so the argument goes, strong leadership is needed. Lyndon Stratton, for example, argues that anxiety grows where there is little concern for the communal nature of church and that leaders are the ones who keep this in focus by setting the right posture and tone towards others. His leadership manifesto offers an alternative picture of a 'healthy church community' arguing that worship wars develop where efforts to repair failed relationships are built on the wrong foundations. Only by prioritizing the commonality of different congregations and traditions in Christ will the impetus for the commitment and care we need to have towards others in order to end the worship wars be found. He emphasizes co-operation and humility, so that what matters most for a Christ-centred ecclesiology is that those with whom I disagree are also people whom God loves, and therefore people whom I should love. Worship wars develop where we close ourselves to this possibility.

---

10 Byars, *The Future of Protestant Worship*, p. 15.
11 On this, see Simon Chan, *Liturgical Theology: The Church as Worshipping Community* (Downers Grove, IL: IVP Academic, 2006).

Stratton identifies three key theological foci which require leaders' investment if this relational dynamic is to be foregrounded: commonality in Christ; acceptance in Christ; and trust in God.[12] Such values ensure respective commitment of congregations to one another, as well as their active willingness to work together, and the recognition that God will work all things together for good. That said, proponents of this view see the success or failure of the project as being about leadership rather than some miraculous work of God:

> Worship issues are leadership issues . . . The church that worships together with one voice does so because leaders understand the community's unique expression . . . Then each believer may understand and embrace what a worshipping community is all about by how leaders lead.[13]

Stratton is not alone. Thomas Long suggests that disputes about worship can be transformed into liturgical renewal through effective leadership. Key to Long's case is the office of pastor as the focus of unity in the Church, precisely because she or he is the driver for its vision. While Jesus is the head of the body, the gift of the leadership and pastoral ministry are, here, the principal mechanism for the Church's growth. Thus, the pastor is central to overcoming the worship wars, using skills of diplomacy and leadership to change culture for good:

> if the pastor doesn't move, worship doesn't move . . . it's the pastor who always must provide the impetus, shape, and direction of change . . . Indeed, in all of the vital congregations, the renewal of worship happened because the pastor of the church had a vision of what worship could be and boldly took steps to put that vision into practice.[14]

Long's pastor has a lot of power, authority, and responsibility in this scenario but Long is not self-consciously a clericalist. He continues: 'even

---

12 Stratton, *Beyond Worship Wars*, ch. 4, in which he roots these three virtues in Romans 15.1–13.
13 Stratton, *Beyond Worship Wars*, pp. 93–4.
14 Long, *Beyond the Worship Wars*, p. 108.

though the initiative for worship-change lies primarily with the pastoral staff, clergy alone cannot and should not carry the full weight . . . key leaders in the congregation should be brought on board.' Though he is much less top-down than Stratton, he is also not egalitarian or communitarian: 'the pastor needs to own and articulate the vision firmly.'

But, despite this clarion call for strong leadership, the worship wars rumble on. This seems to be because, when done well, the ecclesiological model ends up with a friendly tolerance of other traditions and styles, and this effects a surface-level change. Relationships become cordial. But simple tolerance does not lead to a radical transformation of the situation. A bigger vision of worship is needed for that. Furthermore, it has been suggested that the unwavering commitment to the capacity of the leader is a distraction, operating under the genuine belief that a ceasefire can be called by theologically informed, skilful and well-executed people. Indeed, while recent studies have shown that good leadership is important for healthy churches,[15] too much emphasis on the qualities of leaders can miss both the theological substance of ecclesiology (as a miracle worked by the Holy Spirit) and the proper location of leadership within the Church (under the headship of Jesus Christ). Where this is forgotten, leaders move blindly across the battlefield of the worship wars not fully appreciating the differing perspectives and sharing no common orientation. What is needed for the peace talks is an authority and vision for worship that goes beyond fixed traditions and stylistic preferences. Our leaders need to be led. This is, I think, where generous orthodoxy is most helpful, because of its vital appreciation of the work of the Holy Spirit as the initiator and curator of all Christian worship and therefore its relativizing of any exclusive commitment to localized styles of worship. It emphasizes the spiritual substance and the theological orientation of worship. It is this pneumatological approach to which I now turn by, first, considering two related ideas often associated with the work of the Holy Spirit: mystery and participation.

---

15 The Church of England Report *From Anecdote to Evidence* cites good leadership as the top of its list of seven factors that significantly influence church growth. See <www.churchofengland.org/more/church-resources/church-growth-research-programme/anecdote-evidence>.

A Spirit-shaped solution: mystery and participation

In Christian theology mystery is a distinctive species of knowledge rooted in revelation. It describes something that once was hidden but is now uncovered.[16] In Scripture it usually concerns how God is known, explaining the particular mode of God's self-revelation. Important in this is divine simplicity; that God's being and action are united in a way for which there is no human parallel. Where humans have a destructive capacity for duplicity and dishonesty, God is absolutely consistently Godself. Hence why Scripture's writers often infer things about God's being and character from divine actions, and vice versa.

In the New Testament, this mysterious knowledge is coterminous with Jesus Christ, the one who is God (Colossians 1.15), and who does the things that God does (John 5.19–20). When people encountered Jesus, they encountered God (Mark 15.39; John 3.2). Reflecting on this fact, the apostle Paul describes Christ as 'the mystery that has been hidden throughout the ages and generations but [which] has now been revealed to his saints' (Colossians 1.26), declaring that 'the mystery of God's will is set forth in Christ . . . to gather up all things in him' (Ephesians 1.9–10), and that 'the knowledge of God's mystery is Christ himself' (Colossians 2.2, 4.3; Ephesians 3.3–6). Paul commends to the Church the proclamation of Christ's gospel 'according to the revelation of the mystery that was kept secret for long ages but is now disclosed' (Romans 16.25). The point is simple: Jesus Christ is God's self-giving presence to and for creation, and this is mysterious – something God always intended, but which was revealed at a time in keeping with divine purpose so that people may know God's love and love God in return (cf. Hebrews 1.2).

The Christ-centred orientation of mystery alerts us to its unusual texture. Its description is better served by words like encounter than by conventional ideas like understanding, learning or comprehension. Mystery resists any of the sedentariness we might associate

---

16 For a fuller taxonomy, see Stephen Boyer, 'The Logic of Mystery', *Religious Studies* 43.1 (2007), pp. 89–102; and Galen Wiley, 'A Study of Mystery in the New Testament', *Grace Theological Journal* 6.2 (1985), pp. 349–60. See also G. K. Beale and Benjamin Gladd, *Hidden but Now Revealed: A Biblical Theology of Mystery* (Downers Grove, IL: IVP Academic, 2014).

with information-gathering or fact-finding. It is active and personal –
knowledge of a *who* rather than a *what*. This relationality is definitive.
Jesus Christ is lively and gracious, merciful and good; he is saviour and
friend but also the Lord of all creation; he refuses to be exhausted or
manipulated by human intelligence, and thus always invites us to grow
deeper in relationship with him. This is exactly what we mean when we use
the word 'mystery': 'the reality known is always known as enigmatically
larger or deeper than our knowledge of it.'[17] Mysterious knowledge is
measured in depth rather than quantity and is persistent because of
its inexhaustible nature. It is a relationship we continually inhabit and
grow into. We find ourselves captivated in our encounters with Christ,
rather than being simply observers of God's will and purpose. Mysterious
knowledge always implicates the knower, reorientating and drawing the
knower into the bigger story of Christ's redemptive work.

And, according to the witness of Scripture, the Holy Spirit is the agent
of this mystery. It's the same Spirit who is given by Christ to his disciples
(cf. 1 John 4.13). As Paul wrote:

> we speak God's wisdom, secret and hidden, which God decreed
> before the ages for our glory . . . these things God has revealed to
> us through the Spirit; for the Spirit searches everything, even the
> depths of God. For what human being knows what is truly human
> except the human spirit that is within? So also no one comprehends
> what is truly God's except the Spirit of God. Now we have received
> not the spirit of the world, but the Spirit that is from God.
> (1 Corinthians 2.7–12)

The Spirit reveals Christ and thus the Spirit inducts people into Christ's
Church. And as we have seen, the same Spirit enlivens the Church's
worship. The same Spirit enables bread and wine to become spiritually
the body and blood of Christ and makes the waters of baptism a place of
sharing in the death and resurrection of Jesus (Romans 6.4). Hence the
Church's ancient commitment to the prayer of *epiclēsis*, or the 'calling
down' of the Spirit, as integral to sacramental practice. It is the same

---

17 Boyer, 'The Logic of Mystery', p. 91.

Spirit who breathes in and through the words of Scripture, addressing its readers and hearers, so that the Church may be nourished by word as well as sacrament (2 Timothy 3.15–17). In short, the Spirit leads the Church to Jesus.

For this reason, we might confidently state that worship has a mysterious quality: it is something that only makes sense as we participate in it. Like the person of Christ who is its proper focus, worship cannot be understood from some objective vantage point. The kinds of sharpness, caricature and stereotyping of different traditions that have characterized the *worship wars* fail to take this theological point seriously, often standing aloof from the worship offered by others outside of our localized traditions, and thus failing even to try to discern the presence of the Spirit within them. In effect this is the sort of thing done by those who believe that their experiences have exhausted all that the Holy Spirit can do and is doing. Skilled leadership is not the answer to this problem. We cannot convince others of the Spirit's work: it must be handled with prayerful discernment, and thus it must be attentive to God. We must be willing to participate, to taste and see what the Lord is doing (Psalm 34.8). To do that we must open ourselves up to the possibility that God can surprise us. Prayerful discernment is characterized by openness, orientated towards what we know of the Spirit not in our personal experiences alone but in the Trinitarian metaphysics in which we make sense of the Spirit's work. The theological instincts inherent to generous orthodoxy alert us to what is most important in this task and it's to this that I now turn.

Towards a generous, orthodox theology of worship

At the outset of this chapter, I stated that generous orthodoxy is a rule that guides the posture Christians adopt towards one another, liberating them *from* anxiety over differing worship styles and localized practices *for* mutual enjoyment of and participation in the Spirit's work across various Christian traditions. This has been my experience of generous orthodoxy, both at St Mellitus College and further afield in dioceses in the north-west of England where there is a rich heritage of both the

Catholic and Evangelical traditions. The power of generous orthodoxy in my experience rests in the mutuality of generosity and orthodoxy, how they are understood theologically, and subsequently how they are held together. For the rest of this chapter I want to consider this further by outlining the theological foundations of each in the light of the preceding discussion. As I do, my intent is to commend the power of generous orthodoxy to explicate a Christian theology of worship and to bring us into closer fellowship with one another in the Spirit.

Generosity is a species of charity. Which means it is a disposition that takes time to understand and make sense of another's perspective before coming to a final judgement about that person's faithfulness. In the context of the worship wars, generosity requires a temporary suspension of one's own deeply held beliefs, experiences and practices, or at least a lessening of the level of exclusivity with which one holds to them. It means avoiding an anxiety-fuelled caricature and stereotype and being sympathetically predisposed to other traditions. To do so is to approach the same scenario with an almost entirely opposite attitude: with interest instead of suspicion; with the desire to comprehend rather than reject; viewing others as spiritual kin to be loved rather than as a threat to be overcome. Charity does not mean affirmation or agreement, but it does call us to imagine the possibility that worship of God can happen in ways that are stylistically and liturgically quite different from one's own, and that none the less those ways of worshipping are real and genuine, Christ-centred and Spirit-enlivened. When I teach liturgical theology to candidates for the ordained ministry, I often put it like this: 'Please assume that I am a Christian, and that that means I love the Lord Jesus Christ and worship the triune God and seek to live a life worthy of the term "disciple", and I will do the same for you . . . until either one of us gives the other no shadow of doubt that they are not, in fact, what they say they are.' Generosity leaves room for a final decision about the liturgies of other traditions, but it doesn't rush to get there. In fact, it exposes Christians to *mystery* in the sense discussed earlier: the possibility that any existing knowledge, understanding and experience of Christ may be expanded in community with others, even those who are very unlike me in every way other than their commitment to him. Generosity is rooted, therefore, in the doctrine of God: it makes allowance for Christ to be present and active by the Spirit in ways that are outwith the current experience and expectations of the community of which I am part.

Generosity is only possible from a human perspective because, as we have said, worship is not first and foremost determined by human beings. Rather, all Christians worship in the power of the Spirit in response to the gospel of Christ whatever style they adopt (John 4.24; Philippians 3.3). To refuse generosity towards other traditions is to deny the possibility of the Spirit's work beyond one's own; it is, therefore, a theological commitment that demonstrates a faulty doctrine of God, in which the ungenerous presumes to have exhausted the Spirit's possibilities. Even if one does not outright refuse to be generous and opts instead to tolerate the existence of other liturgical styles, one is entangled in a similar problem: though the possibility of the Spirit's work elsewhere is acknowledged, to refuse to be generous is, in effect, to limit our experience and understanding of it. Generosity summons Christians to immersive participation in worship regardless of stylistic differences or personal preferences. It is to approach the global Church with the question, 'What is the Holy Spirit doing among these sisters and brothers? And what is there of God for me to learn along with them?' To borrow a metaphor, it is to allow the Holy Spirit to be the pacesetter and for Christians to strive to keep up (Galatians 5.25).

However, answers to these questions can quickly become vague if the approach is untethered from the agreed identity-conferring commitments of Christian faith, the things that help Christians explicate what Church is and what it is not. It's easy to see worship through anthropological or sociological lenses and for localized traditions to be interesting examples of contextual evolution. But, as the earlier discussion of the worship wars has indicated, the key focus here is the essence of the Church and so the approach must be primarily theological. So, as well as the dominical sacraments and the preaching of Scripture, I have in mind confessional statements like the Nicene Creed – the fourth-century document that remains the agreed cross-denominational benchmark for Christian faith to this day.[18] The Creed is meant to be a shorthand for the

---

18 For more on this, see my *Faithful Living: Discipleship, Creed, and Ethics* (London: SCM Press, 2019).

witness of Scripture, telling us about the triune nature of God and God's acts and giving us a framework in which to think and speak faithfully. In particular, the Creed helps us to conceptualize a Trinitarian metaphysics, augmenting Scripture's witness to the Holy Spirit as the one sent from the Father and the Son, who creates and gathers Christ's Church through baptism and nourishes it through word and sacrament. Another name for this kind of faithfulness is *orthodoxy*, which is about the Church measuring it's proclamation against what is known of God revealed in Jesus Christ by the Holy Spirit.

To attempt to discern the work of the Holy Spirit, therefore, requires that we think into this credal framework. In fact, to attempt to be *generous* without some reference to *orthodoxy* is to evacuate the words 'Holy Spirit' of any meaning at all, to expunge the identity of the Third Person of the Trinity from the gospel of Jesus Christ. And if that is the case, then our generosity towards others is rooted in little more than pietistic 'niceness' and limp anthropocentrism. But if, as we saw earlier, it is the Holy Spirit who ministers among God's people by revealing to them the mystery of God in Christ and drawing them into the community of faith in prayer and worship, word and sacrament, then our generosity is actually strengthened for being orthodox in its foundation. Indeed, to press the point further, orthodox teaching on the person and work of the Holy Spirit commits Christians to considerable generosity not for their own sake but because the triune God in whom they believe is entirely free, refusing to be limited by the experiences of particular groups but doing a new thing in the worship of all God's people (Isaiah 43.19, Psalm 22.3). To borrow a different metaphor, like the wind, the Spirit blows wheresoever he wishes (John 3.8). Any appeal to orthodoxy, therefore, is a recognition that the Third Person of the Trinity is at the same time consistently free and particularly discernable.

Discernment focuses on substance rather than liturgical style, though the two are indirectly related. It is much less concerned with the way something is done than it is with the meaning, purpose and direction that it is meant to enact. Generous orthodoxy therefore takes its cue from the Nicene Creed as it looks for evidence of the Spirit's distinctive work in curating worship that leads people to Jesus. This is in contra-distinction to any other spirituality we might encounter in liturgical settings (1 Corinthians 12.10). Thus, the basic way *orthodoxy* helps us to answer the questions posed by *generosity* is by raising an additional set of questions that focus our attention: does what we see and experience in the worship offered by others lead to Jesus Christ, witnessed and attested in Scripture? Does it conform to the teaching of Christ? Does it seek to glorify Christ as our crucified and risen saviour, Lord and friend? If the answer to these questions is yes, then we can be reasonably confident that it is the Holy Spirit at work regardless of the liturgical style or local tradition, and thus our generosity has led to something theologically and spiritually important. To discern that will always require time and attention, and, more importantly, active participation in the liturgy of others: we must taste and see.

Commitment to generous orthodoxy contains a summons to a more theologically rich and Spirit-centred account of worship. To respond to this summons offers both a comfort and challenge: that the Holy Spirit is the guarantor of our worship and thus can be trusted to lead us Christward is a great relief, but therefore we may find ourselves surprised and uncomfortable at the places and the people among whom Christ is at work by that same Spirit. We may find ourselves called to repent of our prejudices, to put down our weapons and walk away from the worship wars and become inhabitants of the peaceable kingdom where all violence ceases and those who worship Christ in the power of the Holy Spirit are united as sisters and brothers (Isaiah 11.1–9). We may find ourselves having to readjust liturgical practices in our own tradition, giving way to more faithful expressions that allow us to rehearse the story of Christ with greater clarity or coherence in our own contexts. To grow in relationship with God and experience more of the fullness of Christ is to go beyond the limitations of current experiences and traditions – no matter what they be – and seek the Lord where he may be found (Isaiah 55.6). This takes the prayerful obedience and commitment of the whole people of God, and is, therefore, nothing short of a miracle.

10

Devotional dogma and dogmatic worship

LINCOLN HARVEY

1 Introduction: a practice-based approach to definition

All concepts prove difficult to define *definitively*. What we mean by the word 'God', for example, can vary greatly, and even when we attach theological verbs like 'creates' or 'saves' they don't provide much assistance until we know *which* God we are talking about.[1] That's because these verbs are themselves underdetermined until we link them to a specific agent, which explains why the triune name is so important in Christian discourse. 'Father, Son and Holy Spirit' fixes our attention on the gospel narrative, by which the meaning of the concept 'God' – and predicates like 'saves' and 'creates' – are determined. In short, our theological concepts trade on the concrete event that defines them.[2]

'Generous orthodoxy' is another such concept. It too needs to be grounded before we can decipher its meaning, otherwise it is likely to remain somewhat nebulous, with nothing to anchor its definition. Of course, a lack of definition could prove beneficial, if only because the plain sense of the adjective makes it sound like the sort of thing any Christians could sign up to. 'Generous' clearly signifies a charitable posture, which aligns it neatly with the classical virtues, and so any

---

1 Robert W. Jenson, *The Triune Identity: God According to the Gospel* (Philadelphia, PA: Fortress, 1982; repr. Eugene, OR: Wipf & Stock, 2002), p. xi.

2 Or, as Jenson puts it, 'The proposition "All gods save" is indeed indisputable but only because it is wholly empty.' Robert W. Jenson, *Systematic Theology, Vol. 1: The Triune God* (New York: Oxford University Press, 1997), p. 56.

attempt to pin the concept down could undermine this spirit of common benevolence, effectively unearthing deep-seated disagreements about the contested reality that the umbrella term had happily captured. Or to put that differently, can generous orthodoxy stand up to critical scrutiny?

Let me be clear from the outset. I believe generous orthodoxy does stand up to critical scrutiny, although it will involve us doing some difficult – and in places uncomfortable – work to justify that conclusion. To begin that task, I will first look to situate the phrase in our day-to-day practices, offering a brief account of what it is like to work at St Mellitus College. Having thereby sketched the practical outworking of generous orthodoxy, I will then analyse the reality there described. This analysis will generate an awkward question, which centres on the apparent discrepancy between our approach to worship and our approach to teaching. Having flagged up this potential inconsistency, a conciliatory proposal will be ventured. This proposal will allow us to continue to celebrate the reality of generous orthodoxy, while removing the evident irregularity, thereby ensuring that our worship and our teaching are handled in the same way. The conclusion will be as follows: *within the economy of the triune God, generous orthodoxy is a celebratory outworking of the unity of distinct church traditions through their common obedience to the singular person of the bishop.* Of course, that statement will make little sense at this juncture. However, by the end of the essay it will.

2 Setting the scene: working at St Mellitus College

Over the last ten years, I have had the good fortune to work at St Mellitus College, and I count myself lucky. It really is a wonderful place for a theologian to work. That is because our students gather week by week from their different churches, with the common intention to study theology in the context of corporate worship. We therefore sing God's praise and say our prayers before grappling with the Christian gospel, only attempting to decipher the best way to witness to the resurrection of Jesus having adored him first. And that seems the right approach to me. Christians are called to study dogmatics devotionally.

With this being noted, I have always found it difficult to find the right words to capture the reality of working at St Mellitus. An apparent detour will provide us with a route into this latest attempt, and it will raise an important point which I will develop later in the essay.

St Mellitus College was founded in 2007 under the oversight of Bishop Richard Chartres, the former Bishop of London. Bishop Richard is the kind of bishop the Church needs, in that you can easily imagine him back at Nicaea in 325 or in some Carolingian Court in 809, or even in Sector 47 of the Zargon Empire in the year 6345 CE. That is to say, Bishop Richard possesses the knack of bringing the entirety of ecclesial time into the present moment, which is precisely what any bishop should do. They should never be reducible to contemporary reality, but are instead called to minister out of the fullness of the Church's time. In short, bishops are the entire Church *present*.

To put the point another way, I am suggesting that the Church is most basically personal. Strip away our buildings and committees, our mission action plans and charitable endeavours, and what you will find is a communion of bishops gathered by the Spirit around the resurrected Christ in the celebration of the sacrament. This means Bishop Richard *was* London during his incumbency, in that London Diocese is a communion of local churches, where the priests stand in for the bishop as they feed the faithful – vicariously presiding at the Eucharist, so to speak, hence 'vicars'. In practice, this means the bishop functions as the personal point of unity between all the neighbourhood churches, ensuring that the manifold congregations are united in their distinction by their personal relation to the serving bishop. As a result, whether a local church identifies itself as Anglo-Catholic, Charismatic, conservative Evangelical, or some such tradition, it will remain one with the others through their distinct communion with the episcopal office holder. And this is important to note. We will circle back to the point later.

When St Mellitus College was founded, Bishop Richard wanted to break the norm. In the Church of England, theological colleges have tended to be aligned to one particular tradition. Evangelicals go to these ones, Anglo-Catholics head to those ones, and the Charismatics study elsewhere. Of course, this tactic reaps many benefits, not least in enabling the students to celebrate their own tradition in the company of fellow beneficiaries, thereby inhabiting their tradition in its fullest expression and learning more about it within the security of their own identity. The danger, however, is equally obvious. Christians from different traditions will remain at arm's length, and so they can often remain misunderstood, with this miscalculation rarely providing a stimulus for unity. Of course, this may be an unfair critique, though exceptions may only prove the rule. Besides, the underlying point doesn't depend on accuracy: Bishop Richard wanted St Mellitus to be different to this perceived norm. The college was not to be aligned to one ecclesial tradition.

Right from its inception, the college has therefore meant to function as an extension of the bishop's personal charism of unity, being populated with students who are drawn from across the ecclesial landscape, never becoming the sole preserve of one tradition within the Church of England. Anglo-Catholics, Charismatics and Evangelicals have therefore always made up our numbers, meaning that we are one college defined by our intentional diversity.

The benefits of this approach soon became clear, though they have never been taken for granted. Staff and students get to learn alongside those who are different, with friendships being formed across historic divisions, and mutual understanding established through the brokering of personal disagreements. Students thereby get to see how we all worship the same Lord, sensing the common integrity that runs through our differences, with fascinating convergences emerging as a result. For example, Anglo-Catholics and Charismatics discover their shared understanding of the Spirit's work in worship, while also discovering that they understand the Spirit's act in different ways. Catholics celebrate his freedom to be faithful to the transformation of the eucharistic elements, while Charismatics celebrate his spontaneous outpouring amid the surprises of prayer ministry. Both traditions expect the Spirit to be freely active in their gatherings, but that discovery binds us together despite our different beliefs about what he primarily does. In short, genuine diversity is celebrated on the common ground of the Spirit's freedom.

However, something else should be noted. Bishop Richard wanted to ensure that the college's diversity remains within limits. That is why the virtue of 'generosity' is run alongside 'orthodoxy'. The bishop never wanted us to be the sort of institution that prioritizes scepticism and suspicion over faith, thereby privileging deconstruction and dissolving the confidence of our students as a result. Instead we are to use our intellectual faculties constructively, with the aim of understanding the Christian faith at a deeper level. We therefore teach with confidence, believing that Jesus is risen from the dead, that the apostolic witness to him bears true testimony, and that the towering figures who have gone before us can help us to work out what needs to be said to make the gospel intelligible today.[3] Or to put that otherwise, we trust that the gospel is the most beautiful idea in the world.

In many respects, our buildings bear witness to our institutional vocation. Take London, for example. With its towering spire, beautiful chancel, ornate pulpit and stained-glass windows, any visitor can see that our building is a church. Yet there can be few churches like it. Our London Centre houses a well-stocked library, accessible amenities, academic and administrative offices, and a cafe area, as well as its own subterranean marvel: spacious lecture halls, seminar and break-out rooms, with each providing a well-equipped space within which students and staff can embark on the theological task. The architectural combination is therefore striking. Our building says that the college is a place *where the Church can think*. Just so, our ethos – that is, our desire to serve the Church faithfully as a confident academic faculty – is architecturally expressed. Institutional vision and institutional facilities coincide.

However, life at St Mellitus is never easy. Our stark differences are always evident, and these often come to the fore during times of corporate worship. Worship – as the etymology suggests – centres on what we most value, and so it is always difficult to find yourself in a service that is alien to your norm. What you most cherish can appear to be overlooked or downtrodden, as God is praised in ways more familiar and habitual to others. With the benefit of hindsight, it might have been easier to duck this issue and instead sink to the lowest common denominator. But that would only have alienated everyone, and all of the time. We therefore made the decision that when Mass is said, it is said properly; when Charismatic services are held, they are done well; Book of Common

---

3 As Jenson argues, each generation's task is essentially 'working out what needs to be said to be saying the gospel'. Jenson, *Systematic Theology, Vol. 1*, p. 14.

Prayer, Services of the Word, Sung Evensong, prayer ministry, Compline and so on are all done with integrity. In short, we want to honour the different traditions by inhabiting them fully. And I think that is a very good idea, although that doesn't necessarily make it right.[4]

3 Raising the question: devotional dogma, but undogmatic worship

I have long since spotted an apparent inconsistency at St Mellitus College, and it should already be evident from the description just offered. The practice of generous orthodoxy appears to treat worship and belief differently, and so it is in danger of uncoupling Christian worship from Christian dogma, thereby ignoring the ancient adage that 'the law of prayer is the law of belief'.[5] That is to say, we readily accept that Christian beliefs must be regulated – in the sense that there are boundaries within which we are invited to think – but at the same time imagine that our worship is different. To illustrate this point, I will share a brief anecdote.

When I was ordained as a priest, one of my uncles told me that Jesus was an extra-terrestrial, no more than an unexpected visitor from a faraway galaxy who had bewildered a startled people before returning to his home planet. Jesus thereby left us with a mistaken impression of who he really was, and rather than recognizing his alien status we wrongly thought he was 'divine'. Just so, the Christian religion rests on a case of mistaken identity.

In some respects, this is a reasonable notion, and I continue to admire the strength of my uncle's conviction. However, I also know that it is not what the Church believes, and in that regard the thesis amounts to little more than a private opinion, with almost no authority outside my uncle's own head. That is to say, his conjecture carries little weight for the Christian, because we have been taught that the faith centres on

---

4 A sharp-eyed reader will have noticed the list of traditions makes no mention of 'liberals'. The reason is simple: 'liberalism', as I understand it, isn't itself a style of worship, indicative of a way of devotion, but can instead transcend these different traditions to a certain extent. Thanks to Fr Simon Cuff for helping to clarify this point.

5 The unattributed adage that *lex orandi lex credendi* – that is, the law of prayer is the law of belief – indicates the way 'the school of [Christian] logic was the church's liturgy'. Jenson, *Systematic Theology, Vol. 1*, p. 92

the divinity of the Son. The point to note is therefore simple: Christians acknowledge that the Church teaches the baptized how best to think about Jesus.

To take one example: the Nicene Creed provides us with a rule for belief, which functions as a condensed exegesis of Scripture and thus places limits on our subjective opinions. The Creed is authoritative in that plain sense, meaning that if you find yourself reading your Bible in a way that prevents you from saying this creed – that is, you keep your fingers crossed or lips sealed – then the Church thinks you are reading the Scriptures wrongly. Church dogma trumps private opinion.

Robert Jenson has made this point, arguing that our public confession of the faith is precisely that, public not private. Which is to say:

> A creedal recitation is not an expression of the current inventory of my religious opinions; I have not looked inside myself, discovered that I currently think God to be 'Father', 'Almighty', etc., next discovered that you currently make exactly the same inventory, and so joined you in self-expression. The personal commitment made by reciting the creed is rather that I declare allegiance to the continuing community which stipulates its faith by this text.[6]

Of course, Jenson has skirted the issue of which version of the creed we should recite, although his substantive point remains. Christian belief is defined publicly, and is never a matter of private opinion and personal preference.

None of this seems contentious to me, although I appreciate the concerns of others.[7] In baptism, I joined a community that has thought about the gospel for a long time, and so this community wants to initiate me into its established ways of thought before inviting me to make up my own mind. Catechesis, instruction and public declarations follow, all of which are meant to introduce the novice to the Christian faith. Of

---

6 Robert W. Jenson, *A Large Catechism* (Delhi, NY: American Lutheran Publicity Bureau, 1991), p. 15.

7 Many theologians rightly question the dominance of particular demographics in the creation of 'orthodoxy', but without denying that Christian belief is public. The vital question is *which* voices constitute that public.

course, everyone remains entitled to their own opinion, but the Church effectively asks us to do our research first. We should learn what it has previously meant to be Christian, before trying to define that adjective for ourselves.

Despite the widespread consensus that Christians need to be taught dogma, we can often assume that the same does not apply to worship. Recall the liturgical smorgasbord that characterizes St Mellitus. Some staff and students prefer contemporary worship, with its modern choruses and guitars, inspirational sermons and periods of prayer ministry, while others prefer a formal liturgy accompanied by organs and hymns. The different styles vary greatly, and there appears to be little need to justify our preferences, maybe because it is hard to see how one form of worship can be justified without causing offence to others. As a result, our doxological preferences become a matter of taste, with each of us opting for the style that appears to scratch our spiritual itch best. Or to put that more bluntly, the sovereign authority is our own subjectivity.

With this being recognized, the apparent discrepancy is now in view. Our collective thinking is disciplined, but our corporate worship is not. Or to put that yet another way: the doxological implications of ortho*doxy* are ignored – and that should cause concern. As usual, Karl Barth can help us see why.

Barth thought that worship is inherently dangerous, because it is the primary arena in which our sin comes to the fore.[8] His commentary on Romans hammered this point, arguing that the God of the gospel arises 'like a boxer's closed fist' in the face of religion.[9] Barth thereby claimed – somewhat counter intuitively – that our religion is an expression of *unbelief*, in that we adopt ritualized practices that are designed to help us reach the light at the end of the tunnel.[10] Worship therefore involves us gathering our best offerings, be that slaughtered calf, first fruits of

---

8 In what follows, I am indebted to Matthew Myer Boulton, *God against Religion: Rethinking Christian Theology through Worship* (Grand Rapids, MI: Eerdmans, 2008), pp. 25–135. I also trace material from Lincoln Harvey, *Jesus in the Trinity: A Beginner's Guide to the Theology of Robert Jenson* (London: SCM Press, 2020).

9 Karl Barth, *The Epistle to the Romans*, 6th edn, trans. Edwyn C. Hoskins (Oxford: Oxford University Press, 1968), p. 259.

10 See, for example, the section entitled, 'The Meaning of Religion', in Barth, *Romans*, pp. 240–56.

the land, some epistemological achievement, pious act, or supplicatory posture, in the mistaken belief that we can thereby polish ourselves up and strong arm our way into the realm of the gods. Religion is therefore little more than an attempt to deal with God on the basis of a 'Therefore'.[11] 'Oh Lord, we present you with this, that and the other, *therefore* you must bless us.' And precisely so, worship – according to Barth – is inherently sinful, because we mistakenly situate God at a distance, thereby making him an object of our intentions, who we can then *approach* in better or worse ways, which are always the wrong way and for a simple enough reason.[12]

Barth concluded that religion is unbelief because the Light is not at the end of the tunnel; he shines in our midst, Jesus Christ and him crucified. In effect, the only thing that could separate us from God would be if we somehow managed to destroy him, but that is exactly what God has chosen for his life in Christ. And because God has eternally chosen the event of separation as his life, nothing can separate us. There is therefore no distance for the religious person to travel and no time for the religious person to prepare, which is precisely the KRISIS of the Christian religion.[13] God has already pronounced his great 'Nevertheless'.[14] 'You are a sinner, *nevertheless* I shall bless you in my presence because of my crucified Son.'

Because Barth thought the inescapable presence of God is a 'judgement that pardons'[15] – that is, it is all about grace – he knew that we also have to say something positive about worship. If religion is the epitome of our sin – in that it rests on the presupposition of our estrangement from a separated and distant God – then it must also be the epicentre of God's

---

11 See, for example, Barth's analysis of being 'reckoned', in Barth, *Romans*, p. 123.

12 Again, I am here indebted to Boulton, *God against Religion*, pp. 25–135.

13 As Jenson summarized Barth's argument: 'Sin is helpless. It cannot achieve its goal, the establishment of a life separated from grace. For grace gets there ahead of it and grace is exactly God's victory over this attempt.' Robert W. Jenson, *Alpha and Omega: A Study in the Theology of Karl Barth* (New York: Thomas Nelson and Sons, 1963; repr. Eugene, OR: Wipf & Stock, 2002), p. 105.

14 For an example of Barth's use of this word: 'This means the marks of human unrighteousness and ungodliness are crossed by the deeper marks of the divine forgiveness; that the discord of human defiance is penetrated by the undertones of the divine melody "Nevertheless."' Barth, *Romans*, p. 95.

15 This is expressed in paragraph 61 of *Church Dogmatics* IV/1, where Barth moves almost seamlessly from *The Judgment of God* to *The Pardon of Man*.

gracious act towards us. Thus, in the Eucharist, for example, we will still bring our votive offerings, that is, the bread and wine, 'the work of human hands', but we do so in the knowledge that God will graciously take and transform these elements into his *already* done work for us, who is Christ and him crucified. In effect, our eucharistic offering is transformed by God into God-for-us in the act of God undoing our unbelief. Christian worship is set 'against itself', because God is unstoppably present.[16]

If Barth's diagnosis is kept in mind, we can sharpen the question we are asking of generous orthodoxy. By celebrating different approaches to worship – and thereby relegating worship to the aesthetic realm of brute subjectivity rather than church discipline – have we unintentionally done with our neighbours what Barth says we do with God: are we treating them as an object-at-a-distance and making a false virtue out of this mistaken division? Or to put that point more positively: as with God, so with neighbour; there is no space to traverse between Christians in worship because it is precisely the point where we are genuinely one in Christ.

4 Approaching an answer: the search for episcopal blessing

We can now see that generous orthodoxy doesn't appear to add up. Our thinking about God is authorized publically, but our worship of God is authorized privately, thereby leaving us disunited at the exact point where we should be one. The consequent task is to find a way to publicly authorize our worship, and my argument will be relatively simple. The underlying premise is that, just as 'dogma is to private opinion, so liturgy is to popular devotion'.[17]

However, please note something in advance. In making this case, the role of the bishop will become prominent so that we find a way for our current liturgical differences to be maintained. That is to say, one form of

---

16 Robert W. Jenson, *A Religion against Itself* (Louisville, KY: John Knox Press, 1967).

17 This is the place to note my substantial debt to Romano Guardini's work, where the link between formal liturgy and popular devotion is analysed and space created for the emergence of *new* forms of worship. For the quoted phrase, see Romano Guardini, *The Spirit of the Liturgy* (Chicago, IL: Biretta, 2014), p.7.

liturgy – for example, formal or informal – will not be elevated over the others, because the aim is to get all of them publicly authorized. In effect, the term 'liturgy' indicates not so much a prescriptive set of words, but an episcopally authorised act of worship.

To reach that conclusion, we first need to take a run-up, and to do that we must answer a different question: 'How we can trust that the gospel we have heard is accurate?'[18] None of us are exempt from answering this question, because at some stage we will have heard a message about an event that happened two thousand years ago, when certain people experienced the once-dead Jesus to be risen. But how can we be confident that the message we have heard has not been corrupted during the time it took to make its way from them to us? Jenson can again help us, providing an analogy to solve the dilemma. It centres on the children's game called 'telephone'.[19]

In this game, a message makes its way around a group of children in a series of whispers, with the fun centring on the corruption of the original message as it circulates the room. Analogously, we are situated at a distance from the first gospel whisperer unsure if their message has been mistakenly changed. Of course, if we were the first generation of Christians this wouldn't be a problem, or at least it could be easily overcome. We could visit one of the apostles and enquire as to the meaning of the gospel, checking out whether what we have heard aligns with what they have witnessed. For example, we could ask Peter what happened by the lake or question Paul about his interrupted journey to Damascus, thereby discovering what the good news of Jesus Christ really means. But once the apostles began to die out, there would appear to be nowhere left to turn. As a result, the Christian community needed a 'surrogate' for the apostles.[20]

With this problem in mind, we can see why the Church established a threefold structure to underwrite its witness, thus guaranteeing that the continuing message could be constantly measured against the apostles'

---

18 On this, see Jenson, *Systematic Theology, Vol. 1*, pp. 23–41.

19 For an example of Jenson's use, see Robert W. Jenson, *Lutheran Slogans: Use and Abuse* (Delhi, NY: American Lutheran Publicity Bureau, 2011), p. 27.

20 Jenson, *Systematic Theology, Vol. 1*, p. 23.

faith.[21] For example, the Church canonized certain texts, with the New Testament – as 'canon', literally a measuring stick – thereby becoming the prime authority, bearing faithful witness to the lordship of Christ in tune with the apostles' teaching. Scripture thus became 'the norm without a norm', being commissioned as the final adjudicator in any theological controversy, so that the Church which canonized it immediately submitted its judgements to it. However, it also became clear that Scripture can be understood in different ways, with its meaning rarely proving transparent.[22] The Church therefore needed to legislate authoritative readings of Scripture, not least because the Bible 'cannot defend itself against misinterpretation'.[23] The Church therefore wrote a series of credal statements, which are meant to function as condensed summaries of the scriptural whole, thereby ensuring that there is a common standard of theological exegesis. If the way you read Scripture is out of kilter with the creeds, you are reading it wrongly.

At the same time, the Church also needed office holders to speak *as* the Church, in the sense of being able to hold fellow Christians accountable to the credal interpretation of Scripture. It therefore began to single out the office of the bishop, authorizing bishops – in magisterial form, so to speak – to oversee the Church's teaching within a specific jurisdiction, and thus ensure that what is being preached from the pulpit is faithful to the Scriptures and the creeds, and thereby in harmony with the apostles. So, to return to Jenson's analogy, the whispered message is accompanied by a handwritten note, typeset summary and a person with good hearing as it begins to journey from person to person, with the good hearer being tasked with listening in at the points of transmission to guarantee that the current speaker is following the twofold script. As a result, it becomes a lot more likely that the message we hear has remained faithful to its

---

21 As I will note shortly, history is messier than this polemical account suggests. As Barth said, we are always dealing with '*Dei providentia et hominum confusione!*' Karl Barth, *Dogmatics in Outline* (New York: Harper, 1959), p. 86.

22 As Luke Zerra argues, canonization 'does not mean scripture presents the most *developed* instances of gospel-speaking, but that it presents *unchallengeable* instances of gospel-speaking'. Luke Zerra, 'Escaping the *Libido Dominandi*: Authority and Accountability in Jenson's Ecclesiology', *Pro Ecclesia* 28.2 (2019), p. 195.

23 Zerra, 'Escaping the *Libido Dominandi*', p. 196.

original version. The Church's proclamation can be trusted because it is authorized.

Now this is obviously a limited analogy, and church history is much messier than this account suggests. For example, those who have been judged heretical have been able to draw on the Scriptures, nod to the creeds and enjoy the blessing of their bishops. As a result, only Jesus Christ can be our final insurance that the gospel message is really about himself, with his Spirit alone guaranteeing the Church's faithful witness to the resurrection of the Father's only Son. Of course, that conclusion is circular, although not all circles are vicious. To trust the gospel is finally to trust in God. Or, to put that otherwise, ecclesial authority is always a charism and faith the appropriate mode of knowledge.[24]

So far, so good – or at least that's how the argument reads to me. However, I want to underline the role that the bishops play in the account just ventured. The scriptural canon, for example, is created somewhat haphazardly – albeit through the inspiration of the Spirit – but the agreed texts are only signed off by an assembly of bishops in 397 at Carthage. The creeds are similarly the product of the episcopal mind, with hundreds of bishops gathering at Nicaea, Constantinople, Chalcedon and the like to formulate dogmatic statements. Finally, it is bishops who ordain bishops, thereby creating – however broken or unbroken – a personal line back to the apostles. In short, the threefold mechanism of church authority depends on the authoritative oversight of bishops. Or to return to an earlier point: the Church is most basically personal, with each bishop called to bring the whole of ecclesial time into the present.

So what about worship? Can it be similarly authorized? Of course, the Church already possesses a range of authorized prayers, which are given to us in the belief that we need to be taught to pray just as much as to think. For example, I live under the discipline of the Church of England, which provides me with a Book of Common Prayer and *Common Worship* to help in my devotions. I suspect some colleagues and students assume that I pray these liturgies because they suit my temperament, in that I like a bit of order, a set menu and everything in its place, although nothing could be further from the truth. I would never choose to wade

---

24 Zerra, 'Escaping the *Libido Dominandi*', p. 199.

through formal collects and set prayers, with psalm after psalm and passages of Scripture set by the lectionary. If I was king, things would be different. Nonetheless, I have accepted that I need to learn how to pray just as much as I need to learn how to think, and so I trust the Church's decision that these liturgical resources are key to that. But what about Christians who don't use authorized texts?

First, I think there are very good reasons to break with the formal liturgies on occasion, most of which centre on adapting to our missionary context. However, any divergence from established norms should be undertaken carefully. For example, the Church has long since recognized the importance of praying with Israel, thereby immersing ourselves in her psalms, as well as hearing from her Scriptures. Confession and the assurance of forgiveness likewise seem vital, as is a distinct time of Bible study and intercession that is shaped by the Church's calendar so we don't skip elements of the story and get stuck on the bits we prefer. And, of course, it is hard to find a good rationale for omitting the Lord's Prayer. As a result, if we put our heads together, we could probably work out the essential aspects of a Christian act of worship and translate it into a form appropriate for today, although we may end up with the same sort of liturgy we have already been given. Nonetheless, whatever new patterns of worship emerge – and however informal they are – there remains a simple enough way to make these liturgies genuinely *public*. In short, we seek our bishop's blessing.

The bishop – accountable to other bishops under God, and with an eye on the apostolic mission of the Church – can authorize a public act of worship, having exercised due diligence to ensure it coheres with our scriptural and credal faith and is appropriate for our context today. If the bishop is happy with our worship, then it is hard for anyone – except other bishops! – to find fault with the liturgy that we use, whether it be formal or informal, because, as Jenson says, episcopal blessing will mean we have found the 'right *sort* of thing to be doing'.[25] In short, it will be authorized.

And so that is what we should do. Of course, the mechanism of authority might not be perfect, but it remains genuinely church because

---

25 Jenson, *Systematic Theology, Vol. 1*, p. 32.

it is genuinely personal. It also reminds us why the Church needs good bishops and – most importantly – why we should all pray for them too. It also clarifies that the apparent discrepancy identified in generous orthodoxy is only that – *apparent*. Our various acts of worship have always been authorised by the bishops who oversee our work. Our thinking and devotions are public.

5 Concluding statement: a definition of generous orthodoxy

And so we finally return to my formal definition: generous orthodoxy is a celebratory outworking – within the economy of the triune God – of the unity of distinct church traditions through their common obedience to the person of the bishop.

11

Remembering we were Gentiles: A generous orthodoxy from the margins

WILLIE JAMES JENNINGS

We were Gentiles: Christian faith begins with this truth. We were those who were as Ephesians 2.12 says, 'without Christ, being aliens from the commonwealth of Israel, strangers to the covenants of promise, having no hope, and without God in the world'. Christian faith emerged at the margins of Judaism, at the margins of promise, and fully within the vulnerability of being Gentile in a religious world not our own. To be Gentile in a Christian framework is already to accept marginality. This reality of marginality, however, has never truly entered into how we understand Christian faith and, more devastatingly, it has never been a part of how we understand Christian intellectual life.

From the very beginning of Gentile Christian faith, we have stumbled with this scandal – of faith in another people's God whom we understand to be our God as well. We quickly dismissed this marginality in favour of interpretative frames that emphasized the universality of the gospel and of a God who loves all peoples and the entire creation.[1] This is of course true, but in bypassing the significance of marginality we bypassed something crucial to being Christian and to the way in which God's love comes to be seen and God's identity comes to be understood through us.

Very early, we are not sure when or where, Christians grew impatient with the actual story of our faith, that we were the outsiders to the

---

1 Daniel Boyarin, 'Answering the Mail: Toward a Radical Jewishness', in *A Radical Jew: Paul and the Politics of Identity* (Berkeley, CA: University of California Press, 1994), pp. 228–60.

covenant of promise who were included by fleshly grace and divine desire found in Jesus Christ through the Spirit. We offered an alternative reading of Christian reality that made Gentile Christians the whole point of the matter, made us the centre of the story, and sent Israel to the margins. That legacy of sending Israel to the margins profoundly shaped Christian intellectual life. What we might call now a Christian intellectual and racial hegemony had its seeds in the Christian refusal of marginality. This chapter explores the contours of what that refusal means and what accepting it now might mean for Christian intellectual life and the embodying of a life-giving, life-affirming orthodoxy.

No room for the view

Acts 15 shows us a road that was not travelled. We can see this in the words of Peter:

> After there had been much debate, Peter stood up and said to them, 'My brothers, you know that in the early days God made a choice among you, that I should be the one through whom the Gentiles would hear the message of the good news and become believers. And God, who knows the human heart, testified to them by giving them the Holy Spirit, just as he did to us; and in cleansing their hearts by faith he has made no distinction between them and us . . .
>
> Therefore I have reached the decision that we should not trouble those Gentiles who are turning to God, but we should write to them to abstain only from things polluted by idols and from fornication and from whatever has been strangled and from blood. For in every city, for generations past, Moses has had those who proclaim him, for he has been read aloud every Sabbath in the synagogues.'
> (Acts 15.7–9, 19–21)

This portion of the story of Acts 15 brings us into the unprecedented, if not in Israel, then surely with the followers of Jesus. Gentiles become believers not only in the God of Israel but in Jesus. Not only do they follow the way of Jesus but they also had the Spirit of God dwell in them just as the Spirit dwelt in the Jewish followers of Jesus. So the Gentiles

emerge as a profound theological question for the Jewish believers –
what will we do with them, with their faith? Gentile believers are an
occasion for rethinking, and for an intellectual expansion of how to
mark the actions of God. Unfortunately, the admonition to 'not trouble
the Gentiles' could not capture the newness that was already being
announced in Antioch where Jews and Gentiles were forming faithful
community together (Acts 13). This was the first road that was not
travelled where the Gentile question might have opened up a new way
to imagine Jewish faithfulness as a shared project of Jew and Gentile. Yet
the road not travelled that concerns us here is the position of the Gentile
in the conversation of Acts 15.

We are not speaking. We are being spoken of. We are not present in
power, but in hope of acceptance. We are not determining what faithfulness to God should look like for us and our peoples, we are being
discussed in order to determine *for us* what faithfulness to God should
look like *for us*. If we imagine this story in Acts 15 from present-day
sensibilities then we might see this as a moment of Jewish hegemony, but
that would not be very helpful, because Gentiles are in the vast majority
even in the differences between their multiple peoples. Gentile presence
in Jewish life in the time of this text is an existential threat to Torah
and temple faithfulness as the people of Israel must remain on guard
against the crumbling of their ways of life underneath the weight of the
quotidian power of Gentile life. We can understand the concerns of those
who wanted to make sure that these Gentile believers understood what is
entailed with Jewish faithfulness. *The Gentile is in the position of one who
could destroy a world even as they enter that world.*

The Jewish disciples of Jesus understood this, which in part explains
the subtext of Peter's words: let's not trouble the Gentile believers because
we don't want them troubling us, that is, disrupting our way of life.
There is a profound cultural anxiety that moves through this chapter
and through the entire book of Acts as Jewish communities rightly
fear a cultural crumbling affect from Gentiles outside their community
and a corrosive affect from inside their community from this new sect
that commingles with Gentiles. Yet what is also clear from this story
is that Jewish believers are being asked to think their history, expand
their historical consciousness in such a way as to include Gentiles in a

new way. This is not to suggest either historically or theologically that Gentiles were absent from Israel's historical self-understandings, nor am I trying to wade into old or new arguments about how the universal and the particular were configured in biblical Israel's understanding of the redemptive work of the Messiah. These disciples of Jesus are grappling with the actions of God in and among Gentiles and seeking to align those actions more clearly with what they understand God to be doing through them on behalf of Israel. How is the Jesus mission, which they understood to be in the long history of God's actions for Israel, bound up with Gentiles having received the power of the Holy Spirit? But the more crucial point for us is that Gentiles are now being positioned inside the history of Israel. The greater disruption is of our own historical consciousness – we Gentiles are inside Israel's story, characters in their play and scenes in their drama. *Gentiles are in the position of thinking themselves inside another people's story, trying to make sense of their lives in that story.*

The position of the Gentile in Acts 15 is an odd sort of marginality and vulnerability – one in which we lack narrative control but are present as potential destroyers of story, one in which we are being allowed to forego full cultural and theological assimilation while bearing the power of an assimilation that has always menaced Israel.[2] There is a cultural and theological assimilation that we will accept because we are after all inside the promise of God for Israel and their hope, and in this way we submit to a new theological grammar beyond the logics of our gods. In so doing, we choose Israel's God over the gods of our peoples with all the accusations and condemnations of cultural and theological betrayal. We become traitors to our own peoples. We have become wanderers on a strange new theological landscape, caught between the old gods and the God of Israel, caught in ad hoc theological thinking, trying to grasp and translate the contours of this new faithfulness.

Somewhere in the history of the early Church we rejected our position. Whether this rejection grew from becoming impatient or annoyed with

---

2 Michael Wyschogrod, 'Paul, Jews, and Gentiles', in *Abraham's Promise: Judaism and Jewish–Christian Relations* (Grand Rapids, MI: Eerdmans, 2004), pp. 188–201. Wyschogrod suggests that the principles of the Noachide law, which is the Torah for the Gentiles, are being articulated in Peter's advice here, which means that what is being advised here is not for Gentiles to seek to become Jews.

hearing the truth of our marginality or if it grew from an active attempt to recast God as disconnected from Israel and only involved with them inconsequentially or certainly not eschatologically, or some combination of both, it resulted in an intellectual posture that refused to think from the position of marginality and set Christian intellectual life inside that refusal. This is the road not travelled – an intellectual life attuned to three dynamics: silence, sensitivity and story.

The silence that begins in the Bible has been denied in the legacy of a Christianity that ignores that silence in how we read the Bible and teach others to read the Bible. It is the silence of Gentiles in the conversation of biblical Israel with its God. The Acts 15 story has often been characterized and is still often characterized as the first church council, as though it were we Gentiles making the decisions about our own future. So Acts 15 is lined up with church councils from Nicaea all the way to the Second Vatican Council as the continuing deliberations of Gentiles about life with God. This is just one example of a wider problem of erasing Jewish centredness in how we understand Scripture. As Naomi Seidman notes in her brilliant work, *Faithful Renderings: Jewish–Christian Difference and the Politics of Translation*, Christians very early began translating Jewish texts in ways to minimize Jewish centredness.[3]

Such minimizing of Jewish centredness grew as Gentile Christians distorted the internecine interpretative struggles of Jewish diaspora communities. Their struggles to make sense of the prophet Jesus and his significance for Israel's life and destiny was the soil in which a pattern of reducing Jewish presence *in the very practice of interpretation* would take hold of Gentile Christian existence. We translated Israel out of an interpretative struggle and translated ourselves as Gentile Christians into the centre of interpretation. Moreover, we translated ourselves into the centre of the text as its true possessors and thus as the authentic owners of the text.[4] The biblical text became a text without a people in order to become the text of Gentile Christians. I am not saying that

---

3 Naomi Seidman, *Faithful Renderings: Jewish–Christian Difference and the Politics of Translation* (Chicago, IL: University of Chicago Press, 2006). Also see Kathleen Biddick, *The Typological Imaginary: Circumcision, Technology, History* (Philadelphia, PA: University of Pennsylvania Press, 2003).

4 Susannah Heschel, *Abraham Geiger and the Jewish Jesus* (Chicago, IL: University of Chicago Press, 1998).

Gentile Christians from *Christian* antiquity throughout the history of the Church denied Jewish presence in the Bible or that we denied that God spoke to Israel. We denied the silence. We denied that the Bible first reveals to us an exclusive conversation between God and God's people and among God's people, which *is itself revelatory of God and pedagogically crucial for Christian intellectual life.*

The silence teaches. It shows us that the first step towards exercising faithful thinking after God that is orthodoxy is listening. Not just any kind of listening, but listening with the sense of an outsider who was being brought in by grace and by the sheer willingness of God's people to see God's expansive love. Christian listening to the Scriptures as it now stands exists in a legacy of denial which means that it exists in a legacy of distorted listening. We formed a reality of listening that loves the Scripture but shuns the people of Israel, rooted in a history of hatred for those same people. How is it possible to form a legacy that claims to love the word of God but hates the people to whom and through whom that word has come to us? Christian listening to the world lacks this pedagogy of silence through which this sense of marginality would do its proper work, forming an intellectual disposition that remembers, discerns and honours the contours of a conversation that formed outside us. Such a disposition would have allowed us to move wisely into that conversation, recognizing the importance of being seen as one aiming to enter in.

The entering in is key to recognizing diaspora life and essential to capturing the sensitivity necessary for theological reflection. Gentiles were a threat to the life of Israel. We were the enemies of Israel and of Israel's God. We bore a destructive assimilating power rooted not only in sinful disobedience and allegiance to the worldly powers but also in sheer numbers that could, if unchecked, drown Jewish identity in waves of Gentile ways of life. Yet God through mercy and grace transformed us by the Spirit and set us on a path of a different reality of assimilation. We entered the dynamic of thinking our lives between Jewish promise and prophecy, rethinking and reweaving our ways of life to match life with Israel and Israel's God. Yet this was a dynamic quickly ignored as Christian communities formed with segregationist impulses alive and well. This meant that Christian intellectual life formed without its founding sensitivity to its own powers and problems with assimilation.

We have not been trained to sense our lives inside another people's story, and without that theological sensitivity training we lack the ability to move with diaspora acuity in how to open ourselves to new worlds while not losing ourselves in them or inviting people into our worlds without destroying them in the process.

The gospel story is Israel's story first. Yet we stand in a legacy that weaponized the universal and turned Israel into a minor figure in their own story. T. F. Torrance used to say that Jesus is the Messiah of Israel and the head of the Church.[5] This is not a statement about dual vocations, but about the historical trajectory through which we must think the present moment. To be Christian is to be part of a people formed to give witness to the story of Israel and give witness to Israel of the expansion of their own story through Jesus of Nazareth. Christian witness to the world is first witness to Israel. Gentile faith is first a question to Israel before it is an answer to the world, and to both the words are the same. This is our God. This life inside story is decentred life. We are not in control of the narrative and we resist other narratives that wish to control our lives or that offer themselves as tools of control for us to use. To be inside the gospel story reorients the stories of our peoples towards the God who created and loves them and destines them for life together with the triune God. Our individual stories and the stories of our peoples in all their complexity matter to God, but no longer may they claim the captain's chair, guiding and directing us to our future. Yet the gospel story that we inhabit was intercepted by another story – Christian colonialism. The Christianity that entered colonial waters from the fifteenth century onwards carried an intellectual life and a vision of orthodoxy unschooled in silence, sensitivity, or story.

A sick centredness

The Christians who came to the new worlds had been formed over centuries in Gentile hubris. This was a way of seeing and living the faith that imagined a strange and diseased centredness. They saw themselves at the centre of the gospel story. One could argue that seeing humanity

---

5 T. F. Torrance, *The Mediation of Christ* (Grand Rapids, MI: Eerdmans, 1983), pp. 12–56.

at the centre of the gospel story is correct, yet this was not a centre calibrated to humanity qua humanity; this was a centre organized around the particular bodies of these proto-Europeans who narrated the story of God and the story of God's work in the world *essentially* through their bodies. This is by far the most decisive effect of supersessionism – to unleash into the Christian imagination a sick centredness, one that infects and permeates Christian intellectual activity from interpreting Scripture, to forming and disseminating doctrine and liturgy, to engaging in other ecclesial practices. Such centredness not only killed Jewish presence in the Christian imagination but also imagined a God with a narrowed focus – only on the Church and only through the Church on the world.

These Christians entered worlds heretofore unknown to them with a powerfully intoxicating sense of providence – God had led them to the new worlds. This sense of providence, however, was already distorted having collapsed in on their bodies, leading them to believe that they embodied the blueprint for maturity, for the maturing of mind, body, spirit and the built environment. They thought and felt their centredness as a grave responsibility given to them by God. That diseased centre formed what I have called a pedagogical imperialism that thinks Christian witness from the idea of being first and foremost teachers to the world.[6] These Christians, however, sought to teach the faith in worlds that they were struggling to understand. It is the mixture of that struggle with their arrogant posture that set the stage for the formation of racial identity and the emergence of whiteness.

These proto-Europeans, in their attempts to grasp the density of the new worlds, turned their descriptive analyses of indigenous life into an ontology of difference that would be organized hierarchically with themselves as the pinnacle of human maturity and salvific reality. Whiteness emerged as the designation that creates designation and a descriptor that enables description, that is, it emerges as the fount of all evaluative logics. Whiteness as a way of seeing and evaluating flowed through a Christian intellectual life that was encased inside the imperial operations of colonialism. The taking of the land, the subduing of the

---

6 Willie James Jennings, *The Christian Imagination* (New Haven, CT: Yale University Press, 2010), pp. 112ff.

peoples and animals, and the turning of everything towards commodi-
fication nurtured not only ethnic chauvinism for the many European
nations that would enter the colonialist enterprise but also formed an
educational enterprise that was obsessed with control – of bodies, minds
and behaviour.

That educational enterprise facilitated the formation of theological
orthodoxy in the new worlds both in terms of appropriate thought
patterns and ways of speaking as well as forms of behaviour and
comportment. Theological orthodoxy formed inside technologies of
control and became expressions of them as Christians from the old
world established a Christianity fitted for conquest. The idea of making
disciples was inextricably bound up with the idea of remaking the world
into the image of the European. It would, however, be a mistake to see
this obsession with control aimed exclusively at indigenous life and
environments. It also redounded to the colonialists themselves who saw
the need to cultivate in their children the capacity to handle the gifts of
the colonies and the responsibilities of their power in the new worlds.
The need to educate, bound to the desire to control and seed the ability
to control, found its most powerful manifestation in the operations
of slaveholding Christianity with its pedagogy of the plantation. The
pedagogy of the plantation refers not only to the educational efforts that
took place in the new world on plantation, Hacienda, Encomienda and
Doctrina, but also for the ways these sites set the template for envisioning
education more broadly aimed at both the formation of society and the
formation of men to lead that society.[7]

As I note in my book *After Whiteness*, the dominant central image
around which education in the faith and education in general formed
was that of a white self-sufficient man who would embody three virtues –
possession, mastery and control.[8] Education that forms this man even in
those who are not men or white would become the guiding aspiration of
theological and Western education. These three virtues once embodied

---

7 Alan Durston, *Pastoral Quechua: The History of Christian Translation in Colonial Peru,
1550–1650* (Notre Dame, IN: University of Notre Dame Press, 2007). Also see Joanne
Rappaport and Tom Cummins, *Beyond the Lettered City: Indigenous Literacies in the Andes*
(Durham, NC: Duke University Press, 2012).

8 Willie James Jennings, *After Whiteness: An Education in Belonging* (Grand Rapids, MI:
Eerdmans, 2020).

would yield a person fit in body and mind for their environment. They would be one not given to emotional extremes and therefore one who was self-possessed and in possession of the necessary knowledge to perform their task. Moreover, they would also be one able to handle possessions and the processes of more accumulation. Possession and self-possession imply mastery – so the one formed in mastery would operate with the knowledge and the skills necessary to complete his tasks. Possession and mastery yield control both in terms of a person's ability to control themselves in the midst of contention or chaos as well as being poised to take control of one's environment – from people to land and in whatever arena of life that presents itself. Such people who have been cultivated in self-sufficient masculine form are able to place themselves in service to a task and a world being created that is greater than themselves but is inseparable from their power.

The aspiration towards self-sufficient masculinity was the engine inside the formation of theologically orthodox minds. This was education in the faith that was itself in the service of forming masters. Yet this was a much wider reality than simply forming young men who could run plantations, but forming young men who could run institutions from business to government to military units to nations. Wider still, this educational endeavour formed an orthodoxy in the Western world obsessed with control – of bodies, minds and behaviour – and one that would become an abiding characteristic of whiteness. If we might define orthodoxy as a way of life that involves a way of thinking and living and evaluating then modern colonialism formed a theological orthodoxy permeated with whiteness as also a way of thinking, living and evaluating. Woven together they are a profound signature of the legacy of Gentile hubris.

That Gentile hubris infected the orthodox imagination and bequeathed to Christians formed on colonial sites a mangled legacy of education where the good of learning of the gospel was mixed with the horror of learning to turn a relentlessly derogatory and suspicious gaze on their own peoples' ways, cultures, rationalities and wisdom. It was Christianity that inspired the idea of cultural backwardness in its modern forms as we cultivated Christians to measure their peoples by how well they followed European form in thought, mannerism, dress and sensibility. Cultural assimilation as part of the history of Western missions is not new news, but we have not fully considered its deep inroads into the orthodox imagination and what this legacy means in terms of the continuing performance of an orthodoxy. This legacy has robbed us of a legacy of a faith formed through humility and a Christian witness established through learning. It turned the educational life of a Christian on its head. We have turned what should have been our strongest disposition – of adaptability, malleability, flexibility and performing an assimilation without loss – into the burden of so many people who have become Christian, who must struggle to discern how they may be Christian and not reject their own people in total, how they may be Christian without entering a trajectory towards whiteness, and how they may think deeply inside a Christian way without becoming European or Western.[9]

The kind of orthodox imagination we need is one that challenges the long trajectory of Gentile hubris by returning us to the margins from which sight of our life in God is clearest. Christians need to configure our intellectual life from the trajectory of marginality to rightly situate ourselves in the story of God and thereby open up new ways of envisioning not only what it means to think as a Christian but also what positionality we Christians inhabit as we offer witness to the living God. Yet, why use the idea of marginality at all, given its now centuries of enactment through the operations of colonialism? As I noted in another essay, marginality is a form of positionality that historically represents the spatial ecology of a 'centred' Western world.[10] As is now clear, that spatial ecology formed in the womb of modern colonialism ironically using the idea of Israel and theologies of election as the abiding tropes through which to articulate approvingly the colonial remaking of worlds. Would it not be better simply to jettison our current spatial ecology all together especially given its historical connections to Christianity and Christian theology?

To end the forms of marginality constructed through colonialism and whiteness requires we unravel its remade world. Restoring the trajectory of Gentile marginality begins that unravelling by turning us towards a

---

9 Jennings, *The Christian Imagination*, pp. 207ff.

10 Willie James Jennings, 'To Be a Thinking Margin: Reframing Christian Intellectual Life', in *Enfleshing Theology: Embodiment, Discipleship, and Politics in the Work of M. Shawn Copeland*, ed. Robert J. Rivera and Michele Saracino (Lanham, MD: Lexington Books, 2018), pp. 153–64.

different kind of intellectual posture and a different work. We remember. Ephesians 2 reminds us to remember the nature of being outside. Marginality carries hermeneutic import. It opens an essential lens through which to read the world, one that brings us near the way Jesus invited his disciples to envision God's own looking at us from the places of humiliation. Jesus positioned the looking of God from the places of poverty, incarceration, sickness, abandonment and death. It was from those places that Jesus calibrated the work of discipleship. This is marginality crucial to the overcoming of marginality.

Having been drawn into the very life of God through the journey of Jesus, we find ourselves moving not only from outsider to insider but insider to outsider – towards whoever has been left destitute and at the mercy of agents of death that seek to steal more life from the living. Yet even the position of service can reinscribe the racial centredness born of colonialism. The movement of service towards those at the margins must be guided by the pedagogy of remembering that not only places Jesus at the sites of need but also at the site of learning. Jesus is God learning of God's creation, entering fully into the joy of coming to know the quotidian realities of life. Jesus of Nazareth learns of his people and of their ways with the land and of their life with God. He listened and he learned and then he spoke. Jesus presents a faith found first in the listening before the speaking, a faith performed in the learning before the teaching. In contrast, we have presented a Christianity that glories in the teaching and shuns the learning, and in so doing we have presented an orthodoxy that denies its true architecture, the way of Gentile learning. We are those who learned of our God by overhearing the great Shema, and in such hearing we heard the call of love.

12

Blessing the other: Jesus, Elijah, Elisha and generous orthodoxy

MARK SCARLATA

Luke 4.24–30; 1 Kings 17.9–16; 2 Kings 5.1–19b.

At the inauguration of Jesus' ministry in the Gospel of Luke he is confronted by those from his native village of Nazareth. Having declared that Isaiah's Jubilee vision of release, healing and restoration has become a present reality (Luke 4.17–21), Jesus is faced with astonishment from those friends and family who have known him throughout his life. 'Is this not Joseph's son?' (4.22), the crowd asks in disbelief having heard his 'gracious words'. What begins as an inspiring, communal encounter between the neighbours of Nazareth sharply turns into confrontation when Jesus reveals to them the nature of his calling and the nature of God's salvation in the world.[1]

His first response confounds villagers' expectations that he would perform miraculous signs and wonders similar to those they had heard stories of him performing in Capernaum (4.23). This is the community that had raised Jesus since he was a little boy. He had played in their homes, shared their bread – he was a part of the home team. Those from the tribe take care of their own and if Jesus was healing elsewhere surely he would do the same, if not in greater measure, for those who loved him, protected him and helped him grow up to be a man. But rather than being restricted by his network of relationships in Nazareth, Jesus cites

---

1 See Jacob W. Elias, 'The Furious Climax in Nazareth (Luke 4:28–30)', in *The New Way of Jesus: Essays Presented to Howard Charles*, ed. William Klassen (Newton, KS: Faith and Life, 1980), pp. 87–99.

two Old Testament narratives which illustrate the nature of his calling to the lost sheep of Israel and to the Gentiles.

Jesus recalls the stories of Elijah blessing the foreign widow from Sidon and Elisha healing the Syrian commander, Naaman, from leprosy. No doubt the people of Nazareth would have been familiar with the spectacular miracles of each prophet and that Elijah was prophesied as the forerunner of God's coming salvation (Malachi 4.5–6). They were not, however, prepared for how these narratives would upend their perceptions of God's generosity to those outside his covenant people.

This confrontation and response at the beginning of Jesus' ministry offer valuable insights into the nature of God's kingdom but also provide a framework for how we might understand and practise a generous orthodoxy within the Christian faith. This chapter will examine the theme of crossing borders in order to bless the other as a posture for how Christians might encounter those of differing theological or ecclesiological views while maintaining credal orthodoxy. Jesus' use of the Elijah and Elisha stories set the paradigm for his own ministry as one that brings the good news to Israel, but also extends beyond tribal boundaries to offer blessing and healing to the Gentiles. This is further alluded to in the ministry of the disciples in Acts 10—11 when Peter is also pushed beyond his own ethnic and religious boundaries. This pattern from the Old Testament prophets offers a model for how a generous orthodoxy among Christians can bring about the unity, while maintaining the diversity, of the Church today.

According to Hans Frei, the battle between 'liberal' and 'evangelical' scholarship of his day was promoting divisions that needed to be overcome with a kind of 'generous orthodoxy' that could encompass both voices in order for there to be fruitful dialogue.[2] Hunsinger sums up Frei's approach by writing, 'It is as though Frei sensed in his theological bones that generosity without orthodoxy was empty but that orthodoxy without generosity was blind.'[3] Frei recognized the need for an approach to discussing Scripture, doctrine and Christian practice that was rooted

---

2 Hans Frei, 'Response to "Narrative Theology: An Evangelical Appraisal"', *Trinity Journal* 8 (1987), pp. 21–4, p. 21.

3 George Hunsinger, 'Hans Frei as Theologian: The Quest for a Generous Orthodoxy', *Modern Theology* 8:2 (1992), p. 123.

in a commitment to the historic faith of the ecumenical councils of Nicaea and Chalcedon. He also argued for reading the Bible with a *sensus literalis* that was employed by the earliest Christian traditions.[4] The formal narrative structure of the Gospels did not need to be deconstructed by historical-critical methods, but could be read through a literal sense that formed a 'traditional consensus' among early Christian readings.[5] Like Paul Ricoeur's argument for reading Scripture with a 'second naïveté',[6] Frei rooted himself in what he believed were orthodox readings of the Gospels in their *sensus literalis* that allowed for multiple interpretations but were grounded in the high Christology of the text.

Frei's understanding of generous orthodoxy spoke to the divisions between the liberal and conservative factions of his day. His hope was to offer a middle way that allowed for disagreement yet maintained the unity of the Church. Though debates between historical-critical and *sensus literalis* readings of the Scripture continue, we still find the need for open dialogue between different Christian approaches to Scripture, doctrine and tradition that does not lead to division. Frei was right to call for a 'generous orthodoxy' that would allow for Christians both to question traditional assumptions and to speak from a conviction of faith. This generosity of engagement can be embodied by a deep commitment to the historic faith of the Church and to the life of prayer and worship.

Generous orthodoxy offers an approach to theological and biblical studies in the context of theological institutions, secular universities or in relationship to different traditions within the global Church. Frei's vision of generous orthodoxy offers a starting point that moves towards a Christian commitment to engage with, and allow room for, the flourishing of traditions other than one's own. Whether Protestant, Anglican, Catholic, Orthodox or Pentecostal, each expression of Christian faith can offer a unified vision of Christ if there is a willingness to go beyond the borders of our tradition, to relinquish control and to be open to the

---

4 H. Frei, 'The "Literal Reading" of Biblical Narrative in the Christian Tradition: Does It Stretch or Will It Break?', in Frank McConnell (ed.), *The Bible and the Narrative Tradition* (New York: Oxford University Press, 1986), pp. 36–77.

5 Hans Frei, 'Literal Reading', pp. 67–71, pp. 36–43.

6 Paul Ricoeur, *The Symbolism of Evil*, trans. Emerson Buchanan (Boston, MA: Beacon Press, 1969), pp. 351–5.

possibility of blessing the other as Jesus and the prophets were willing to do.

Elijah and the widow: going beyond our borders

The first story that Jesus recalls is that of Elijah, who appeared during the reign of Ahab the king of Israel. The narrative of 1 Kings 17, like many Old Testament stories, is sparse in detail. We are told nothing about Elijah except that he is associated with a place called 'Tishbe in Gilead' (1 Kings 17.1). We are not told that he is a prophet but his name means 'YHWH is my God'. We might be surprised that no further detail is given about Elijah's authority or his relationship with YHWH, yet Robert Alter reminds us that 'an essential aim of the innovative technique of fiction worked out by the ancient Hebrew writers was to produce a certain indeterminacy of meaning, especially in regard to motive, moral character, and psychology'.[7] He goes on to argue that deliberate gaps in the narrative open up the process of revision and discernment of multiple possible interpretations. In the story of Elijah the gaps of the unknown become partially revealed, but what is clear is that the battle between the prophet and Ahab/Jezebel is the embodiment of YHWH's conflict with Baal and an echo of Moses' clash with Pharaoh.[8]

Israel is a place of famine. The three-year drought has taken its toll on a parched land. The root of the problem is presumed to be Ahab's sin in worshipping the false gods of the Canaanites and being led away by Jezebel (1 Kings 16.31). The drought is a physical sign of God's judgement on Ahab and the land. Rather than the abundance and fertility promised through covenant obedience, the people suffer under the brutal realities of death and starvation. It is into the midst of such a harsh setting that the narrative draws attention to the life-giving word of the Lord as spoken to the prophet. Yet God calls Elijah to go beyond the suffering Israelites to the outer-most boundaries of his land, his home, to Zarephath in Sidon,

---

7 Robert Alter, *The Art of Biblical Narrative* (New York: Basic Books, 1981), p. 12.

8 Terrence Fretheim, *First and Second Kings* (Philadelphia, PA: Westminster John Knox Press, 1999), p. 95; Hartmut Gese, 'Bemerkungen zur Sinaitradition', *ZAW* 79 (1967), pp. 137–54; cf. Moshe Garsiel, *From Earth to Heaven: A Literary Study of the Elijah Stories in the Book of Kings* (Bethesda, MD: CDL Press, 2014).

which marks the northern-most territories. Elijah is compliant to God's command to 'go and live' in a foreign land.[9]

Sidon was an ancient Phoenician port city that marked the northern border of Canaan (Genesis 10.19). Jacob spoke of it as the boundary of Zebulun (Genesis 49.13) and Joshua included it as part of the land promised to Israel (Joshua 13.6) for the inheritance of Asher (Joshua 19.28), but it was not taken in the conquest (Judges 1.31; 3.3). At this point in Israel's history, Zarephath is beyond the borders of Israelite territory, but it is also the land of the enemy, the home of Jezebel (1 Kings 16.31). This is where Elijah must go to dwell.[10]

Elijah finds himself pushed to the outer limits of his tradition and experiences the discomfort of confronting what is foreign. He has stepped out of his tribal heritage. It is a strange and unsettling place, yet the word of the Lord calls him there so that he might bring blessing and life in a time of famine and death. In this land the people worship Canaanite storm god Baal. He is the god of fertility, the rainmaker, but the drought caused by YHWH demonstrates his ultimate authority over the heavens and the earth. There Elijah encounters a nameless woman who is not from his ethnic or religious background but she acknowledges that YHWH is the Lord God (1 Kings 17.12). Brueggemann calls her a 'cipher for the powerless, uncredentialled, disadvantaged, and hopeless'.[11] She is not only helpless but she is a Canaanite, a presumed enemy of YHWH.

In the Old Testament, the widow was one of the most vulnerable figures of society. In a patriarchal world she was without a legal defender or protector. As part of the covenant agreement, YHWH gave specific commandments for their protection and care (Exodus 22.22; Deuteronomy 24.17–18, 19–22; 27.19). The widow, the orphan and sojourner were those on the fringes of society and vulnerable to abuse, and they were those whom Israel was commanded to protect.[12]

---

9 See J. T. Walsh, *1 Kings*, Berit Olam Series (Collegeville, MN: Liturgical Press, 1996), pp. 228–30.

10 See Phyllis Trible, 'The Odd Couple: Elijah and Jezebel', in Christina Büchmann and Celina Spiegel (eds), *Out of the Garden: Women Writers on the Bible* (New York: Fawcett Columbine, 1994), pp. 166–79, p. 178.

11 Walter Brueggemann, *1 & 2 Kings*, Smyth & Helwys Bible Commentary (Macon, GA: Smyth & Helwys, 2000), p. 210.

12 See Anna Norrback, *The Fatherless and the Widow in the Deuteronomic Covenant* (Turku: Abo Akademis Förlag, 2001). Cf. Paula S. Hiebert, '"Whence Shall Help Come to Me?": The

One might expect that Elijah, the central power figure of the narrative, would be the one to bless the powerless widow. He is YHWH's advocate for the defenceless who are suffering under the intransigence and sin of Ahab. Yet at the moment of his request for water and bread, we are struck by the reciprocal act of hospitality by the widow. She could have blamed the man of God for the famine, her suffering and her impending death but, instead, she trusts that YHWH is a God who can save despite her circumstances.

Elijah comes to this foreign world as a sign of YHWH's abundant blessing to the poor that reaches beyond the covenant people. One of the key terms repeated throughout 1 Kings 17 is 'word'.[13] The word is to be obeyed, whether it is YHWH's word or Elijah's word. Faith listens to the word that comes from God himself or as it is expressed through his prophet and responds despite where the command leads. Elijah is willing to go to the foreigner and he is welcomed with hospitality. In response he brings both food and life to the weakest and those on the margins of society. The widow has faith and comes to understand that the 'word' is also in the prophet's mouth (1 Kings 17.24). In a time of drought-induced famine caused by the oppressive and abusive structures established by Ahab and Jezebel, the word of YHWH brings new life.

The widow, though a Gentile, confesses YHWH's name (1 Kings 17.12), but in a polytheistic culture it would not have been uncommon to acknowledge the gods of other lands. In this case she references her knowledge of the God of Israel. Even though she is not a worshipper, she is respectful to the prophet and deferential towards his God. Yet Elijah's actions towards her demand an extreme trust and faith as he says that he must eat first and then she and her son. The extravagance of the blessing is noteworthy since this is not a one-time provision, but it represents God's perpetual blessing on those who trust in him.

Elijah reassures the widow that God will provide with the classic Old Testament formula, 'Do not fear.' The assurance is one that confirms the

---

Biblical Widow', in Peggy L. Day (ed.), *Gender and Difference in Ancient Israel* (Minneapolis, MN: Fortress Press, 1989), pp. 125–41.

13 Walsh, *1 Kings*, pp. 234–5. Cf. Thomas L. Brodie, *The Crucial Bridge: The Elijah-Elisha Narrative as an Interpretive Synthesis of Genesis-Kings and a Literary Model for the Gospels* (Collegeville, MN: Liturgical Press, 1999), pp. 70–3.

power of YHWH to bring about salvation and blessing. Fear of death is set aside when God presents the real gift of bodily provision that sustains life. The oil and the bread that do not cease to provide for the widow become a blessing to her and to her whole household. The effect of her hospitality and willingness to sacrifice what little she had becomes the vehicle for her experience of YHWH's blessing and the blessing of all those who are touched by the power of her faith.

The blessing, however, soon turns to curse with the death of the widow's son. How could God call Elijah beyond the borders of his land to bless a Gentile widow only to bring death? The second narrative builds on the hope of the first and establishes the authority of the prophet. The accusation of the widow that Elijah has brought judgement upon her because of her transgression (1 Kings 17.18) is a mistaken theology. She sees divine punishment and suffering in the world in direct relation to one's sins, but in this instance her 'transgression' may point to the fact that she is outside God's covenant community. Yet Elijah refutes such beliefs as he turns to accuse YHWH, 'O LORD my God, have you brought calamity even upon the widow with whom I am staying, by killing her son?' (17.20). Elijah then takes the boy and lays upon him three times, which is a prophetic act of transference as the prophet's spirit is transferred to the boy.[14] The widow's response is marked by her honouring Elijah as truly a 'man of God' who carries the word of YHWH.

Though Elijah miraculously revives the son, the widow's question still lingers, 'Why have you brought my sin against me?' No answer is given in the text, but the biblical authors seem to allude to the widow's hospitality and faith as a means for Gentiles to participate in God's blessing despite being outside the covenant community. If this is the case, then the widow's question is answered by the fact that the prophet brings the son back to life. YHWH will bless those who trust in him and extend grace to all peoples (Genesis 12.1–3). The example of the widow, however, must be held in tension with the other Gentile woman of Sidon, Jezebel. The unbelief and sin of the queen *is* held against her

---

14 Regarding different theories on Elijah's actions, see Stuart Lasine, 'Matters of Life and Death: The Story of Elijah and the Widow's Son in Comparative Perspective', *Bibint* 12 (2004), pp. 117–44, pp. 122–5.

and so Jezebel's son, Joram, will die under God's judgement (2 Kings 9.21–26).[15]

The biblical narrative of Elijah makes use of this tragic period in Israel's history. The people had been led astray to worship false gods under Ahab and Jezebel. The dryness of the land is a metaphor for the spiritual dryness that had consumed Israel. The God who desires to bless his covenant people cannot because of their idolatry. Instead, the God who blesses sends his chosen servant to bring sustenance and life to a Gentile widow beyond the borders of Israel.

This story was retold by the Israelites and passed down because each generation was 'endlessly amazed that God, through his human agent, can override killing scarcity with lavish abundance'.[16] Brueggemann employs Martin Buber's phrase 'abiding astonishment' to describe this miracle story, which offered each new generation an enduring witness to the continuing provision of YHWH to those who are faithful, whether Jew or Gentile. Elijah is sent beyond the borders of his tradition to bring blessing. This is the story that Jesus uses to define his own ministry and it can be used as a model for generous orthodoxy alongside the story of Elisha.

The healing of Naaman: an invitation to wholeness

The second narrative that Jesus recalls is that of the healing of Naaman, the Syrian general who is stricken with leprosy. 'Leprosy' in Hebrew can refer to various types of skin disease that were contagious and considered dangerous since they could spread quickly throughout a community. Without the aid of modern medicines, the only possible way of dealing with such threatening diseases was through exclusion and isolation until it was resolved.

We are told that Naaman is a 'great man' and a 'mighty warrior' (2 Kings 5.1) in the nation that was one of the chief threats to God's people.

---

15 Jopie Siebert-Hommes, 'The Widow of Zarephath and the Great Woman of Shunem: A Comparative Analysis of Two Stories', in Bob Becking and Meindert Dijkstra (eds), *On Reading Prophetic Texts: Gender-Specific and Related Studies in Memory of Fokkelien van Dijk-Hemmes* (Leiden: E. J. Brill, 1996), pp. 231–50, p. 238.

16 Brueggemann, *1 Kings*, p. 211.

Syria (Aram) was a more powerful nation than Israel and raids across the northern borders were common. There is no doubt that Naaman insti-gated many of these battles and earned his reputation as a formidable general, but in an unexpected twist to the narrative we are told that 'by him the LORD had given victory to Aram'. Nothing further is said about God judging Israel through the Aramean conflict, but the statement highlights the fact that YHWH is Lord over all nations and can bring healing and wholeness to all peoples.

Naaman is the proud warrior, but he is also the leper, the social outcast, always living on the edges of his success and kept from becoming too arrogant. His counterpart in the story is the young, nameless Israelite servant girl who was possibly a casualty of Naaman's successful raids (2 Kings 5.2–4). In spite of her circumstances, she offers the voice of faith in the midst of her own tragedy. The childlike trust of the girl highlights the deep-rooted arrogance and pride of the general who, though he heeds her voice, proceeds by his own accord.

Naaman goes to Israel not to see the man of God but to see the king (2 Kings 5.5–7). A powerful general on a diplomatic trip goes to meet with men of prestige and influence. A state visit with a request means that Naaman will bring luxurious gifts of gold and silver as if he can purchase a blessing. He learns, however, that the healing of the God of Israel does not come through bribery or payment, but through the prophetic activity initiated by the word of YHWH.

Naaman is directed towards the prophet Elisha's home. He must cross his own borders into foreign territory if he is to be healed. He is an uninvited guest and with a distinct lack of hospitality the prophet does not come out to greet him. Instead, he sends a messenger (2 Kings 5.10). Unlike Elijah, Elisha's calling is not to venture into foreign territory but to welcome the foreigner into his land. The seeming disinterest of the prophet is an affront to the great general who cannot believe that his only requirement is to wash in the Jordan river seven times. After a fit of rage, he finally relents and obeys the simple command and his skin is restored. The Hebrew wordplay on 'child' (*naar*), used first to describe the Israelite girl, is seen in the description of Naaman's skin being like that of a 'child' (2 Kings 5.2, 14). It is through childlike faith that Naaman is encouraged to seek the prophet in Israel and it is in childlike trust that he is healed.

His skin is the outward sign of an inward transformation that recalls the faith of an unnamed Israelite girl.

Naaman's confession articulates the truth that emerges from the miracle, 'Now I know that there is no God in all the earth except in Israel' (2 Kings 5.15). The declaration of a foreigner that YHWH is the only God echoes the Psalmist's cry, 'Let the peoples praise you, O God; let all the peoples praise you' (Psalm 67.5). The revelation of YHWH's glory on the lips of Naaman is a sign of the fulfilment of God's kingdom made present on earth. But the reality of that presence for Naaman means that he will also be restored to full social and political duties when he returns to his homeland where the Syrian god Rimmon is worshipped.

The response of Elisha is noteworthy, as Brueggemann argues:

> Because he healed the general he does not now intend to control him. The prophet respects the fact that the general must return home, must re-enter his old life, even if he is a changed man, changed in a way his cohorts cannot observe. There is no coercion on the part of Elisha.[17]

The lack of coercion demonstrates the prophetic call and obedience to the God who is over all the nations. Elisha does not intend to restrict worship of YHWH to his own terms but allows for an expression of faithfulness to be present on foreign soil. Though Israel's cultic life is governed by Torah, the prophet recognizes that conformity to a particular form or place of worship cannot be dictated to foreigners. Instead, soil from the land will prove sufficient to offer YHWH sacrifices and Naaman will be pardoned when worshipping in foreign temples since his heart is now bound to YHWH (2 Kings 5.17).

The stories of the widow and the Syrian general reveal the universality of YHWH's reign and his willingness to bless beyond the borders of Israel. The prophetic work of Elijah and Elisha remind us of how

> Israel remembers and imagines that human history is the place where divine power to transform is given from time to time. And

---

17 W. Brueggemann, '2 Kings 5: Two Evangelists and a Saved Subject', *Missiology* 35 (2007), pp. 263–72, p. 269.

those times, enigmatic and inexplicable, constitute the news of an alternative world that is not under royal administration. That alternative world is genuinely human; it is peopled by humanness beyond the usual arena of the credentialed.[18]

It is the sacramental encounters between human beings that bring about YHWH's blessing where there is faith and trust. Through Elijah and Elisha the word and blessing of God goes out to the other by crossing borders. Whether the prophet is sent out or stays at home, the outcome is the same. YHWH accepts the faith of the non-Israelite and extends his blessing to bring hope, healing and restoration.

The mission of Christ and generous orthodoxy

The mission of Christ in Luke's Gospel demonstrates a willingness to bring blessing beyond the boundaries of Israel.[19] Though Jesus is called to the lost sheep of Israel, he identifies himself with Elijah and Elisha's acts as a sign of the Messiah who will listen to the word of God, bless the Gentile (Luke 7.1–10), and raise the dead (Luke 7.11–17). The miracles Jesus performs in his itinerant, prophetic ministry mirror that of the two great prophets who were not unwilling to cross borders, or to bless those who crossed into their territory, to bring God's salvation to those outside the tribes of Israel.[20] The healing and restoration of Christ is one that moves beyond traditional ethnic and religious divisions and offers new life to both Jew and Gentile.

The acts and miracles of Jesus also look forward to the coming movement of the Spirit in Acts and the sending out of his disciples to cross similar borders so that Jew and Gentile might live in fellowship

---

18 Brueggemann, '2 Kings 5', p. 264.

19 John C. Poirier, 'Jesus as an Elijianic Figure in Luke 4:16–30', CBQ 69 (2007), pp. 349–63, p. 361, contends that Jesus is not alluding to a mission to the Gentiles in his reference to Elijah and Elisha. Though Jesus does not use the illustration to demonstrate God's rejection of Israel, the reference to blessing the Gentiles as part of his mission cannot be excluded. Cf. Bart J. Koet, Five Studies on Interpretation of Scripture in Luke–Acts, SNTA 14 (Leuven: Leuven University Press, 1989), pp. 44–52.

20 See John P. Meier, 'From Elijah-like Prophet to Royal Davidic Messiah', in Jesus: A Colloquium in the Holy Land, ed. Doris Donnelly (New York: Continuum, 2001), pp. 45–83.

together. Just as Jesus embodies the prophets Elijah and Elisha, so too does Luke see the same manifestation of the Spirit in the disciples as they are commanded to go to the Gentiles with the gift of the Holy Spirit.[21]

In Acts 10—11 Peter is called to bring the gospel to Cornelius, a Roman centurion, and despite Peter's reluctance he goes and confesses his understanding that 'God shows no partiality, but in every nation anyone who fears him and does what is right is acceptable to him' (Acts 10.34–35). Cornelius and the others receive the gift of the Holy Spirit and the sacrament of baptism into Christ. After Peter reveals what has happened to the Jews in Jerusalem a famine is predicted by Agabus echoing the famine of Elijah's day. Rather than waiting for rain from the heavens, the New Testament looks forward to the outpouring of the Spirit on all who believe.

The acts of Jesus and the apostles find their roots in an ancient prophetic tradition that rejected Israelite xenophobia or self-obsessed tribalism to offer a model of God's desire to bless all nations. The Old Testament narratives begin with obedience to God's word when called to cross borders into foreign soil. These may be physical or metaphorical borders, but they demonstrate God's desire for his people to go beyond familiar territory, or to welcome strangers into their own territory, in order to bring his blessing and hope.

In a similar manner, a generous orthodoxy between Christian traditions can be founded on a willingness to go to the outer edges of one's theological or doctrinal convictions to encounter those with different beliefs or practices. The willingness to cross borders into other traditions is the first step to encountering the other. It is there that we meet people in a sacramental encounter, rooted in Jesus Christ, and founded on deep humility in recognizing the other's intrinsic value.

In the stories of Elijah and Elisha we see each prophet's willingness to listen to the word of God and to respond by encountering the other with a genuine care for the intrinsic value of the person regardless of his or her background or beliefs. Traditional power dynamics are undermined in each narrative and are replaced by a mutual trust that becomes a conduit

---

21 Larrimore C. Crockett, 'Luke 4.25–27 and Jewish–Gentile Relations in Luke–Acts', *JBL* 88:2 (1969), pp. 177–83.

for God's blessing. The prophets, Jesus and the apostles offer an alternative to social, political and religious divisions by responding in faithfulness to God's word, which creates a sacramental encounter without giving up their own theological convictions. So too does a generous orthodoxy offer a confidence in one's own tradition while respecting the individual value of others.

A second point that emerges from these narratives is the willingness to bless without coercion or manipulation. Whether it is in the stories of Elijah and Elisha, the gift of God that comes through genuine human encounter is not supplanted by underlying personal agendas. Elijah could have demanded that the widow follow the God of Israel, but he did not. Elisha could have made demands on Naaman after his healing, but he did not. God's blessing comes out of a faithfulness in one's tradition with an openness to the movement of the Spirit in inexplicable ways. Following these examples, a position of generous orthodoxy does not have as its goal the conversion of the other to one's own traditions, beliefs or practices. Instead, there is an intentional movement away from one's own tribal allegiances in order to meet with another human being face to face.[22]

At the inauguration of Jesus' ministry we are offered two Old Testament stories that describe the prophets crossing social, political and religious boundaries in order to make known the salvation of God. Neither prophet gives up their theological convictions but, rather, they set aside traditional power dynamics and ethnic divisions in obedience to God's word that results in blessing the other. For Elijah it is the discomfort of entering into foreign territory; for Elisha it is welcoming the foreigner into his own territory. In both cases, the example of the prophets, and the example of Jesus' own ministry, offer a model for how we might cross theological or doctrinal boundaries within the Church. We need not seek to convert, manipulate or change others but, rather, we encounter others in humility as we experience our own discomfort in crossing boundaries. This kind of generous orthodoxy can engage in theological debate or in matters of ecclesiology, but seeks first the sacramental encounter that comes when Christ and the manifestations of his salvation are present.

---

22 See E. Levinas, *Time and the Other*, trans. Richard A. Cohen (Pittsburgh, PA: Duquesne University Press, 1987), pp. 82–94.

13

Rooted and sent: Generous orthodoxy as an expression of God's mission in the world today

HANNAH STEELE

It might not be surprising that a chapter on the subject of mission begins with these oft-quoted words from the end of Matthew's Gospel: 'Therefore go and make disciples of all nations' (Matthew 28.19, NIV). Here at the climax of the gospel story is the expectation that the Church's future is to be one of multiplication, diversity and ultimately generosity. The call to the 11 disciples gathered on the mountain side is one of outward movement towards the world in generous proclamation of the good news of the risen Jesus. The great commission is a rallying cry to venture beyond the boundaries of the known and the accustomed into the unknown, the unaccustomed and possibly the uncomfortable. This command reiterates the words Luke places at the start of the book of Acts: 'you will be my witnesses in Jerusalem, and in all Judea and Samaria, and to the ends of the earth' (Acts 1.8, NIV). This outward trajectory at the opening of the book of Acts similarly indicates the nature of the Christian mission that would unfold as this growing group of disciples receive the gift of the Spirit at Pentecost. This fledgling church, inspired, directed and at points propelled by the Spirit, follows this predicted movement from the religious centre in Jerusalem to the continent of Europe. Lesslie Newbigin suggests that Jesus' word in Acts 1.8 is not a command to be obeyed but rather a statement of the reality of the Spirit-filled life:

Please note that it is a promise, not a command: it is not 'You must go and be witnesses'; it is 'The Holy Spirit will come on you

177

and you will be witnesses'. There is a vast difference between these two.[1]

In many ways both this and the great commission serve as anticipations of the gospel's incarnation and translation into the many cultures, contexts and locations of the world. The gift of the Spirit is seen here not only as a gift for believers but one ultimately for all nations, echoing the Abrahamic promise of blessing to the whole world. The great commission speaks of the generosity of God – the scope of his love is not just for Israel but it reaches even to the ends of the earth.

However, the great commission is also a call to orthodoxy, a narrowing of focus on to the person of Jesus. The apostles gathered on the mountain are to make disciples of Jesus alone. They are not free to make disciples of anyone else. These disciples were soon to learn that obedience to this exclusive call was costly and hard. In writing on the nature of conversion, Michael Green observes that early Christian conversion was unique in the way that it required exclusive allegiance to Jesus alone, something he suggests was influential in both the rapid growth and subsequent persecution that followed.[2] The great commission is indeed unashamedly christological in its focus. However, it is also unapologetically ecclesial in nature since its intention is not the gaining of converts but the formation of a community of disciples. The goal of the great commission is not individualistic but corporate, involving teaching and obedience and ultimately the formation of communities of faithful followers of Jesus. Ecclesial boundaries are laid as baptism becomes expressed as one of the defining marks of the new Christian communities birthed out of this commission. The great commission presents both a broad vision – making disciples of all nations – and also a narrow one – baptizing them in the name of the Father, Son and Holy Spirit. It is both generous and orthodox.

It is in this way that the discipline of missiology can provide us with an essential and intriguing window on to the concept of generous orthodoxy.

---

1 Lesslie Newbigin, *Mission in Christ's Way: A Gift, a Command, an Assurance* (Chester Heights, PA: Friendship Press, 1988), p. 16.

2 Michael Green, *Evangelism in the Early Church* (London: Hodder & Stoughton, 1970), pp. 144–7.

Arguably mission itself is rooted in this very concept. Bosch's definition of mission as 'the participation of Christians in the liberating mission of Jesus . . . the good news of God's love, incarnated in the witness of a community, for the sake of the world', reflects the great commission's call both to breadth of scope and narrowness of focus.[3] Mission is a rallying cry for both generosity and orthodoxy. At the heart of it is the proclamation of the gospel, which is good news for all the world, but it is the good news of Jesus Christ, risen from the dead, and his alone. Mission, therefore, is the Church's primary call to be both rooted and sent: rooted in the gospel of Jesus Christ and sent into the world. This echoes the risen Jesus' own words to his disciples: 'As the Father has sent me, I am sending you' (John 20.21, NIV). The Church is sent into the world in the manner and pattern in which Jesus is sent into the world; indeed the Holy Spirit is given here for that very purpose; 'And with that he breathed on them and said, "Receive the Holy Spirit"' (John 20.22, NIV). The Church is sent in the same spirit of generosity but it is sent in a way that is conformed to the manner and pattern of Christ. As Paul reminds the Philippians, 'your attitude should be the same as that of Christ Jesus' (Philippians 2.5). The Church is a sent community, but it is also a community that gathers into fellowship in Christ, fellowship that is marked by baptism and a shared meal in his name. These centripetal and centrifugal dimensions of the Church's missionary nature find a home in the concept of generous orthodoxy. However, the argument can also be made that while generous orthodoxy is rooted in the missional nature of the Church it can also act as a safeguard for the practical outworking of this very missiological imperative. If at the heart of the concept of generosity lies the call to diversity, multiplication and perhaps even innovation, its inherent connection with orthodoxy acts as an anchor ensuring that which is novel responds to the prophetic work of the Spirit, given for this very purpose, and not the changing tide of cultural preference. This chapter, therefore, will explore how generous orthodoxy might be rooted in missional theology while also considering what wisdom it might offer to our contemporary practice.

---

3 David Bosch, *Transforming Mission: Paradigm Shifts in Theology of Mission* (Maryknoll, NY: Orbis Books, 1993), p. 519.

In February 1952, C. S. Lewis wrote a letter to the *Church Times* in which he pleaded that Catholics and Evangelicals should unite against the forces of modernity and, instead of focusing on what divides them, consider the source of their unity. Lewis's conviction was that these two great traditions both shared commitment to the 'supernatural nature' of the gospel which modernity sought to undermine, most particularly 'creation, the Fall, the incarnation, the Resurrection, the second coming, and the . . . Last things'. What Lewis had in mind here was not some version of lowest-common-denominator theology but rather 'a commitment to a "thick" or maximalist form of Christianity'.[4]

Andrew Walker has brought this concept into contemporary thinking about ecclesiology by suggesting that the charismatic movement of the 1960s and 1970s expressed something of the 'deep church' to which Lewis pointed. My conviction is that generous orthodoxy has also continued this trajectory within the Church of England, particularly through the work of St Mellitus College. For Walker, reimagining Lewis's deep church for the twenty-first century became a way in which the Church could seek to marry together the 'new things God is always doing' and the 'old things', the 'historic givens of the faith'.[5] In rooting itself in the orthodox foundations of the faith, Walker imagines the Church to be capable of connecting with contemporary culture in such a way that it can speak its language, responding to its contours, without capitulating to its whims or becoming captive to its values. It is in this way that the notion of deep church echoes through the concept of generous orthodoxy with its dual emphasis on contemporary innovation and rootedness in the past. Such wisdom is vital for our contemporary practice.

In recent decades, faced with what sociologists might term the inevitability of its own decline, the Church of England has sought to embrace innovation, experimentation and creativity with regards to its practice. Such endeavours are demonstrated in the renewed commitment to church-planting, fresh expressions of church and pioneer ministry. In many ways each and every one of these initiatives can be seen as an outworking of a spirit of generosity within mission and a renewed

---

4 Andrew Walker, 'Recovering Deep Church', in Andrew Walker and Luke Bretherton (eds), *Remembering Our Future: Explorations in Deep Church* (London: Paternoster Press, 2007), p. 2.

5 Walker, 'Recovering Deep Church', p. 20.

desire to fulfil the great commission by seeking to reach the 'ends of the earth' within post-Christendom Britain. At the heart of such concepts of ecclesiological innovation lies an incarnational approach to mission. Lamin Sanneh, in his writing on the Church in postcolonial Africa and the subsequent 'historic shift in Christianity's theological centre of gravity', remarks that where the indigenous name for God was adopted, Christian growth has been most remarkable and extensive.[6] To Sanneh, this is part of the incarnational particularity of the Christian gospel, that it is able to incarnate itself, taking root, within any cultural context. This approach echoes Padilla's conviction that not only is contextualization of the gospel possible but that it is crucial to ensure that the message of Christ is not a historical memory but a dynamic presence within our different contexts:

> To contextualize the gospel is to translate it so that the Lordship of Jesus Christ is not an abstract principle or a mere doctrine, but the determining factor of life in all its dimensions and the basic criterion in relation to which all the cultural values that form the very substance of human life are evaluated. Without contextualization the gospel will become tangential or even entirely irrelevant.[7]

Within the context of pioneering or planting, this incarnational approach to contextualization is understood generously in terms of a movement of giving away. The concept of *Missio Dei is* often cited as the theological rationale for pioneering and planting and can be understood as the motivation behind such endeavours being focused outwards towards the world. In this way the Church's missionary life is understood less in terms of a list of activities and more in terms of an orientation towards the world, a posture of generosity.

Sam Wells suggests that an incarnational approach to mission could be understood as an attitude of *being with* people, rather than the traditional approaches to mission that have sought either to *work for*

---

6 Lamin Sanneh, *Whose Religion Is Christianity? The Gospel Beyond the West* (Grand Rapids, MI: Eerdmans, 2003), pp. 10, 18.

7 C. René Padilla, *Mission Between the Times: Essays on the Kingdom*, 2nd edn (Carlisle: Langham, 2013), p. 113.

people (in a traditional mode of social engagement) or *work with* people (adopting a more collaborative approach). For Wells, the notion of *being with* advocates an attitude of presence, engagement and focus on the other – 'enjoying people for their own sake', rather than a contractual exchange.[8] In ecclesial terms, Michael Moynagh suggests that we might understand the Church in terms of a gift that needs to be released to others in order to fulfil its true identity.[9] This act of missional generosity means that there is inevitably an element of letting go for the giver, allowing the recipient to appropriate the gift in possibly new and surprising ways. Jonny Baker suggest that while this pioneering approach to mission is risky it is nevertheless crucial if unchurched people are to encounter Christ:

The gospel always comes culturally robed so, without this letting go, the gospel will not be free to find new indigenous robes and language. In contrast with this, the local insider is to speak up and to speak out boldly finding God in the cracks and corners, the signs and symbols of their own context, to feel proud about using the resources of their culture and location, of taking the risk of robing the gospel in new language and clothes.[10]

Such perspective highlights the reciprocal nature of mission, which has become a recurring theme within contemporary approaches to missiology and a welcome redress to the missionary as power-holder and knowledge-giver approach. In a similar way, Rowan Williams highlights the mutuality of the incarnational approach to mission where the giver is also the recipient. It is arguable that the Church which gives away the gospel is also the Church that finds its own understanding of it enhanced and even deepened:

---

8 Sam Wells, *Incarnational Mission; Being with the World* (Norwich: Canterbury Press, 2018), p. 12.

9 Michael Moynagh, *Church in Life: Innovation, Mission and Ecclesiology* (London: SCM Press, 2017), p. 149.

10 Jonny Baker, 'Prophetic Dialogue and Contemporary Culture', in Cathy Ross and Stephen B. Bevans (eds), *Mission on the Road to Emmaus: Constants, Context and Prophetic Dialogue* (London: SCM Press, 2015), p. 205.

It is sound theology to say that there are things we shall never know about Jesus Christ and the written Word unless we hear and see what they do in ever-new contexts. Mission is not only the carrying of good news; it is the willingness to hear the good news as the Word goes abroad and is embedded in culture after culture.[11]

This incarnational approach to church planting and pioneering suggests that a tension exists between the missionary Church's form being determined by both the message it brings and the context in which it is seeking to engage and take root. For Newbigin, the very concept of contextualization itself is based on a dialectic between an ecclesial community that seeks to live according to the truth of the gospel while at the same time identifying authentically with those around them. And yet Newbigin articulates profoundly the challenge of such generous and incarnational approaches to mission, expressing the age-old conundrum of the contextual model:

> Everyone with experience of mission knows that there are always two opposite dangers, the Scylla and Charybdis, between which one must steer. On the one side there is the danger that one finds no point of contact for the message as the missionary preaches it, to the people of the local culture the message appears irrelevant and meaningless. On the other side is the danger that the point of contact determines entirely the way that the message is received, and the result is syncretism. Every missionary path has to find the way between these two dangers; irrelevance and syncretism. And if one is more afraid of one danger than the other, one will certainly fall into its opposite.[12]

However, this is once again where the concept of generous orthodoxy may act in service to the contemporary missiological model by providing an impetus to *both* diversity and conformity. This impetus can be best

---

11 Rowan Williams, Foreword, in Andrew Walls and Cathy Ross (eds), *Mission in the Twenty-First Century: Exploring the Five Marks of Global Mission* (London: Darton, Longman & Todd, 2008), p. xi.

12 Lesslie Newbigin, *A Word in Season* (Grand Rapids, MI: Eerdmans, 1994), p. 67.

expressed in terms of the apostolic nature of the Church and the way in which the Church is both sent to proclaim the gospel afresh in each generation and is also rooted in the foundation of the apostles and the prophets. The Church in mission is called to proclaim the same gospel as the first apostles, namely that Christ has risen from the dead. With reference to our starting point of the great commission, the call upon the missionary church is not simply *to go* but to gather and to teach, baptize and make disciples. There is a drawing inwards movement which also accompanies the outward trajectory of mission. Within the global scope of the missionary call upon the Church, there are inherent ecclesial threads that serve as signposts and boundary markers ensuring that what is proclaimed afresh is indeed what has always been proclaimed. We might also express this in terms of the apostolic nature of the Church and the dynamic link between first-century witnesses and our contemporary mission today.

In this way the apostolic mark of the Church has both implicit and imperative functions, being both descriptive of what the Church is and prescriptive of what the Church will become. Generous orthodoxy provides a way in which emerging and inherited expressions of church can also learn from one another in a spirit of mutuality and receptivity. Generous orthodoxy is not a postmodern commitment to 'live and let live' but rather a commitment to a humble posture of learning from one another. In this way, innovative and fresh waves of Spirit-inspired missionary endeavour can breathe new and sometimes unsettling life into our comfortable ecclesial forms. However, those new forms are also encouraged to remain anchored within the wider tradition, avoiding what Lewis termed 'chronological snobbery' and seeking to learn vital lessons from history. There is, after all, very little that is genuinely new. In *On the Reading of Old Books*, Lewis suggests that familiarity with the past enables those in the present to maintain a sense of critical distance from the urgency of the present, perhaps even acting as a precaution against the endless pursuit of novelty for novelty's sake allowing us to 'keep the clean sea breeze of the centuries blowing through our minds'.[13]

---

13 C. S. Lewis, *God in the Dock: Essays on Theology and Ethics* (Grand Rapids, MI: Eerdmans, 1979), p. 202.

In this way inherited and emerging forms of church can learn from one another. The traditional can be renewed by the vigour and creativity of the pioneering while the new can learn from the established, prevented from the presumption that novelty always trumps the old. Paas even suggests that in all spheres of missionary activity partnership becomes the only way to 'prevent duplication and harmful competition'.[14] Perhaps generous orthodoxy is truly what a mixed economy means.

However, there is one further step we can make in exploring what the concept of generous orthodoxy can add from a missiological perspective. While I have sought to argue that the great commission itself is rooted in generous orthodoxy and that it can also act as an impetus to a mixed economy, it can also be argued that generous orthodoxy is a vital expression of mission in the twenty-first century.

One of the rationales behind Lewis's plea for deep church was a form of pragmatism based on the reality of the Church's current plight. Lewis pleaded with Catholics and Evangelicals to unite in adversity and join forces against the common foe of modernity. Perhaps such a pragmatic argument can be made in our own time also. If the statisticians are correct and the Church of England is staring down the barrel of its own demise, what sense is there in remaining within the silos of our separate traditions? Surely the missional purpose of church is better served by a unified approach. Walker goes so far as to suggest that the third schism facing the Church is its response to secularization, and its preoccupation with division from previous schisms means that the Church is capable of being caught asleep on its watch. Thus an appeal can be made that Lewis's cautionary warning speaks into our present context also. Walker advocates with some urgency that 'in order to prevent the Third Schism becoming Christianity's final divide, orthodox Christians will have to come together and put aside their differences'.[15]

However, there is also a theological rationale for unity that far overrides any pragmatic one, as sensible or justifiable is it may be. In reflecting on

---

14 Stefan Paas, 'Experimenting with Mission and Unity in Secular Europe', in John Gibaut and Knud Jorgensen (eds), *Called to Unity for the Sake of Mission* (Oxford: Regnum Books International, 2014), p. 186.

15 Andrew G. Walker, *Notes from a Wayward Son: A Miscellany* (Eugene, OR: Wipf & Stock, 2015), p. 263.

the passing of a hundred years of the ecumenical movement, Gibaut and Jorgensen propose that the rationale for unity is not strategic pragmatism but gospel significance:

> The 'engine' or driving force is mission because we have come to realize that the world will not believe that the Father sent the Son if the messengers of the Good News are divided (John 20.20–23). Spiritual unity is not enough; the world must see that we love one another.[16]

The missionary Church is not well served by division and lack of co-operation. Disunity disrupts and distorts the mission of the Church. Jesus' words to his disciples as he washed their feet were that through the demonstration of love for one another 'everyone will know that you are my disciples' (John 13.35). Love in action and gospel witness go hand in hand for those who would dare to follow Jesus.

Indeed, one of the earliest expressions of the missionary nature of the Church was in its demonstration of *koinonia*, and the forging of a common life between those who were previously divided within the first-century world. Michael Gorman adopts this approach in his writing on Pauline churches, maintaining that gospel witness was primarily expressed through the common life of the Church, as they did not merely believe the gospel but lived it together in the world.[17] Arguably the nitty-gritty reality of this communal and participative life was one of the predominant challenges facing the Church as it sought to establish a common ecclesial life, but Jacques Matthey argues that 'love expressed in celebrating God and sharing bread together at the same table, in sharing goods and resources, showed visibly that religiously or ideologically justified rules of separation had no absolute power'.[18] Such koinonia has both present and future dimensions. In its unified life the Church in the present foreshadows the future life of the kingdom inaugurated by Christ.

---

16 'Introduction', Gibaut and Jorgensen, *Called to Unity for the Sake of Mission*, p. xviii.

17 Michael Gorman, *Becoming the Gospel: Paul, Participation and Mission* (Grand Rapids, MI: Eerdmans, 2015).

18 Jacques Matthey, 'Foreword', in Gibaut and Jorgensen, *Called to Unity*, p. xiv.

Arguably in the New Testament the call to koinonia is part and parcel of Christian discipleship. The apostle Paul urges the Philippians to have the mindset of Christ in their shared life together (Philippians 2.11–5). These verses are often used as the foundation for an incarnational approach to mission, but it is interesting to consider that the context in which those verses are given is an appeal to unity within the Church. Similarly, in Ephesians Paul makes the bold claim that in the unity between Jew and Gentile, slave and free, the wisdom of God is made manifest within the cosmic realm (Ephesians 3.10). Such strong statements indicating the eschatological orientation of the unified ecclesial life point to a vital Christian unity based not on the pragmatism of the Church in decline but on the outworking of the gospel within the world today. Such unity must not be misunderstood as uniformity or bland similarity, but a potent and distinctive living out of the call to make, teach and baptize disciples of the living Christ in all the spheres of human society. As Karkkainen reflects, 'the unity of the church does not . . . reduce difference to uniformity. In the New Testament the church is neither a zone of intimate sympathy among the like-minded, nor a space of live-and-let-live.'[19] Generous orthodoxy provides a way of pursuing such radical unity without necessitating uniformity, of allowing distinction of expression and form while preserving commitment to the foundational witness of the risen Christ. It is a commitment not merely to tolerate the other but to learn from the other since that very act of learning may prove crucial to the missiological task.

A commitment to generous orthodoxy does not simply mean that Christians of different traditions are called to stand together in the face of the challenge of secularization, nor that they are simply to love one another as an expression of the gospel, as potent and critical as those two calls are. Generous orthodoxy also suggests that Christians are called to learn from one another and in so doing they may find renewed insight into the calling of the worldwide Church to be the herald of the gospel and Christ's coming kingdom. Peter's encounter with Cornelius in the book of Acts serves as a salutary reminder of a generous approach to

---

19 Veli-Matti Kärkkäinen, 'Growing Together in Unity and Mission', in Gibaut and Jorgensen, *Called to Unity*, p. 69.

encounter with those who are different. In witnessing the Spirit falling upon uncircumcised believers, Peter and those with him are 'astounded that the gift of the Holy Spirit had been poured out even on the Gentiles (Acts 10.45). Peter's encounter with 'the other' is transformational in his own understanding of the scope and reach of the gospel, a conviction that proves to be critical in the subsequent missionary journey of the Church. Stanley Hauerwas expresses this in the following way:

> Christians . . . must trust that the God who sends them to the ends of the earth is bringing forth something new in his redemptive action, in which they participate. This includes a trust that those to whom they witness will learn the gospel in a new and different light, drawing it out in ways hitherto unimagined.[20]

For Hauerwas, therefore, mission can also have a preseverative function on the life of the Church, preventing any particular tradition from assuming that its own particular way is the only way there is. Mission prevents us from remaining in our ecclesiastical silos.

This approach moves us deeper into an explicitly missional rationale for generous orthodoxy. Not only is the authentic partnership and unity of the Church a demonstration of the new life of the kingdom of God, but without it the missional effectiveness of the Church might be seriously hampered. This is the approach Paas also takes in his reflections on the Church's need to rethink itself in a post-Christendom mindset less focused on growth and expansion and instead seeking to renew its prophetic voice as a minority movement within contemporary society. Paas maintains that rather than remaining siloed in its particular tradition out of perseveration, the Church needs intentionally to seek interaction with those who are different in order both to fully understand and be able to respond to the huge and complex challenge that secularization presents to the Church. For Paas, the present missionary challenge in Europe is so multifaceted that 'co-operation, networking and constant interaction are crucial to open up the hermeneutical space

---

20 Stanley Hauerwas, *Approaching the End: Eschatological Reflections on Church, Politics and Life* (Grand Rapids, MI: Eerdmans, 2013), p. 59.

that we need for a better understanding of this challenge'.[21] It is in this context that generous orthodoxy can function as a gift within the life of the Church, enabling the precious ability to see our contexts through the perspective of another. Such a posture entails humility, and the possibility of discomfort and challenge may yet also lead to a deeper understanding of how we might face the challenges and opportunities of our contemporary missiological moment. In all this, the call upon the Church to be one rings out with missiological significance since its very corporate life is a reflection of the good news that calls and summons all, and the new life to which all are invited and compelled to enter. While sharpening praxis and honing evangelistic skill remain ever crucial in our post-Christendom world, the missional mandate simply for the Church to be the Church remains central.

It is the missionary nature of the Church that constantly compels the church to engage with new frontiers, people and places. It is the missionary nature that prevents the Church from becoming ossified, tied to its current forms and practices, inflexible and incapable of change. It is the missionary nature of the Church that compels it to extend a hand to the other, curiously wondering what it might learn through the exchange. It is the missionary nature of the Church that means there is always space for more at the table.

It is in responding to the great commission that we are today caused to ask audacious questions about the shape and form of Christian witness in our Church today. However, generous orthodoxy ensures that, as bold and necessary questions are asked, they are explored while remaining anchored within in the apostolic tradition, enabling us to ask daring questions without fearing we might veer into sectarianism by default. Those of a more pioneering disposition might be encouraged to seek from the institution vital lessons from the past missionary endeavours to ensure that mistakes are not repeated in cyclical fashion. Those of a more preservation mindset might be encouraged to learn from the innovation and creativity of those who imagine church could potentially look quite different for a twenty-first-century context. In this way, those who are different from us become not obstacles to missionary endeavour

---

21 Paas, 'Experimenting', p. 188.

or stumbling blocks to the preservation of tradition but rather those from whom we can learn so that our own sense of calling and conviction is both sharpened and honed to face the contemporary challenges and opportunities of witness in a post-Christian culture.

WE HAVE A VISION OF A WORLD IN WHICH EVERYONE IS TRANSFORMED BY CHRISTIAN KNOWLEDGE

As well as being an award-winning publisher, SPCK is the oldest Anglican mission agency in the world.

Our mission is to lead the way in creating books and resources that help everyone to make sense of faith.

Will you partner with us to put good books into the hands of prisoners, great assemblies in front of schoolchildren and reach out to people who have not yet been transformed by the Christian faith?

To donate, please visit www.spckpublishing.co.uk/donate or call our friendly fundraising team on 020 7592 3900.

Graham Tomlin is Bishop of Kensington and President of St Mellitus College. He served as Chaplain of Jesus College, Oxford and Vice-Principal of Wycliffe Hall, Oxford, where he taught historical theology within the Theology Faculty of the university. He was the first Dean of St Mellitus College. He is the author of many books and articles, including *The Power of the Cross: Theology and the Death of Christ in Paul, Luther and Pascal*, *Looking through the Cross* (the Archbishop of Canterbury's Lent Book for 2014), *The Widening Circle: Priesthood as God's Way of Blessing the World* and *Luther's Gospel: Reimagining the World*.

Nathan Eddy is Interim Director of the Council of Christians and Jews, the UK's oldest interfaith charity. He earned his PhD in Hebrew Bible at Northern College, Luther King House, in Manchester, and managed the past two years of the Generous Orthodoxy project at St Mellitus College, where he has taught Hebrew and Bible. He lives in London and serves in a local United Reformed church as part of the ministry team.